DEATH OF A PIRATE

ALSO BY ADRIAN JOHNS

Piracy: The Intellectual Property Wars from Gutenberg to Gates

The Nature of the Book: Print and Knowledge in the Making

DEATH OF A PIRATE

BRITISH RADIO AND THE
MAKING OF THE
INFORMATION AGE

ADRIAN JOHNS

W. W. NORTON & COMPANY | NEW YORK · LONDON

For information about permission to reproduce selections from this book,
write to Permissions, W. W. Norton & Company, Inc.,
500 Fifth Avenue, New York, NY 10110

For information about special discounts for bulk purchases, please contact
W. W. Norton Special Sales at specialsales@wwnorton.com or 800-233-4830

Manufacturing by Courier Westford
Book design by Chris Welch
Production manager: Anna Oler

Library of Congress Cataloging-in-Publication Data

Johns, Adrian.
Death of a pirate : British radio and the making of
the information age / Adrian Johns. — 1st ed.
p. cm.
Includes bibliographical references and index.
ISBN 978-0-393-06860-3 (hardcover)
1. Pirate radio broadcasting—Great Britain—History.
I. Title.
HE8697.65G7J64 2010
384.54—dc22

                                        2010024525

W. W. Norton & Company, Inc.
500 Fifth Avenue, New York, N.Y. 10110
www.wwnorton.com

W. W. Norton & Company Ltd.
Castle House, 75/76 Wells Street, London W1T 3QT

1 2 3 4 5 6 7 8 9 0

TO ELIZABETH

CONTENTS

LIST OF ILLUSTRATIONS

(PAGE NUMBERS REFER TO PHOTOGRAPH INSERT)

DEATH OF A PIRATE

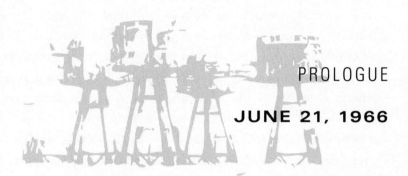

PROLOGUE

JUNE 21, 1966

The Ford Zodiac edged cautiously down the lane. High hedges loomed to the left, and overhanging branches brushed the roof. It felt barely wide enough for the big car to pass. On the right, a row of old cottages. At the last of them the Zodiac coasted quietly to a halt, nestling into a parking space to the side of the road.

A man got out from the passenger side. He felt the cool, still air of a midsummer's night in the country—a pleasant change from the clamor and grime of London. It had rained earlier, but now the sky was clear and the pale walls of the seventeenth-century thatched cottage in front of him shone faintly by the light of the crescent moon. Nobody was about at this late hour. The only sound was of voices, softly audible from within the cottage itself.

He looked at his watch. Almost eleven o'clock: they had made good time. Even after stopping to get directions—they had been lucky enough to find a furtively courting couple at the pub who knew the village well and could point them to the exact house—it had still taken less than two hours. As the low rumble of a man's voice reached them from an open window, the passenger stopped. He listened, then started forward.

"Smedley's here," he whispered. "I recognize his voice."

As he strode toward the cottage, Reginald Calvert glanced back and beckoned the driver to come with him. Calvert was a well-built thirty-eight-year-old northerner, open-mannered and energetic, but at this moment he felt agitated and distracted. He had dressed warmly for the season, in an attempt to mitigate the lingering side effects of a smallpox vaccination. A brown tweed coat covered his blue three-piece suit, and he had even pulled on fleece gloves as he rushed from his flat in the capital earlier that evening. But his mission was urgent and brooked no delay. So he had come anyway, accompanied by an acquaintance named Alan Arnold. The men did not know each other well, but Arnold too had an interest in their task tonight. And Calvert, whose eyesight was weakened by cataracts, had wanted him to drive.

The two had left Arnold's home at about nine, taking Calvert's sedan rather than Arnold's E-Type. The Ford was slower, but it was one of the few private vehicles in Britain at that time to carry a radio-telephone, and Calvert needed to keep in touch as they drove to the village. They had chatted as they drove about what the outcome of their journey might be. Heading into the tiny Essex village of Wendens Ambo—at first they missed the house and had to turn around—Arnold saw no reason to doubt that it would be good.

Inside the cottage, Oliver Smedley had risen to get himself a drink. In his mid-fifties, Smedley moved with military bearing and an assured air bespeaking a man of conviction. He was still wearing the gray suit and tie that he had put on in the morning to go to his office in London. From the living room where he had spent the last few hours talking on the telephone, he strode through the hall to the dining room. These rooms, all small and low, stood in a line along the front of the cottage, facing out onto the lane. The living room was the largest, with a sofa, an armchair, and a gas fire standing in the old fireplace. But three adults would fill the room. To the rear, through doors that led out from both the dining and living rooms, was a conservatory running the length of the three rooms. As Smedley began to pour, he continued to chat about the events of the day with his twenty-three-year-old housekeeper, assistant, and occasional mistress, Pamela Thorburn. His voice drifted out through an open window.

The knock that answered it surprised them both. It was not aggressive, but firm and resolute. Then it came again.

Calvert had not waited for the radio engineer to catch him up, but had marched straight up to the cottage door and knocked, as if suddenly resolved on something. Now he waited for someone to answer, Arnold standing slightly behind him. A moment later the door began to open. Behind it stood Thorburn.

For what happened next we are reliant on the testimony of Thorburn herself, corroborated at points by Arnold.[1] As they described it, she looked blankly at the newcomer for an instant, then seemed to start as she realized who he must be. She made a movement to shut the door. But Calvert preempted her. He pressed forward with startling speed. Suddenly he was flushed, furious—"demented," Arnold would later say. He threw open the door and barged in, colliding with the astonished Thorburn. She fell back a little, but recovered her footing and tried to push the intruder back. It was too late. He was stronger and heavier, and had the benefit of surprise. Calvert made it into the hall. She found herself struggling with him, pushing at him and scratching his face. A cut opened above his good eye.

"Where's Smedley?" He grabbed her arm. "I'm going to take him to the police."

She tried to free herself. "Be sensible," she stalled: "go and bring a policeman here."

Arnold, shocked by what was happening, moved into the cottage behind Calvert. "You look upstairs," Calvert ordered. Arnold went to obey. As Calvert looked up after him, Thorburn saw her chance. She broke away, ducked under his arm, and lunged for the telephone that sat on a table in the living room. She got as far as dialing 9 before Calvert saw what she meant to do. He grabbed at the telephone cord and yanked it out of the wall. Thorburn fell back, staggering into the bathroom and colliding with the wall. As she got to her feet, she felt the phone handset hit her on the shoulder. They scuffled, knocking over the table and an electric heater. The lamp fell to the floor. Thorburn called out for help to Arnold, who had reappeared empty-handed. But he was rooted to the spot in apparent horror. The shouting got louder. "Where is that bastard Smedley?" Thorburn later recalled him saying. "I'm a desperate man—don't you know what he's done to me?"

At that moment Calvert spotted what he thought must have been his quarry's escape route. The French window into the conservatory was standing open. He thrust Thorburn aside, dropped the phone, and sprang forward into the dining room, heading for the open door. "He's gone this way," he told Arnold. It took Thorburn a moment to grasp what was happening. Then she followed and pulled on his shoulder to hold him back.

"He isn't there," she cried. "And why don't you get the police if you want them to have him?"

Calvert stopped, and for a moment they confronted each other in the hallway. As though struck by the thought that Smedley was indeed not there, Calvert suddenly reached for a statuette of Napoleon, one of several in the room. Thorburn froze as he hefted the ornament. "If I can't get him," he announced, "I'm going to take you. Are you coming willingly?"

Thorburn backed away. "This is ridiculous," she retorted. "Of course I'm not." She was still determined above all to prevent Calvert going into the dining room.

"All right," Calvert started to say, "if that's the way you want it . . ." But suddenly something else caught his attention. Calvert's eyes darted to a spot behind her where the door to the conservatory stood open. A triumphant note entered his voice. "There's the bugger!" He pushed Thorburn aside. She fell against the dining room door. Tossing away the bust, Calvert leaped forward, toward his real quarry.

SMEDLEY HAD BEEN lucky. He was in the dining room when Calvert first knocked at the cottage door. As Calvert pressed forward into the hall he had moved and looked to the right, which meant that Smedley was behind him. The struggle with Thorburn then took the two of them into the lounge, giving Smedley a precious moment to duck out unnoticed into the conservatory. Almost instinctively, he did so.

Collecting his wits, he turned to his right, moved quickly down the passage, and went through another door. It led directly into his bedroom. There he reached up, pulled down a gun case from the top of the cupboard, and silently opened it. Inside was a double-barreled twelve-bore shotgun. Smedley loaded cartridges into both barrels. With no time to pause, he hefted the gun under his right arm and stood up.

Rather than go straight back into the house, Smedley went out into the garden. He headed for the neighboring cottage that stood to one side of the lawn, looking for a way to call the police. Even before he reached it, a man emerged. It was another stranger. But Neil Warden was no threat. A friend of the housewife who lived there, Evelyn Pithers, he had been visiting to check on her well-being at the request of her husband, who was away on business. He was just taking his leave when Smedley accosted him. There was no time for introductions. "Ring the police," he ordered, already turning back toward his own house. "I have big trouble."

The sounds of Thorburn struggling with Calvert rose up again as Smedley crept back into the conservatory. He released the safety catch and headed slightly to his right as he reentered the house. There, at the entrance to the dining room, he turned. He saw Calvert for the first time.

And Calvert saw him.

ARNOLD HAD ROUSED himself from the state of horror that at first held him transfixed. He ran out of the front door of the cottage, intent on finding help and somehow stopping the chaos. A few yards into the lane, and the tranquillity of the rural night enveloped him once again. He slowed to a halt, his eyes adjusting to the gloom. Arnold stood still in the middle of the lane, panting slightly and wondering what to do. Already the survivor of two heart attacks, the idea of violent confrontation appalled and terrified him. He felt helpless, indecisive, and confused.

At that moment a sharp, harsh *Bang* cut through the silence. There was no mistaking it. A gunshot.

Snatched back to the moment, Arnold spun round and made for the house once more. The front door had swung shut again. He pushed it open. As he entered, Calvert staggered across the doorway. Arnold had a brief glimpse of a ragged, red-lined hole in his chest. Then Calvert half-turned, pitched forward, and fell to the floor face-first.

There was a sudden, eerie calm—a moment of stasis after the furor. The silence was weighty after the brutal sound of the shot.

It took Thorburn a second or two to see Smedley, take in the gun, and realize that Calvert had been shot. She bent down and checked him. He was alive but unconscious, his eyes half-closed and his breathing shallow and rough. Bubbles of blood had already appeared about his mouth. His skin had taken on a blanched tone, and the rattle of each breath filled Arnold with dread. Thorburn rose and went for a cushion. Gently raising him, she placed it under his head. Then she laid a coverlet over his chest.

Arnold too was astonished and horrified. He stared at Smedley and their eyes met. "My God," he said. "This is murder."

Smedley made a movement. Fearing that he was about to turn the gun on him, Arnold retreated. He ran out again to the street, desperate now to find help. He went first toward the car, then turned, trying to collect his wits. Then he walked to the house next to Smedley's, where he found a door open. Inside were Warden and Evelyn Pithers. They were already terrified after their previous exchange with Smedley. Warden was talking into a telephone.

"Get help," Arnold told him. "A man's been shot."

"I'm on to the police now," the man replied.

"For God's sake," Arnold pressed, "get help quickly—a man is bleeding to death."

Smedley now appeared at the door, and Arnold retreated again. The engineer ran back to the cottage. Calvert was still prostrate on the floor, unconscious. Arnold breathed out as Smedley reappeared. He was still carrying the gun.

"I need a drink," Arnold declared. Thorburn stepped past the prone man and poured a whisky. He downed it, and then a second.

While Thorburn continued to check Calvert's fading pulse, Arnold drifted agitatedly between the prone man and the street outside, desperate to see the lights that would signal the approach of help. It seemed to take a long time. But in fact the ambulance took only a few minutes to get to the cottage. It drew up at 11:18 pm, two men jumping out and marching past Arnold into the hall. The first medic knelt and removed one of Calvert's gloves to check for a pulse. He looked up at Smedley, who was still clutching the shotgun. "What's happened here?" he asked.

"I've shot him," Smedley said flatly. "Is he dead?"

"Yes. I'll wait for the police; you go and call a doctor."

In fact, a doctor was already on his way. As soon as he had called the police and ambulance, Warden had phoned the local GP out of concern for Pithers. The physician turned up at eleven thirty. At almost the same moment the local constable, Christopher Kearney, arrived, followed shortly after by Robert George, a sergeant from the nearest sizable town, Saffron Walden. The doctor confirmed that Calvert was dead. Just after midnight, they were joined by Detective Constable Frank Mann from more distant Harlow, a dreary New Town on the outskirts of London. And two hours later Detective Superintendent George Brown arrived from the opposite direction, having driven from the county town of Chelmsford, thirty miles away. Brown took charge. The long, painstaking, and intimately modern process of bureaucratizing violent death began.

Mann handled the physical evidence. He also took photographs. Early the following morning he would gather clothing and artifacts from Calvert's body at the mortuary, along with physiological specimens, and take them all to Scotland Yard. Twice more in the next week he would return to take more photographs, and to draw the ground plan that is reproduced on page 2 of the photograph insert. Only on one of those later visits would the police think to look in the car. When they did, along with a packet of butterscotch and an unopened bottle of cider, they found a package. In it was a draft for a business partnership—some kind of entertainment venture called "UK Good Music."

Brown, meanwhile, paced slowly and carefully through the ground floor, noting damage to the furniture and minutely observing the positions of objects dislodged in the fight. The detective read both with an expert eye. A broken bust told him how it had been thrown— its force, velocity, and trajectory. An overturned lamp betrayed the course of a struggle. A scraped wall spoke of a woman falling back before an assailant. Brown reconstructed from angles, patterns, and shards the clumsy history of a fracas.

Three hours later, tired but resolute, Brown attended the postmortem. Calvert had died from lacerations to his lung and liver, caused by a gunshot wound sustained at close range. He noticed only one unusual thing: a strange device that Calvert had been carrying in his pocket. It was the size and shape of a fountain pen, but it could never have been used for writing. Instead of ink it contained a small canister of gas.

Before he could go to bed the detective had one more duty to perform. Brown drove to Saffron Walden police station and charged Oliver Smedley with murder.

SMEDLEY HAD BEEN taken to the station by PC Kearney at 2 am. Before that, he had sat quietly and to all appearances rather desolately in the living room of his cottage, feet from Calvert's body, as the police worked. It was Kearney who asked him what had happened.

"I shot him," Smedley repeated.

"And you?" Kearney turned to Arnold. "Do you live here?"

"No," Arnold replied. He gestured toward the body. "I came with him."

"What happened?"

"I don't know." Arnold shrugged. "We came to the house and this man went mad and shot him."

Leaving Arnold aside, PC Kearney sat Smedley down in the dining room and started again, trying to coax more from him. Shock was beginning to set in. Smedley, who had had the presence of mind to put the gun down carefully in a corner and to warn that it was still loaded, was suddenly looking shaken. But Kearney had Pamela Thorburn sit down at Smedley's side, and soon he began to respond. As the initial horror of the shooting receded, the words flowed more freely. Scraps and hints began to cohere. Sergeant George recited the standard caution and let him continue. As he did, Smedley would get up and pace the room, only to sit down and put his head in his hands at the memory. "Any rational man would now be quiet and say no more," he remarked. But he went on.

At first, Smedley's words focused on the events of the night. He had realized it was Calvert as soon as he heard the door open, Smedley said. He knew too, he added, that this was a man capable of violence. "I knew he came here to kill me: I had a message yesterday to say things were getting dangerous." Smedley told how he had crept into his bedroom, fetched the gun, and returned just in time to see Calvert apparently about to hit Thorburn over the head with the bust. When he saw Calvert make to lunge at him, he had fired instinctively, not thinking to warn or wound. "What a terrible tragedy," he added, glancing at the body in the hall. Calvert had a wife and two daughters. "But I feel I was doing right in what I did. He came here to get me. . . . He did not come 40 miles just to have tea." He was already recovering confidence in his actions. "I feel morally right and I am not worried because he was a very violent man."

But there soon began to emerge—at first haltingly, in fragments, then in more extended measures—another story altogether. It began, apparently, some time earlier, days before the knock on his cottage door.

"This is the outcome of something that happened in the week" Smedley explained—"a joke which turned sour." He turned to Kearney. "You see, we had an expedition the other day.

"It was to do with pirate radio stations."

WHEN DAWN BROKE the next day, the tale that Smedley had begun to tell was already on its way to becoming a national sensation. Radio news reports opened with the revelation. The tabloid press too pounced on the opportunity. The nation's economic woes and political feuds were suddenly relegated to the margins. Within forty-eight hours, lurid stories of kidnappings, conspiracies, and threats were filling the front pages. At the peak of a pirate radio boom, one of the country's foremost pirates had been killed.

The enterprise of pirate radio was a signature phenomenon of the sixties in Britain. Offshore commercial broadcasters—immediately and lastingly dubbed "pirates"—had proliferated since the start of the decade, challenging a formal monopoly that the British Broadcasting Corporation had enjoyed ever since the 1920s. Dedicated to the latest pop music at a time when the BBC was tightly constrained in its ability to broadcast records, pirate radio became massively popular at all levels of society. It seemed set to flourish. It was already shaping a new generation's musical taste, favoring the Beatles, the Rolling Stones, the Who, and the latest American soul. But the enterprise was an unstable one, vulnerable to any North Sea storm or high court decision. After long delays, Europe's governments were converging upon measures that threatened its future. Some of the pirates, at least, were bound to fail. By mid-1966, a scramble to survive was in the offing. The jockeying for position had already begun. Everyone was waiting to see who would win and who would lose. Fleet Street capitalized to the maximum on this anxiety.

By the time Smedley faced the magistrates at Saffron Walden a month later, a fairly consistent tale had emerged out of the welter of scandalized rumors. It focused not on Smedley himself but on the man he had shot. Reginald Calvert appeared to have been a desperate man whose recklessness had led to his own death. The legal proceedings followed the same line, giving this account weight and authority. It was soon accepted as true. And it had immediate consequences. For if this was what pirate radio entrepreneurs were like, then the country had to act to end their operations. Sure enough, after years of inaction the Cabinet in Westminster suddenly announced decisive action to silence the pirate stations. The death of Reginald Calvert was set to catalyze the biggest changes to British radio since its inauguration forty years earlier.

To this day, sound broadcasting in the United Kingdom retains the imprint of the transformation it underwent at that time. What had been a continuous historical trajectory was brought to a halt, and a fundamental change imposed. The direction that broadcasting would follow in the aftermath would be markedly different, affecting popular culture itself—not only in Britain but well beyond. Our musical sensibilities, our practices of listening, and our moral assumptions about creativity all bear the imprint of that moment in 1966.

The story of desperation that emerged in mid-1966 proved resilient. Yet it remains only one version of the events of that midsummer night. It left much about the incident itself unclear. More important, it entirely obscured the historical currents that gave rise to the tragedy and would help explain it. Those currents—the real causes, perhaps, of Reginald Calvert's death—were as far-reaching as its consequences. They extended back to the invention of broadcasting itself in the 1920s, and they included the most important processes in twentieth-century political and social history. Much of *Death of a Pirate* is devoted to revealing those deeper currents.

In one sense, then, this book is about the significance of a moment. It tells a story of how ideology, pop music, and demimonde entrepreneurship led to tragedy, and through that tragedy to the transformation of a medium. We shall see that not everything that was reported about that incident should be accepted at face value—and that includes some of the evidence on which the story told in the previous few pages rests. The image of a desperate and violent man intruding into a country cottage was powerful and compelling at the time, and it remains so today. But perhaps all was not quite what it seemed.

In addressing this moment, the book is also about a process. To discover that process, it ventures farther afield as well as further back: as far afield as Normandy, Berlin, Geneva, and Chicago. Decisions made and practices forged in these places created the possibility of pirate radio. For some, they made such radio not merely a money-making enterprise but an urgent moral imperative. As they coalesced, so pirate media came to challenge a well-entrenched, centralized public service, and to do so in the name of popular freedom.

That challenge has its own parallels today. Our networked society faces its own hordes of pirates, proclaiming once again virtues of

1

A PIRATE PEOPLE

On Saturday, December 20, 1922, promptly at nine o'clock in the morning, a tall, impeccably dressed man with piercing eyes walked up to the doors of Magnet House, the headquarters of the General Electric Company (GEC) in the busy London thoroughfare of Kingsway. As it was not a working day the building was quiet, but an obliging attendant showed him up to the second floor. The office there was deserted and sparse—just a table, a telephone, and a pile of accumulated mail. But the newcomer tried to make himself at home as best he could. "The new company," as the doorman called it, might not be expected until Monday, but its incoming general manager already had much to do. He had to create not just a new corporation, but a new kind of enterprise: one devoted to something called "broadcasting."[1]

John Reith was thirty-three. He hailed from Glasgow, the engineering heart of the empire, where his father had been a senior minister in the Free Church of Scotland. That combination of technical and moral conviction—steel, in both its senses—distinguished the son, too. Almost ten years younger than his six siblings, he emerged from an emotionally austere childhood to become an engineer and factory manager. During World War I he was wounded in the face by a German bullet. Being unfit to return to the front, he traveled to the United States, where he managed an arms factory in Philadelphia.

Reith increased its production from fifty rifles daily to five hundred, even while introducing important technical improvements. He also found himself in demand as a public speaker for his exhortations to America to enter the conflict. But after 1918, with his return to Britain, he became frustrated at the task of reviving a declining engineering plant in Glasgow. He resigned his position to come down to London and enter politics.

There followed a period of irresolution while Reith sought a future for himself. But in his private diary he expressed undimmed confidence: "I believe there is some high work for me in the world," he wrote, "but that it won't come till I have reconciled myself absolutely to God's way of working." He at first seemed inclined toward Labour, telling one MP that the Old Testament virtues of his father's church were the best foundations for political life. But by late 1922 he was seeking patronage from the Conservatives. It was during this quest that he chanced upon an advertisement in the *Morning Post* for positions in a concern so new that it did not yet even exist: a British Broadcasting Company. What it might amount to he was not sure, but he put in an application anyway, taking care to highlight the Scottish background that he shared with Sir William Noble, the GEC executive and ex–Post Office man who would be making the appointment. On December 13, Noble interviewed him, and the next morning gave him the job. As Reith later recalled, he still "hadn't the remotest idea what broadcasting was."[2]

If Reith had little notion of what broadcasting might be, he was not alone. Radio was the technology of the hour. An extraordinary surge in public interest in the medium had taken place since the armistice. But using it to send out transmissions to all and sundry, who might be expected to have receiving sets in their homes and listen in as they wished, was a form of communication without any precedent in history. Many of the fundamentals—its technical character, its day-to-day practices, its norms, its regulation, and perhaps above all its economics—had yet to be determined. Amid much intense debate, the major companies in Britain's radio industry had agreed over the previous summer to pool their patents and create a single consortium charged with this formative task. It was this syndicate that Reith was about to take control of.

Reith set about his responsibilities with the same conviction that he had shown in marshalling the Philadelphia rifle works. He had already interviewed staff (all four of them) before he arrived at GEC that Saturday morning, barely a week after being offered the position. And by then Reith had also made one of the most significant decisions he would take in shaping British broadcasting. Naturally, his company would "observe Sundays." That meant it would restrict itself to a curtailed schedule on the sabbath of sober, even austere programming centered on religious services and music by such composers as Bach. This policy—so self-evident to Reith himself that adopting it scarcely amounted to making a decision at all—would be critical to both the development of a distinctive culture of public broadcasting and the possibility that rivals to it might prove popular. The "Reith Sunday," as it would become known, isolated a moment of calm and reflection in the helter-skelter rush of modern life. Piracy would owe a lot to it.

WIRELESS BROADCASTING WAS unbounded and undirected. There was no obvious way to know who was receiving it, where, how, and to what effect; nor was there a way to prevent anyone in particular from doing so. A single program could reach an unknowable—but clearly large—audience simultaneously. The advent of this medium, with properties so unlike those of writing, print, the telegraph, or even the telephone, therefore posed radically new questions. And as the 1920s wore on, so these questions had to be tackled against a background of new uncertainty about what had once seemed political and economic fundamentals. The turmoil of the General Strike of 1927, followed by the Crash and the Depression, cast doubt on what had long been established verities about laissez-faire and free trade. The result was that as it took shape, broadcasting itself came to be seen as providing a model for a new kind of economic culture. Its institutions and practices, many thought, showed the path from social malaise to a bright national future. The first radio piracy arose in the midst of this ferment. It too seemed to have implications that extended far beyond broadcasting itself.

The phenomenon of piracy in general—the expropriation, in some manner, of intellectual goods—is much older than broadcasting. It was first spoken of in the mid-seventeenth century, as the upheavals of the English Civil War and Glorious Revolution were fomented by newspapers and the excesses of Grub Street. The term caught on and became commonplace in the 1700s. At that point it spread to other fields of creative endeavor. During the Industrial Revolution there were pirates of music, of spectacles, and of medicines. Inventors and engineers habitually decried the hordes of pirates waiting to steal their devices. By the high point of British industrial supremacy in the Victorian era, piracy was an internationally recognized sin with a global impact. And so it would continue in the twentieth century.[3] But radio was different, and radio piracy would be radically unlike anything that had gone before. So far, piracy had always been a matter of reproduction. Pirate printers replicated books; musical pirates reproduced notes on staves; pirate engineers appropriated machines. But the first radio pirates did not physically produce or replicate anything. They were pirate *listeners*.

The furor over pirate listening arose from the sheer popularity of wireless among the general public in the early 1920s. Across the UK, continental Europe, and the United States, countless amateur enthusiasts, many of whom had been introduced to radio while in military service, launched themselves into homemade projects to transmit and receive signals. Their magazines—*Wireless, Amateur Wireless, Modern Wireless, Popular Wireless Weekly,* and others—had hundreds of thousands of readers.[4] The extraordinary phenomenon encouraged visionary proclamations for a future of social harmony and peaceful progress. Many pronounced that the ideal nature of science itself was finally set to become a reality.

One such was Oliver Lodge, a prominent pioneer of wireless science and a staunch advocate of the amateurs. Not coincidentally, Lodge was also a champion of spiritualism, and of ether theories of electromagnetic radiation. These theories invoked an all-pervading medium to account for the propagation of light and other forms of electromagnetic wave radiation, such as X-rays and radio waves. They had a long pedigree in the history of science, extending back at least to Newton. Although it is commonly thought that Einstein's special relativity rendered ether theories unviable, in practice they remained plausible to respected physicists and especially radio engineers well into the 1920s. And this mattered, because convictions about the ether correlated with those about popular research and creativity. For Lodge, and for the mass of amateurs whom he represented, the ether through which an announcer's voice reached citizens' homes was the physical concomitant to the ideal universality of science. A natural commons, it allowed an "interchange of discoveries between the nations," as "scientific discoverers throughout the world virtually pool their resources and communicate to each other their results." If secrecy was "alien to the spirit of science," then radio was science's natural vehicle as well as its most compelling subject. The conjunction of wireless and mass popular science, Lodge concluded, stood to bring to an end the whole long history of human error and conflict. Partly thanks to its cultivation in the British Empire, "the ether welds the worlds together into a cosmic system of law and order."[5]

Sentiments like Lodge's were by no means hard to find in the heady days of the early 1920s. Yet when it came to the nascent enterprise of broadcasting, they posed profound questions. And, given that powerful individuals and companies were already proposing to launch broadcasting ventures, those questions had to be answered urgently. Two problems loomed especially large for the constitution of this peculiar new endeavor. One was economic viability. Both the initial costs and the continuing expenses of broadcasting were going to be substantial. Transmitters, aerials, and studios must be erected, and staff trained and paid; there would inevitably be fees for copyright and performance rights licenses too. The capital costs alone were likely to be well over £100,000, and in fact by 1925 experience would show that this was an underestimate. By then the enterprise of broadcasting required at least £600,000 in annual revenue (roughly $30 million in today's money) to be viable.[6] It was not easy to see how costs of this

magnitude could be met, given that there was no way to restrict access
to the signal to paying customers. One possibility was advertising. But
the Post Office, which enjoyed jurisdiction by virtue of its control of
wireless telegraphy, was wary of replicating what it saw as the vulgar
commercialism already apparent on American radio. On the other
hand, however, direct state funding seemed almost as inappropriate,
as it would imply political control of the new medium.

The second problem, inseparable from the first, was interference.
In the United States, the proliferation of stations in competition with
each other was already leading to severe mutual interference in major
cities. With several transmitters all seeking to dominate the one permitted wavelength, the prospect was of a mutually destructive "ether
chaos." That prospect haunted officials in London, who were acutely
conscious that their country was far smaller and more densely popu-
lated than the United States. In common with their American counterparts, they believed chaos to be a danger implicit in the physics of
the ether itself.

Two principles, then, were axiomatic for the coming British broadcasting regime: that the state must forestall chaotic interference by
restricting the number of broadcasters, ideally to one; and that that
broadcaster must be neither crassly commercial nor overtly controlled
by the state. In both respects the hallowed openness and democracy
of the medium would become central issues.

Behind the scenes, these debates over finance and control raged
with quiet intensity through the summer of 1922. Several companies
were keen to proceed with transmitting stations. Some, indeed, already
had them. Marconi, the dominant player in the industry since its formation by Guglielmo Marconi himself in 1897, had operated one at
Writtle, an Essex village just west of Chelmsford, since 1920, and it had
put out broadcasts (mainly of gramophone records) since February
1922. From then until its final transmission in January 1923, its star
was Peter P. Eckersley, a brilliant wireless engineer and a natural performer. Eckersley more or less invented the semi-formal radio "talk"
that was to become a mainstay of the BBC in midcentury. Marconi also
had another experimental station, 2LO, in its London headquarters.

Metropolitan Vickers ("Metrovick"), a heavy engineering conglomerate with vast facilities in Manchester, had its own transmitting station there, and wanted to build one in Slough, within reach of London. By mid-1922, the Post Office had received over twenty applications for similar operations. It deferred them all with the explanation that "the ether is already full." But something had to be done. Each manufacturer was protective of its own patented technologies and none trusted the others. Yet they could not be put off forever, and unless some agreement could be reached, their signals would surely interfere and chaos would result.[7]

In the autumn, the government announced a resolution. One broadcaster would come into existence. It would be named the British Broadcasting Company (not, it should be noted, the British Broadcasting *Corporation*—that came later). It would be formed as a combine of the radio manufacturers, and its income would come from listeners themselves. In the first place, they would have to pay a royalty on every receiver they bought; this tax would pay for the initial building of transmitters and studios. In the second, they would be required to buy licenses in order to use their receivers. Its revenue would fund the running costs of broadcasting, and the requirement would therefore be ongoing. This second idea would become central to—indeed, definitive of—British broadcasting for the rest of the twentieth century and beyond. It tied listener and broadcaster into a kind of contract, such that the broadcaster undertook to furnish a "public service," autonomous of commercial or political interests, while the listener undertook to contribute a fair share to sustain that service. But when it was enacted in late 1922, this exchange was unproven. Its fate hung on a simple but unanswerable question: how many citizens would honor the contract?

Citizens who "listened in" without buying a license represented a potentially fatal problem for Britain's broadcasting system. Indeed, this had been recognized from the outset, at the very first of the meetings in which the license policy had been hashed out. Conducted between the rival manufacturers at the neutral ground of London's Institution of Electrical Engineers, the meeting had been chaired by the Institution's president, Frank Gill. Gill knew that if broadcasting were to avoid the peril of ether chaos and become a thriving "service," then the manufacturers would have to swallow their suspicions of each other. The central obstacles to achieving this, he noted in his agenda, were three: patents; protectionism; and what he called "piracy." The first two terms were obvious enough. Forming a single broadcaster would require Marconi, Metrovick, and their fellows to allow each other access to their proprietary devices and "know-how." And a royalty on receivers would necessitate a controversial ban on unauthorized sets. But the third term was new. When Gill noted a risk of "piracy," what he had in mind was not a problem of rival transmitters. Rather, he was referring to the possibility that people would "listen in" to the proposed broadcaster without paying for licenses. This was a real danger, given that there was no way to detect or police the practice of listening. Would conscience alone (plus a certain peer pressure) prod people to pay up? In practice, the proposed system rested on the high-stakes wager that it would. The fate of a new medium would depend on Britons' sense of fair play.

"Broadcast licences" went on sale to the general public in autumn 1922 at 10 shillings each (the equivalent, very roughly, of about £60–£100 today, or $100–$170). Citizens were expected to buy them every year from then on, at their local Post Offices. In principle, they were rather restrictive documents. They authorized their holders only to use BBC-approved receivers to "listen in" to BBC transmissions. They did not permit the use of non-approved equipment, nor other listening; they implied that tweaking one's set was inappropriate. And they explicitly authorized Post Office inspectors to enter one's home to ensure that these conditions were properly observed. That was a major presumption, and it was included for good reason. The Post Office had estimated that 200,000 licenses would be bought in the first year. The BBC's future depended on that estimate being accurate. But the whole scheme, with its overtones of protectionism and monopoly, had already aroused substantial opposition in Parliament and the press. Nobody knew how docile the public would be. The threat of license inspectors—which was in truth a largely empty one—was all that could be done to encourage their compliance. If it failed, and the British public became a nation of listener pirates, then the BBC was doomed.

IT WAS IN this context that John Reith arrived to manage the new company. The workload in its early days, he found, was "almost overwhelming." The demands came in relentlessly. Some concerned the myriad technical questions that had to be answered. In February 1923, Reith recruited Peter Eckersley, the engineer who had made such a success out of Marconi's Writtle station, to deal with these. As the company's first chief engineer, Eckersley became responsible for making sure that the system's new transmitters were built and operated correctly, without interfering with rivals like the Air Ministry. He must also find some way to stop amateurs from interfering with the BBC's own signal. And Reith characteristically instructed him at their first meeting that he should learn to dress better. Other questions, meanwhile, were less technical but equally essential to deal with. Reith faced endless negotiations over copyright and performing rights, continuous conflicts over patents, and long talks with groups representing actors, theater managers, and news companies.

Through all this the company's existence remained fragile. It was, as Eckersley observed, "nobody's child and everybody's whipping boy."[8] The press loathed it, and parliamentarians were often suspicious. So it had little to fall back on when its financial state proved to be critical. Sales of broadcast licenses had lagged badly, such that by the time Reith arrived the crisis was already looming. By early 1923, only 75,000 had been bought, meaning that tens—and more probably hundreds—of thousands of Britons were now "pirates." Soon the Postmaster General himself had let slip that there might be 500,000 of them, and by 1925 the American magazine *Radio Broadcast* was estimating the number of listener pirates at 2.5 million. The government was considering a sentence of twelve months in prison for the offense, it claimed. The central problem was not punishment, however, but detection. And because listening in could not be prevented or detected technologically, that was a political problem, defined in terms of categories of privacy and state access that had acquired fundamental significance in the British constitution. To issue search warrants wantonly, allowing state officials into people's homes on no evidential grounds, would arouse "a tremendous antagonism."[9]

Yet worse still was at hand. Thousands had noticed a loophole in the law—a loophole that threatened to make policing, however intrusive, futile. They realized that it was possible to circumvent much of the cost of the license system without overtly turning pirate. All the listener had to do was declare himself an "experimenter."

In order to gain parliamentary approval for the BBC, the Postmaster General had had to make a critically important concession to anti-protectionist MPs. One of their complaints about the prospective system was that the restrictions it would impose on sets and practices would prevent amateur radio experimenters from researching. Thousands of these amateurs existed by 1922, and they had certainly made pivotal contributions to the advance of radio. Marconi himself was their archetype. At a time when the British public commonly believed technology to be critical to their nation's future, but when a generation of scientifically trained experts had been lost in the trenches, the fate of the empire itself might lie in the hands of these people. So the Postmaster General had bowed to science and the national good. He had guaranteed that an older license, long issued to wireless hobbyists, would remain viable alongside the broadcast license. This now became known as the "experimenter's licence." Although it cost the same as a broadcast license, it permitted the holder to build a receiver out of parts, and to use it in unpredictable ways. "Experimenters" could therefore become listeners without paying the substantial royalty to the BBC that was charged on every ready-made receiver. And rumors abounded that the freedom to select components also made for better-quality sets than the hoipolloi could buy.

As broadcasting came into operation, the number of self-proclaimed experimenters in the land rocketed. In early 1922, about 7,000 experimenters' licenses had been in effect. By January 1923—only two months after the system had gone on the air—the number of applications had passed 30,000 and was fast approaching 50,000. The BBC warned that without a huge increase in the experimenter's fee, *every* British listener would soon be claiming to be an experimenter. The applications process collapsed under the strain. At the same time, the number of broadcast licenses lagged badly behind early hopes, and the market for BBC-stamped receivers slumped. A new Postmaster General, Neville Chamberlain, was forced to call a halt. From now on, Chamberlain announced, no more experimenter's licenses would be issued until the Post Office could be sure that they were going to *true* experimenters.

The extent of the problem was made clear in March 1923, when wireless manufacturers and experts met to discuss it. As the press reported, the "craze for 'broadcasting'" showed no signs of lessening, but the need to solve "the problems of its organization" was becoming "daily more urgent." The participants unanimously condemned "the broadcast 'pirate'—the man who makes his own listening-in set and does not pay the licence." But few were prepared to condemn experimenters. Indeed, many prized them above broadcasting itself. "It is the experimenter who is the person who counts in wireless development," said Leslie McMichael, secretary of the amateurs' umbrella group, the Radio Society of Great Britain. McMichael estimated their numbers at 20,000 and growing fast, and cautioned against cynical assumptions that they were in truth merely listening to the BBC on the cheap. In fact, he suggested, "experimenters do not like broadcasting because it interferes with their own experiments and transmission."[10] The problem for the BBC and Post Office was therefore this: unless pirates could be distinguished from experimenters, action against the former would be politically impossible. The fate of British broadcasting now rested on devising some mechanism for telling experimenters and pirates apart.

Needless to say, this was never going to be an easy problem to solve. Reliably distinguishing who in the general population may discover something useful at some future point—and therefore qualify as an experimenter—was and is a delicate task. It would be all the harder when applied to a field that was itself new, turbulent, and fast-changing. And it became almost impossible when a critical press was lying in wait to exploit the claim of everyman to be a potential inventor in order to combat a competitor for their readers' attentions. Initially, the Post Office had tried to deal with the problem by ranking people as experimenters if they constructed their own receivers, and this had seemed reasonable because prior to mid-1922 constructing a set was intricate technical work. But by the autumn of that year so-called pirate firms had sprung up across the country, selling parts and instructions that made the task easy. Almost anyone could now put together a receiver. That rendered the Post Office's initial criterion nonsensical. Pirate firms made it impossible to identify pirate listeners.

Coming up with some new rule to make this crucial discrimination proved frustratingly difficult. No interested party—not the BBC, not the Post Office, not the radio industry, and certainly not the amateur population—was prepared to run the political risk of articulating and policing any one principle. After all, it would inevitably involve denying the title of experimenter to a major tranche of the population. Post Office engineers even sorted 30,000 applications for experimenter's licenses into sixteen social categories, hoping that a pattern would emerge. But none did. As one BBC official ruefully put it, it might be possible in principle to save the company from the problem of pirate listening, but only at a political cost so high that it would be destroyed anyway.

A second new Postmaster General, the Conservative William Joynson-Hicks (known as "Jix"), now brought matters to a head. No friend to state monopolies, Jix was skeptical of the BBC and mooted establishing a rival corporation to compete with it. The crisis of pirate listening gave him the opportunity to appoint a committee to review the broadcasting system in general. Such committees would later become regular events, not least because from 1927 the BBC's charter would come up for renewal every ten years. But Jix's was no matter of routine. The very enterprise of broadcasting was on the point of collapse, and the BBC felt under mortal threat.

When Sir Frederick Sykes called his panel to order in late spring

1923, his central concern therefore had to be the problem of distinguishing listener pirates from experimenters. Sykes, a Unionist MP and son-in-law of the terminally ill prime minister Bonar Law, had been a pioneer of the Royal Flying Corps in World War I, in which capacity he had established a track record of effective but sometimes rebarbative management of a radical new technology. His quarrels with Sir Hugh Trenchard had dogged the transformation of the RFC into the fully autonomous Royal Air Force, and although Sykes became chief of staff for the new service, Trenchard and his ally, Winston Churchill, soon saw to it that he was sidelined. His appointment now signaled a willingness to entertain radical options, and added to the uncertainties of the company. But Reith managed to get himself appointed to the committee too, after a personal appeal to Jix. There he carried out a determined defensive action to uphold the BBC's position. In the end, he prevailed. The inquiry gave a disappointed Jix no grounds to curtail the monopoly. But it did provide something almost as significant: a victory for the citizen scientist over the broadcaster.

Despairing of the prospect of formulating any viable rule for identifying experimenters, Sykes deduced that the system itself must give way. The experimenter's license would be abolished. It would be replaced temporarily by a "constructor's licence," which carried none of the same connotations of scientific authority. But that license must in turn be phased out before long, along with the royalty on equipment and the protection it entailed. There must then be only one license for all, along with an open market in receivers. Only this would relieve the Post Office of "the difficult and somewhat invidious duty of determining whether applicants are genuine experimenters or not." The popular experimenters had won, because their practices came to be incorporated into the definition of normal listening. Yet the tension between the BBC and popular experiment would endure beneath the surface.

Meanwhile, the authorities too won an important victory. From now on, they could focus all their attention on the newly unambiguous population of pirate listeners.

———

THE SYKES POLICY met with immediate success. The new constructor's license produced a dramatic increase in license sales—they leaped from 80,000 to 414,000 in ten days, a surge that indicated how prevalent dubious experimenters had been. Yet while the committee might have removed the problem of experimenters, it had had little to suggest about the still pressing issue of harder-core pirates. Pirate listening remained the biggest threat broadcasting faced in the UK. Repeated advertising campaigns would be mounted against them over decades. But the decision to stop worrying about experimenters did give the Post Office one important opportunity in the struggle against pirate listening. It left it free to create the first anti-pirate technology of the information age.

In the 1920s, the Post Office and BBC alike assumed that unlicensed listeners would cause so-called oscillation interference. This occurred when poorly rigged equipment underwent a form of electronic feedback, making the aerial into a transmitter. Oscillation produced a distinctive "howl" in the ether that crippled the ability of others in the neighborhood to listen to broadcast programs. Before Sykes, the authorities blamed both pirates and experimenters, but for different reasons. Experimenters were presumably competent, but they still might cause oscillation now and again in the course of their experimentation. But pirate listeners were assumed to use non-approved parts and to fiddle with their sets too, without the competence that experimenters presumably possessed. Some even caused resonance deliberately, using the feedback loop in a bid to boost volume. After all, pirates were presumably anti-social types: the kind of people who declined to pay their share for broadcasting would not care about their neighbors' listening either. So if the Post Office equipped a van with a directional antenna and used it to zero in on an oscillating aerial, it was simple logic to conclude that the owner would probably be a pirate listener—especially after Sykes, when experimenters were no longer at issue. That symbol of British broadcasting, the detector van, took its origin from this reasoning. The first of them were put on the streets in the mid-1920s. Whether detector vans ever really worked would be the subject of much public speculation, and for a long time there were in any case only two vehicles operating. What was not speculative was the persistence of the piracy they were meant to deter.

LISTENER PIRACY POSED more than merely financial problems, severe as those were. Another implication, present from the early days, was that pirate listeners listened *in different ways* from regular, licensed citizens. This was a critically important point because the BBC saw itself as pursuing a mission. Its purpose, Reith believed, was cultural improvement. Indeed, for Reith and his followers this was the point of the corporation itself and the monopoly it enjoyed. It certainly tried to live up to the ideal of a national voice, for example by upholding the basic rhythms of the Church calendar in its programming: Easter, Christmas, Remembrance Day, and, of course, Sundays in general. But more than that, as its staff liked to say, it sought to give the British public slightly better than what it thought it wanted. The BBC existed to "keep on the upper side of public taste." Implicit in this noble ambition was an expectation for what the practice of listening should be. Pirate listening cast that expectation into jeopardy. It imperiled not just the corporation's balance sheet but its very point.[11]

Skepticism about the Reithian commitment to cultural improvement comes easily to twenty-first-century sensibilities, and it was evident at the time. But there is ample evidence that the effort found a degree of welcome acceptance beyond the elites. Writing groups proliferated in the industrial Midlands, and accessible classical music reached working-class listeners through their wireless sets. It appealed to an audience that already existed: cinemas already played classical music, after all, and many households had pianos. In 1938, a survey found that half the BBC's working-class audience tuned in to listen to this music.[12] What was not so clear was *how* they listened.

Listening to the BBC was supposed to be a refined and refining activity. Official publications were liable to exalt the "duties" or "work" expected of the listener. Listening was not something to be done

while in the throes of housework or child care—as late as 1954, the
BBC was still inclined to "deplore" people who treated listening as
"an accompaniment to other activities in the home." The ether, Reith
had said, was a serious matter, and to use it for mere entertainment
would be a "prostitution of its powers and an insult to the character
and intelligence of the people."[13] The *BBC Handbook* regularly advised
listeners to devote that intelligence to its programming as earnestly as
the corporation itself did. They should "cultivate the art of using their
wireless receivers intelligently and artistically, so that the immense
care and trouble that are taken in compiling and presenting the programmes shall achieve their true direction and effect." Not the least
part of this "art" was selectivity. "There would be something quite
wrong with Broadcasting," continued the official guide, "if any individual listener really enjoyed the whole programme from afternoon to
midnight."[14] Any particular listener had a responsibility *not* to listen to
programs indiscriminately. Better to sit in silence, the BBC felt, than
to listen improperly and negate the cultural effects of the programs
one did appreciate.

   This notion of listening as work had an enormously important
counterpart for the BBC's output: the concept of "balance." A bal-
anced program was a schedule in which string quartets, educational
talks, sports commentaries, and dance music all found a place, but
no interest predominated. Different groups, many of them "minori-
ties" (enthusiasts for the sport of fencing, say, or lovers of medieval
architecture), would find interest in its offerings. Balance was what
melded the nation's different "publics," as Reith called them, into one
audience. But if left to private companies, the BBC claimed—and
this claim commanded widespread respect—then the *actual* range of
programming available to those publics would be drastically reduced,
because all stations would target the same audience for the same
advertisers. The BBC's monopoly was thus essential, paradoxically, to
ensure variety and representation. It therefore came to assert that this
quality in programming was essential to the use of the ether for the
public good, and that it could only be achieved by a non-commercial
monopoly. Although in part forced on the BBC by its unique position,

balance became something of an article of faith within the corporation until at least World War II. It remained the crux of the debate
about the nature and future of broadcasting for decades.

The corporation was aware, of course, that in reality listening might
not come up to its standards. While it is true that it made no systematic
effort to investigate and reflect listeners' actual preferences until commercial rivals forced it to, that does not mean that the BBC ignored
the complexities of listening. But it sought to improve its listeners'
behavior, not to cleave to what it already was. It tried to make listening
more active, critical, selective, earnest, and effective. It spent a good
deal of time devising standards, and issued pamphlets by the million
detailing them. In all likelihood every British household encountered
at least one. In the 1930s the BBC also collaborated with groups like
the Left Book Club in attempts to make listening into a group activity,
alongside engaged reading and political reflection. The same impulse
appeared in a more formal cast in the corporation's education and
adult education programming, which was meant to be listened to
en masse in classrooms. There, a particular practice of listening—
focused, silent, attentive—was supposed to become ingrained. It was a
trained skill: the aural equivalent of close reading. At much the same
time, of course, critics like Q. D. ("Queenie") Leavis were advocating the close reading of canonical literature to fight what they saw
as the commercial publishing industry's corrosive effects on public
taste. The BBC's approach to listening bore marked similarities, and
indeed in the 1930s–1950s reading and writing groups often adopted
forms of sociability that they had encountered on wireless shows like
The Brains Trust.[15]

The other major concern about pirate listeners was that they might
listen not just in some other way, but to *something else*. Casual, indiscrim-
inate, half-attentive listening was to be discouraged all the more when
the listener might flit between different stations. This would destroy
balance. And despite the BBC's nominal monopoly on broadcasting,
such choices were always possible. Indeed, there was a sense in which
using one's BBC receiver to listen to non-BBC stations made one into
a pirate listener, because a clause on the broadcast license asserted a

restriction to BBC transmissions. This was, of course, unenforceable in a liberal society. But it was nevertheless present, and it articulated the ideal of the Post Office and BBC themselves.

THE BRITISH BROADCASTING Company survived the immediate crisis of pirate listening, but it did not endure much longer. In 1926, a new set of hearings chaired by the Earl of Crawford led to the company being closed down. The government replaced it with a new kind of institution—one as unusual as the enterprise it was to pursue. In January 1927 this new body, the British Broadcasting Corporation—today's BBC—came into existence.

It would be easy to miss the significance of the change from company to corporation. The new BBC inherited the premises, equipment, and, to a large extent, role of the old. Above all, it inherited its personnel, led by the defining figure of Reith, now newly knighted. Sir John's principled Presbyterian convictions had not weakened, and as his influence grew, so contemporaries came to portray him as a mixture of Mussolini and Praisegod Barbon, the stereotypical political Puritan of Cromwell's age.[16] (Churchill would later memorably dub him "that Wuthering Height.") But the distinctions between company and corporation were nevertheless real and consequential.

The new corporation was a strange beast at the outset. It was established by royal charter, rather than by conventional incorporation. This was done largely to invest it with an aura of dignity and autonomy from party politics, and made it an unusual institution. The charter defined its financial basis in the license fee, its constitution, and its responsibilities, to be carried out under the oversight of five governors and Reith, who became Director General. But it did not expressly confirm that the BBC had a monopoly on broadcasting. And it limited the new institution's lifetime. It was to endure ten years, beginning on January 1, 1927. In future generations, this combination of silence on the central issue and the need for regular renewal would reliably trigger a crisis for the corporation at the middle of every decade.[17]

The new body was no longer a manufacturers' combine structured around patent-pooling. It had no shareholders apart from the state. It was thus detached from the profit motive at a fundamental, institutional level. Instead, "public service," long a prized concept for Reith himself, took on an explicitly defining role. The BBC remained the sole authorized domestic broadcaster, framing that service around transmission to a putatively harmonious nation. But whereas the old company had tried to deny being a monopoly, and the charter declined to identify the new corporation as one, the BBC soon embraced and affirmed the principle. Its monopoly status was precisely what enabled it to carry out its mission, Reith asserted. That mission was the improving of British culture through broadcasting. And it was fitting, therefore, that it would continue to be financed by a broadcast license levied on all who listened to its programs. In this new form the BBC shed some of the opposition that the older company had encountered, and took on the mantle of a nation's voice. It became a success.

Indeed, the BBC was soon being hailed as the archetype of a new kind of institution: the public interest corporation, or public corporation for short. Autonomous from both the state and private industry, but constituted similarly to a joint-stock company, a public corporation served the common good in a domain that it dominated, free of the inefficiencies of competition. It therefore combined, apparently, the best of all worlds. There had been experiments on such lines before, notably the Forestry Commission and the Port of London Authority. But it was the BBC—with the Central Electricity Board, also founded in 1927, in second place—that was from now on always seen as the archetypal case. Indeed, Reith occasionally claimed to have invented the term "public corporation" himself, as part of his rearguard defense before the Sykes Committee in 1923. And almost a decade later, in May 1932, he would proclaim its triumph in a speech to the BBC staff as the corporation took possession of its new headquarters at Broadcasting House. There was much more at stake in the BBC than broadcasting alone, Reith now declared: the institution represented "a new and vitally important experiment in the management of a public utility service." And with the experiment succeeding, "before so many years are out, you will find public services such as the

Post Office, which are now run entirely by the government, and others which are run by private enterprise, taken over by bodies constituted somewhat similarly to the BBC." He repeated this prophecy in a lecture at the Royal Institution, and the press gave it substantial coverage. It presaged, Fleet Street believed, a "fresh drive to develop the public corporation principle under the National Government's auspices."[18] In the late 1920s and 1930s a number of fields of endeavor would indeed be brought under similar kinds of control, including London's transport system (under the London Passenger Transport Board) and air travel (under the British Overseas Airways Corporation). As the London School of Economics scholar of law and politics William Robson put it in 1937, the BBC had proved to be "an invention in the sphere of social science no less remarkable than the invention of radio transmission in the sphere of natural science."

Strictly speaking, a public corporation was not the same thing as a public utility. But the two were generally associated with each other. Reith himself stated that broadcasting should and must be a "public utility"—a phrase used in the original company's memorandum of association—before he could have seen it as a public corporation.[19] He meant that wavelengths were a scarce "public property" that must be employed for the common good (he added that for this reason the BBC should be protected from copyright claims from the recording industry). Public utilities were generally assumed to be natural monopolies of this kind, and Reith's position made broadcasting fit that bill. Broadcasting also conformed to the precedents set by other public enterprises as a feasible response to the threat of "chaos." The Port of London Authority had been launched in 1908 after revelations of the "chaos" and neglect caused to common waterways by a competitive docks industry. The electricity distribution sector too had developed in "chaotic" fashion, until the Central Electricity Board was created. Ports and electricity supply shared the same characteristics as radio: they centered on a shared resource, and were seemingly poor candidates for either unregulated laissez-faire or full state control. The founding of the BBC was therefore a response not just to ether chaos but to economic chaos. In a world of vertiginous economic instability, the public corporation seemed to offer the way forward.

For its advocates, the public corporation combined the best of capitalist efficiency with the rationalization and public service demanded in the modern age. Some saw it as reviving the community spirit of the old medieval guilds, but the consensus was more that it was an institution of the future. It also appealed to the precious conviction held by so many Britons, then as now, that British values were uniquely qualified to create a *via media*. Unlike rampant American corporate capitalism, public corporations could follow the common good rather than the bottom line; unlike the state ventures looming in Fascist Italy, they were autonomous and imbued with empirical common sense. They rendered both nationalization and ruthless laissez-faire capitalism obsolete. The "line of evolution" was clear: across the country, countless enterprises, from small water boards to the largest state enterprise of all, the Post Office, should and would be transformed into public corporations like the BBC. In place of competition, the Labour Party's rising intellectual star Hugh Dalton declared, they would constantly be driven to improve by being held to a "new and more scientific" standard: that of a public informed about performance by "the searchlight of published knowledge." The rise to favor of the concept from 1927 was sudden and universal. "Perhaps no feature in recent thought in applied economics," the young American scholar Lincoln Gordon would soon report, "is more striking than the rapidity with which it has gained favour among almost all sections of opinion." (Gordon would go on to become the major administrator of the Marshall Plan after World War II.) Public corporations, he added, were now backed by "intelligent opinion without exception." And they had begun to arise elsewhere, too: in the United States (the Tennessee Valley Authority), Canada, Australia, and New Zealand.

So Reith's corporation was apparently to be the vanguard of a new political economy, perhaps even a new society. No less a figure than John Maynard Keynes confirmed as much. Having resigned a Treasury position in protest at the heavy reparations imposed on Germany after the war, Keynes had returned to a life of writing columns, supporting the Liberal Party, and lecturing at Cambridge, where his formidable presence attracted a cadre of economists calling themselves "the Circle." His *leitmotif* in the late 1920s was the theme, not of nationalization per se, but of what he called "management." And he pointed to the rise of the BBC to suggest that thanks to this concept the twentieth century must inevitably see "the end of *laissez faire.*" His characteristically resonant speech on this topic, delivered originally in Oxford in 1924 and revised prior to publication two years later, was the closest Keynes came before the late 1930s to delineating the practical scope of his managerial concept. It placed great faith in the disinterest and scientific rationality of public managers, and suggested that the processes of history were leading inevitably to this new, mixed form of life. *The General Theory of Employment, Interest and Money* (1935–36) would eventually extend the idea to the economy as a whole, articulating the grand synthesis that would become Keynesianism.[20]

In the meantime, in 1928 Keynes also worked behind the scenes to draft the Liberal Party's influential report on *Britain's Industrial Future*. The report put the matter in stark terms. The public corporation had rendered all distinction between "individualism" and "socialism" obsolete, it declared. No longer must society face "a choice between nailing to the mast the Jolly Roger of piratical, cut-throat individualism, each man for himself and the devil take the rest, or, on the other hand, the Servile Society of a comprehensive State Socialism." According to the dominant figure in mid-twentieth-century economics, the BBC was the right answer both to social ownership and to social piracy.

THE FORMATIVE YEARS of broadcasting in the 1920s thus generated three major conundrums, none of them easily resolved. They would continue to dog the enterprise long after the end of the decade.

In the first place, broadcasting brought to the fore a problem of citizenship and science. The practice of experiment had a long history in Britain, extending back to the seventeenth century and the same period as the Glorious Revolution. As a result, a proud tradition existed associating civic virtue and independence of thought with the practice of experimental research.[21] In the immediate postwar years, radio enjoyed mass popularity as a subject of experiments by lay people, and they laid claim to this tradition. The initiative to create a public broadcaster funded by licenses cut athwart this ideal, and aroused intense public controversy—about science as well as about the new medium. The amateur radio community retreated from prominence as that controversy receded. It is often assumed that it became a harmless culture of "ham" enthusiasts—a term apparently adopted from the United States, where it may have originated in an analogy to amateur stage actors. Hams were confined to the fateful shortwave band under 200 meters. (Amateurs were assigned this band because it was believed to be useless; in fact, it turned out to be vital for long-distance work.) But they did not die out. And with them survived a distinctly skeptical stance toward the public broadcaster. That stance put broadcasting in Britain at loggerheads with a vision of science itself—and therefore humanity's future—as free, open, and competitive. From then on, tensions between popular science and a single, public service broadcaster would never quite disappear.

In the second place, the constitution of broadcasting brought into question listening as a practice. It was not yet a subject of research— we shall see shortly how that came about. But it was a matter for serious concern. The BBC's mission of cultural improvement implied that listening be critical, engaged, and discriminating. The license system was thought to encourage this, and the broadcaster devoted major effort to elevating standards of listening among its audience. But pirate listeners were incorrigible. They set up receivers without paying license fees, and roamed the ether looking for other signals. Not only did they endanger the public broadcaster by withholding its funding; they were also, it was feared, anarchic in their listening. They might listen in different ways and to different stations. Or they might simply leave the set on while they did not really *listen* at all. Either way, they posed a problem not just of listening, but of knowing about listening. How could an authority gain such knowledge, and how reliable was it once obtained?

2

ETHEREAL ENTERPRISE

The founders of the BBC thought of the ether as a natural monopoly. The 1930s showed that they were wrong. The ether's most significant physical property turned out to be not its limited capacity, after all, but its boundlessness. Radio signals might fade over long distances, and they could certainly suffer interference, but there was no way to stop them short at household walls, city limits, or national borders. That was why pirate listening would continue to be a major problem for decades: there was no way, short of totalitarianism, to police access to the ether. No less significantly, it also meant that broadcasting was doomed to be an international practice as long as it was a wireless one. That meant that the central principle of British broadcasting was something of a myth. From the transmitter's perspective, the BBC might well be a monopoly. But it was not—and could never be—a monopoly from the listener's, simply because radio signals did not stop at the cliffs of Dover.

Britons had been able to hear commercial broadcasting from the Continent long before the BBC was even formed. In the early thirties, such broadcasting proliferated. Before long, stations across Europe were offering Britain regular, scheduled programming. Far from being supplanted by the public service, commercial broadcasting blossomed into a major enterprise. It was above board, popular, and successful. Its managers and technicians proved that international popular radio could be a practical proposition, and they discovered how to make it work. They also proved that it could be very lucrative indeed.

IN THE 1920S and early 1930s, the scope of experimentation in wireless was not limited to fiddling with resistors and valves. It extended simultaneously to financial, organizational, and even cultural initiatives intended to provide for some kind of sustainable system. It is possible to see the history of broadcasting between the wars as a series of experiments of this broader kind, ranging from the early Writtle trials, through the British Broadcasting Company, to tests of wired broadcasting systems in the last days before the outbreak of World War II. Most of the ventures of the period that are the subject of this chapter—ventures in international commercial broadcasting and local "relay" transmission—originated in similar experiments. The impression that a consensus rapidly coalesced around the BBC and excluded further experimentation is as groundless as the notion that it was experienced as a monopoly. Within the BBC itself, indeed, real and substantial divergences continued. Some even questioned whether the corporation should remain devoted to wireless at all.

The first attempt to avoid national restrictions by broadcasting from a ship was one of these experiments. The *Daily Mail* was the instigator. In 1928 the *Mail*, which had always been keen on technological gimmickry, chartered a sailing vessel named the *Ceto* and fitted it with a transmitter, hoping to broadcast music to Britain's holidaymakers from outside territorial waters. In the event, the swaying of the ship made this impossible, so the transmitter was replaced by a massive loudspeaker array. The *Ceto* then voyaged around coastal resorts from Scotland to the west country, with a shipboard compère, one Stephen Williams, blasting music at bemused sunbathers from a few hundred yards out. It may have been a technical failure, but it was a publicity coup. And from then on upstart rivals would repeatedly come to light, although they would generally be smaller-scale and landlocked. Newspapers reported several occasions in the 1930s when so-called pirate stations on the mainland were detected; one of them actually billed itself as "The Old Pirate." A steady trickle of these incidents would continue uninterrupted from the days of the *Ceto* into the 1960s.[1]

Above and beyond piecemeal ventures like these, in the late 1920s and 1930s more substantial and enduring commercial broadcasters sprang up in profusion. The most important of them—and usually the only ones now remembered—were Radio Normandy and Radio Luxembourg. But they were far from alone. In both numerical and geographical terms, the sheer range of stations that a householder in the south of England could tune into in the thirties was remarkable. Signals came from towns and cities across Europe, from the heartland of Spain to the provinces of Yugoslavia. Some could claim a heritage older than the BBC itself: the first scheduled incoming broadcasts had come from the Netherlands as early as 1919, with sponsorship from, naturally, the *Daily Mail*.[2] Others were newly built and could boast the latest equipment, sometimes more modern than the BBC's own. None was by any means surreptitious. The radio receivers that Britons bought in huge numbers had the stations' wavelengths engraved on their dials, and some even assigned them preset buttons.[3] From 1934, listeners could find their schedules published in *Radio Pictorial*—a weekly counterpart to the BBC's *Radio Times*. And because sponsors sometimes underwrote the same programming on different transmitters, they could be forgiven if they thought of commercial radio as constituting almost a rival network.

As the closest Continental country, France was an obvious location for commercial broadcasting into Britain. Among all the Continental stations Radio Paris had the longest continuous history, having started operations back in 1921. In 1925, its Eiffel Tower transmitter had been the source of a well-known broadcast organized by the ex-RAF officer Leonard Plugge with sponsorship by Selfridges, the huge London department store. Later the station would be associated with Plugge's International Broadcasting Company (IBC), until the *Sunday Referee* newspaper supplanted Plugge in what proved a short-lived bid to expand into radio. In the end the French state would take over the transmitter for its own public service. Close by in the French capital, Poste Parisien was floated as an independent operation in 1929, having initially been set up by a newspaper. It had one of the most powerful transmitters in Europe and a studio on the Champs-Elysées. Beyond Paris, Radio Toulouse was another station to broadcast commercial programs regularly from an early date. It used an illegally powerful transmitter, and its interference with the BBC's Sheffield station led to some of the first attempts to regulate cross-border broadcasts. Once again the IBC employed this station, until the erstwhile BBC engineer Peter Eckersley displaced it in 1937 with his own venture. The IBC also made use of Radio Côte d'Azur, which operated under a number of names. Yet another station, Radio-Lyon, was an enterprise of the wily politician Pierre Laval, an occasional prime minister who would end up shot as a collaborator after World War II. Lyon worked with another London concern, Broadcast Advertising Ltd., to organize its English programming.

Beyond France, a wide swathe of other countries also hosted stations. Radio Athlone in the Republic of Ireland was operated in short succession by an Australian magazine and Plugge's IBC. In Spain, EAQ Madrid was a shortwave broadcaster intended to develop a Spanish international service, but the IBC exploited it too, setting up an "IBC Empire Service" in cheeky competition with the BBC's Empire Service. (In the event, Madrid issued IBC programming for only half an hour in the middle of Sunday nights, and the station was suspended during the Spanish Civil War, never to revive.) Other transmitters could be found further afield, in Andorra, for example. Perhaps the most distant of all was more than 700 miles from London, in the northern Yugoslav town of Ljubljana (today the capital of Slovenia).[4]

Starting almost from scratch at the end of the 1920s, within a decade these stations created what amounted to a standard modus operandi for transnational broadcasting. There was remarkable consistency in how they functioned. They were also broadly similar in their programming—it is telling that after his stint on the *Ceto* Stephen Williams could work for Radio Paris, Radio Normandy, and Radio Luxembourg with equal facility. Most programs were a quarter radio experimentation. It was the creation of a retired Air Ministry researcher, London Underground engineer, and inventive gadfly named Leonard Plugge (1889–1981).[5] Plugge had emerged from military life in 1922 with the rank of captain in the RAF (although he was no flier), an expertise in aeronautics, and, like many fellow servicemen, a passionate interest in the nascent field of wireless. In the mid-1920s he undertook a series of well-publicized journeys across Europe, carrying radio equipment with him. At first he took the train, but then he drove a sequence of specially equipped radio cars, which he christened "Aether I," "Aether II," and so on; the last of them was to be "Aether VI." His travels took him as far as the road extended—and then, in the muddy mountains of the Balkans, further. On the first of his odysseys he stopped off at the Eiffel Tower to make that Selfridges broadcast, which would long be remembered as a landmark event. On the second he transmitted regular updates from the road itself, relaying them to Britain via the Paris station. By this time he had made himself one of Britain's best known radio amateurs. For many Britons, Plugge personified the individualism and flair of the popular experimenter. He stood for the virtues they thought they were defending against the regime of broadcast licenses and closed-box receivers.

Returning from Europe, Plugge devised a scheme to profit by selling the schedules of overseas radio stations to the British press. The large community of enthusiasts eager to explore the ether made for a ready audience for these schedules, which he realized he could obtain gratis from the various stations. He set up a company, Radio International Publicity Services (RIPS), to compile the information from some forty transmitters, including several in North America. He even sold these details to the BBC, which published them in a magazine called *World Radio* that it had launched to serve the experimenters' community. Plugge then used the profits from RIPS to launch his own programming venture, which he called the International Broadcasting Company. His idea was to take advantage of the contacts he had made on his journeys to coordinate commercial broadcasting through Continental transmitters. Plugge registered the new company in March 1930, and soon after signed a deal with Radio Toulouse to transmit thirty minutes of music on Sunday nights for a record company. He housed the new company in Hallam Street, right next door to the headquarters then being built for the BBC—and this was not the last time he would cock a snook at the corporation.

It seems that the BBC fondly thought that it would enjoy leverage over its upstart rival on account of his contract with *World Radio*.[6] It was wrong. The IBC expanded rapidly, in defiance of BBC wishes. As it did so, it made use of several transmitting stations. But the most consistently successful stood just across the English Channel, in rural Normandy.

In 1931, Plugge was on one of his car trips across northern France when he happened upon a small studio in a coastal town called Fécamp. It had been created some six years earlier by the overseer of the local distillery of Benedictine liqueur. Fernand Le Grand was another of the amateur experimenters (in French, *sans-filistes*) who had sprung up in the twenties. He was now broadcasting commercially as Radio Normandie from a transmitter just outside the town. Plugge immediately saw an opportunity. He did a deal with Le Grand there and then. Announcing the formation of Radio Normandy, the IBC helped Le Grand boost the transmitter by a factor of 10 to 5 kilowatts (and soon increased it again, to 20kW), and organized regular publicity through the *Sunday Referee*. As it began to attract advertisers, so IBC invested more. A 500-foot aerial mast was built, alongside new studio facilities housed in a faux château. Until overtaken by Radio Luxembourg later in the decade, Normandy was the preeminent commercial broadcaster for British listeners.[7]

The IBC encouraged its presenters to give the impression that theirs was a formidable institution, on a par with the BBC. When Reith's corporation created its own orchestras, for example, they announced an "IBC Orchestra" that never really existed. Similarly, when the BBC launched its Empire Service, the IBC responded with announcements for its own almost entirely nonexistent "IBC Empire Service." At first this kind of thing was fantastical. In reality the IBC filled its programs with records, leavening them with U.S. comedians and the odd dose of astrology. But as the 1930s drew on and Plugge's business generated substantial profits, so the representation increasingly approached reality. At its peak the IBC coordinated broadcasting not just from Normandy and Paris but also from Madrid, Valencia, Barcelona, San Sebastian, the Côte d'Azur, Athlone, and Cork. Radio Normandy developed its own outside broadcast operation. Plugge invested in major expansions to the IBC's London headquarters, where the company grew to have a staff of 180. And Plugge himself—by now a Tory MP—became ostentatiously rich. He entertained spectacularly in his palatial London mansion and kept two huge yachts moored at Cannes. (He needed the second vessel, he explained, to furnish spare parts for the first.)

Because of its need to combine London studios with Continental transmitters, the IBC pioneered the use of recording technologies in broadcasting. Prior to about 1930, broadcasting had almost always been a live affair. BBC announcers were inclined to regard this as a virtue, believing that live talks and live music carried conviction—provided they were done with the requisite art, which the BBC labored to inculcate in presenters and speakers. Live broadcasting suited the kind of assiduous listening that the corporation promoted. But the IBC had no such ambitions. It did maintain presenters at Fécamp and broadcast live programs, but its advertisers wanted to control content and presentation themselves, and to feature stars who were never likely to venture out to a bucolic Normandy château. So the company established its own studio in London with which to record programs for transmission from Fécamp. By the late thirties, its recording technologies were in advance of anything the BBC possessed. The company recorded some 5,000 programs before the war broke out, and after 1945 the studio would survive for decades as a major production venue. The Beatles, the Who, and the Rolling Stones would all record there.[8]

What curtailed the IBC's rise was not the Post Office or the BBC, but the outbreak of World War II. The company swiftly switched its Fécamp transmitter to broadcasting for the Allied armies, but before long the French government first requisitioned and then silenced it. The Nazis then put it to use to broadcast propaganda into Britain.

Storms and Allied bombing damaged the station, and after D-Day the retreating Germans destroyed much of what was left. In London, meanwhile, the IBC's equipment was commandeered for BBC use, and the company's headquarters were crippled in the Blitz. The Nazis even sank Plugge's yachts. After the war, Plugge and Le Grand (who had been interned for a while as a collaborator) would make an effort to restart Radio Normandy, but French government opposition made it impossible. In the end, the old broadcaster never revived. Plugge himself tried and failed with other inventions, and drifted between enthusiasms. His last years were lonely and painful—he spent many of them traveling to avoid creditors, and his daughter was brutally murdered in Trinidad by a Black Power gang. He died in Los Angeles in 1981.[9]

Reith remarked with some contempt that the IBC was never a real broadcaster. His dismissive declaration obscured the point, perhaps intentionally. He wanted to make sure that Plugge's group—and others like it—were not given excessive credence by the government in deciding the future of British broadcasting. This it would have to do in 1935–36, before the BBC's charter expired on its tenth anniversary. But although the IBC owned no transmitters, it did make it possible for transmitters to operate. It tied together diverse groups—presenters, experimenters, technicians, corporations, bankers, and performers—to forge a broadcaster. In that sense its very existence alongside the BBC posed questions about the corporation. Plugge's company pioneered the intricate financial and institutional practices that could make a commercial broadcasting enterprise work.

FOR THE MOST part, the Continental stations of the twenties and early thirties were not "pirates"; that is, they were not in breach of any law or even convention. The great exception was Radio Luxembourg.[10] The city-state at the heart of Europe had operated a station since the earliest days of broadcasting, but in the early 1930s, with French financing—and, the British feared, French control—it drastically increased its power, range, and broadcast output. What made the station piratical was its deliberate refusal to acquiesce in an embryonic international regime to regulate the use of the ether for broadcasting. By defying the authority of this regime, Luxembourg demonstrated possibilities that later pirates too would recall and prove keen to exploit. The station challenged head-on the idea that the international community, acting together, could govern the ether at all.

The idea that the ether could and should be regulated internationally was an inheritance from the assumptions of late nineteenth-century diplomacy. Prior to World War I, the great powers had arrived at a broad modus operandi according to which areas of mutual concern would generally be addressed at major conferences. The principle had been applied with apparent success to many areas of culture, from weights and measures to trade, arms regulation, and geopolitics. The outbreak of World War I would of course cast this practice into serious doubt. But by that point the prospect had already arisen of using it to form an international regime for regulating the ether. And that ambition would not only survive the conflict but be strengthened by it.

The effort took its start from measures undertaken in the mid-nineteenth century to oversee wired telegraphy. As early as 1865, international conferences had given rise to an International Telegraph Union, with an administrative bureau based in Switzerland. It was the German government that moved to extend this Union into the new domain of wireless, and it did so in a spirit of national rivalry. Around 1900, Britain's Marconi Company enjoyed global dominance in maritime radio communications. Marconi capitalized on the reach and power of the British Empire by selling complete systems to shipping companies; that is, its equipment would be operated by a Marconi employee on board, and Marconi land stations were instructed to ignore messages sent on other companies' transmitters. It was effectively seeking to become a global monopoly. The first two international Radiotelegraph Conferences, in Berlin in 1903 and 1906, grappled with this attempt. To do so, they articulated two critically important principles: that land receivers must accept messages regardless of the transmitter's manufacturer; and that different systems must not interfere with each other. The distant origins of international radio regulation thus lay in a marriage of convenience between anti-monopolist sentiments, nationalist anxieties about British dominance, and—in third place—concerns about maritime safety. The second meeting then further mandated that nations send details of all public (that is, non-military) maritime stations to be registered at the ITU's bureau at Berne. A central registry would come into existence, allowing in principle for the reconciliation of conflicting claims to particular wavelengths. This was not yet a legal authority, but the possibility that it might become one was clear to all. And having originated in a context of maritime great power competition, its principles would subsequently become fundamental to broadcasting regulation in the new century. Any hopes that Marconi might have entertained of combating them evaporated in 1912 with the irrefutable demonstration of the importance of maritime communications that was the *Titanic* disaster.

The carnage of World War I both changed the meaning of this effort and gave it new impetus. The war generated a determination in many countries to construct a new system of international engagement that would not repeat the failures of the old diplomacy. The resolve led at the grandest political level to the formation of the League of Nations. The dream that wireless might be a harmonizing force, able to eliminate war once and for all, demanded that the same enlightened collaboration be applied to radio, too. So the United States proposed renewing the effort. America wanted an international agreement on wavelengths immediately after the armistice. But the issues remained complex, and it was not until 1927—the year that the BBC was founded—that a conference finally took place to establish such a regime. Held under the chairmanship of Commerce Secretary Herbert Hoover, it set in place a structure for deciding issues of cross-border radio competition that would prevail for decades. It allocated wavebands to particular uses, and recommended that if two stations in different countries competed for the same wavelength, whichever had begun operations and registered first at Berne should have precedence. The Berne registry thus took on for the first time the role of something like a record of priority, akin to those that had existed in

Carpendale as its secretary. In practical terms, too, the BBC became instrumental to the new regime. It helped create a regular procedure for notifying Berne about stations and their wavelengths, which the bureau would then publish. And Eckersley assisted in setting up a monitoring station and laboratory to ensure that stations did not drift from their stated wavelengths.

It is clear why the BBC made these efforts. An internal memo dated as early as 1928 shows that it was already wary of stations in France, Belgium, and the Netherlands.[11] The corporation monitored Continental transmissions assiduously, and made its first formal complaint about foreign competition in 1931, against Radio Normandy. In pressing for a formal and practical regime to police the international airwaves, it was acting out of semi-enlightened self-interest and seeking to target such ventures. It thus proposed that countries be forbidden from establishing transmitters outside their nationally allotted bands if some other nation complained of interference with its legitimate broadcasters, and suggested that all proposed stations must be registered at Berne three months in advance to allow for such complaints to be made. In 1932, Reith's representatives fought to establish this as policy at the fourth major international conference, held in Madrid as the successor to Hoover's convention. The Madrid conference focused precisely on the proliferation of international commercial stations and culminated in the creation, seven years after the IBU, of the first comprehensive international regulatory body, the International Telecommunication Union. It replaced the old International Telegraph Union and the informal alliances that had existed since before World War I, and embraced much of the protocol that Reith's men had championed.[12]

Yet the BBC men failed in the major part of their mission at Madrid. They had wanted to create a binding international agreement against cross-border broadcasting. But sovereign nations were never going to be easy to recruit into such a regime, especially as their proposal would have allowed a country to stop another's transmissions without having to demonstrate that interference was *actually* occurring. In the aftermath, the new Telecommunication Union took care never to presume to ban outright any country from operating on any wavelength. Yet the BBC continued to press for stronger measures. The following year, 1933, another attempt was made in Lucerne to hash out a scheme that might satisfy all parties. By this point it was Radio Luxembourg that attracted peculiar hostility from the British. It did so because of its unusually brazen willingness to flout wavelength allocations—and to do so in order to transmit into Britain.

Carpendale duly mobilized the IBU against the interloper, and at Montreux, a year before Lucerne, the Union denounced the station's "piracy" of a long-wave wavelength. When the IBU was placed in charge of the Lucerne conference, the BBC took the opportunity to press home its attack, and to generalize it. The result was the strongest statement yet against cross-border transmissions. The international body now rejected "any type of programme which is essentially based on the idea of commercial advertising in the international field." More broadly, the IBU condemned "the systematic diffusion of programmes" into another country over the protests of that country's broadcaster, terming it "an 'inadmissible' act from the point of view of good international relations." It was in this strained context that the Lucerne conference drew up the first allocation tables to attach wavelengths not just to countries but to specific stations. Eight nations refused to endorse the table, and another nineteen wanted changes. By early 1934, when the agreement was supposed to come into effect, Sweden, Lithuania, Finland, Poland, Hungary, Greece, and the Netherlands all still rejected the allocations. Luxembourg could point out that it was hardly alone in its defiance.

Although not strictly enforceable, the declarations that Reith's men had secured did have practical effects. The French government moved against the stations at Toulouse and Paris. Plugge made contingency plans to use a yacht as a station, in case Fécamp should be shut down. But Luxembourg was the principal target. And against Luxembourg the pronouncements proved worse than futile.[13] Using its huge new transmitter—at 200kW, it was ten times as strong as Normandy's—the station now blithely began broadcasting on wavelengths not assigned to it at Lucerne. (One of them had been granted to Warsaw but not

yet put to use.) Luxembourg thus became the one actual pirate station broadcasting into Britain on a regular basis before World War II.
And unlike any other Continental operation, it could reliably reach
the whole British Isles. Its director of English-language programs was
none other than Stephen Williams—the same man who had sailed
around British beaches on the *Ceto* and latterly broadcast for Plugge.
He had lost none of his talent, and he helped make Luxembourg a
roaring success. After initially transmitting in different languages to
various countries on different days of the week, from 1936 the station
concentrated on daily English broadcasts. It rapidly consolidated its
position, until by the later years of the decade Luxembourg had sur-
passed Normandy to become the main source of commercial radio
for British listeners, especially on Sundays. Its ambitions were clear at
a glance to anyone visiting its home: to enter the transmitter building
one passed through doors designed to show that the station meant to
"encircle the world."[14]

The mode of operation that Luxembourg adopted was in many
ways similar to that of Normandy. It too granted a concession to a
London company to sell time to advertisers. The IBC itself repeatedly
hinted that it would get this concession, but in fact it never quite did,
and it seems that the Luxembourg management was keen to avoid
working with Plugge. For a while the *Sunday Referee* was associated
with the station. Yet it too lost out: bowing to pressure from Fleet
Street, the paper abandoned its radio initiatives altogether, leaving
only the Communist *Daily Worker* to report Luxembourg's schedules.
At first, the contract went instead to Radio Publicity, a company involving Williams that had already expelled Plugge from Radio Paris. But
Luxembourg's managers came to suspect that this might be another
of Plugge's companies, and abruptly canceled the concession. They
instead handed the business to a safely Canadian operation called
Wireless Publicity. The shenanigans, needless to say, were rather
involved. What was never in doubt was the profit to be made.

By this time the BBC had spent a decade trying to establish an
international protocol to manage the ether. It had done so in order
to secure its national monopoly, such as it was, from overseas rivals.[15]

Its targets were the Continental stations broadcasting into Britain, with at their head the most important commercial station, and sole "pirate," Radio Luxembourg. At Lucerne it had seemed to be on the verge of success, creating the strongest international front yet against transnational commercial broadcasting. Yet now the BBC went suddenly silent in its campaign against the pirate. Why it did so would be revealed only many years later.

THE CONTINENTAL STATIONS would not have caused so much anxiety to the BBC were it not for a domestic industry that conveyed their programming to households across the country. "Relay" involved using a single receiver station, from which signals emanated through wires to individual households, perhaps via an amplifying station en route.[16] It was yet another product of mid-1920s experimentation. The first relay exchange had opened in a village near Southampton in 1925, created by an avid wireless experimenter and electrical retailer named A. W. Maton. From that beginning the idea spread rapidly. In the 1930s the National Government, dominated by the Conservatives, gave the sector a degree of freedom to relay Continental stations, and their popularity boosted subscriptions. By the middle of the decade about 340 exchanges were operating, with some 200,000 subscribers in all. Major companies headquartered in London had tens of thousands each across the country. Smaller local firms had thousands more. Immune from problems of interference or ether chaos, the industry seemed set for a bright future.[17]

If the BBC was a public corporation, the relay industry presented itself in a subtly but categorically different way. Relay aspired to make the *supply* of entertainment and information into a utility, as opposed to its *generation*: that is, in its vision of the future, people would have information piped into their homes as they already did gas, electricity, and water.[18] That made the industry an ally of the Continental commercial broadcasters, because it saw itself as a neutral channeling agency, ready to provide all comers with a way to reach listeners on an equal footing with the BBC. Its own vision was of a private utility, of course, but the idea immediately raised the prospect of public control: in the mid-1930s, several municipalities proposed establishing utility services in broadcasting on similar lines, perhaps by using electricity cables or telephone lines to channel the signal. The relay industry opposed these schemes as interventionist, and Parliament tended to reject them. But their appeal was well founded. By contrast, it was easy to cast the BBC as outdated, wedded as it was to an apparently limited and inflexible technology. Relay magazines berated it for trying to keep the public in the dark about alternatives that could be multiplied limitlessly if Britain only abandoned the ether.

Relay's claim to be the future of information distribution rested in large part on the ability of local managers to select programming for local audiences. A principal raison d'être of relay, its managers said, was to attend to the tastes of listeners. As one put it, they sought not to improve the listener but to "distract one's thoughts from the worries and trials of the struggle to exist." The point was eminently practical: the "duty" of relay operators consisted of "finding those items desired by the mass of subscribers and ensuring that they shall be received."[19] That is, relay operators should pick and choose from BBC and Continental programs. They took it for granted that they should exercise "careful selection to avoid unpopular stuff." This, they admitted, was "almost equivalent" to giving them the freedom to create their own programs—but the government had reserved that power to the BBC alone, so the industry was cautious never to proclaim it openly.[20]

The point here was of fundamental importance to the nature of broadcasting. The BBC regarded it as virtuous—indeed, as the central principle in its concept of balance—to mix sonatas with talks and variety in a carefully designed whole. Not so a relay officer. When highbrow material emanated from the BBC, he was exhorted not to "let it go" even for fifteen minutes. He must change *immediately* to a different source, lest listeners switch off. Chamber music, opera, commentaries on obscure sports like fencing, and scholarly lectures were high on the relay managers' "blacklist": they must be excised without mercy. "As many as possible of the duller elements in B.B.C. programmes have to be ruthlessly eliminated," one manager insisted. And what would replace them would be the Continental stations. The popularity of their gramophone concert programs and soap operas was so evident in relay circles as to be regarded as "hackneyed." All but explicitly, the BBC's model of attentive listening and cultural improvement was to be cast aside.[21] The BBC naturally drew the line at such editing. In a bid at reconciliation, the corporation at one point offered the relay industry whole sequences of its programs; but it would permit no "deviation" from its designed sequence. The proposal was dismissed as "senseless." On hearing it, a group of relay managers responded with "unprintable invective." One relay engineer from Maidenhead remarked that it was only explicable on the assumption that the BBC thought commercial programs would "unsettle the public mind."[22]

For both practical and economic reasons, the relay industry particularly flourished in urban, working-class districts. Companies found it easier to string wires along terraced housing, and sometimes they could even build systems directly into the new blocks of flats now being constructed. Subscribers preferred it because it was cheaper and offered better reception than a home receiver, especially in built-up areas that were otherwise prone to interference. They had to buy the standard broadcast license, but after that they paid only 1s 6d a week.[23] That was less than the cost of a receiver bought on hire purchase. In all, as one relay manager put it, the poor precincts of industrial cities were "a Garden of Eden for Relay."[24] And managers prided themselves on their close and dynamic knowledge of the practices of the working-class listeners they found there. Because working-class folk were prone to abandon subscriptions, operators had to work to keep them satisfied. They often described their role almost as if it were a form of urban sociology.

This intimate social knowledge was critical even to setting up a relay operation in the first place. Would a given precinct make a good location? The first thing to do was to drive through the district, taking note of clues that would allow an accurate, even numerical, assessment of what was called its "Relay value." Curtains, for example, were "extremely useful" indicators. "They are the outward stamp of the class and social standing of the people who live behind them." Serried ranks of identical curtains were a bad sign, because they told of a district of boarding houses and rented flats. But clean and varied curtains (however cheap their materials) bespoke financial probity and discipline. The color of paint was telling, too. A row of houses all one color might be owned by a single person or company, which would want to wrangle free service in return for permission to extend wires. Then again, managers should time their drive for 7:30–8:30 am to catch the men going to work, or 4–5 pm to catch the children leaving school: "The more noise they make and the more they are all over the streets," observers learned, "the better the district for Relay." Such behavior indicated close-knit communities in which word of the service would spread through everyday conversations. A local market hinted at the same kind of sociability. Well-kept household gardens, on the other hand, might be a bad sign: getting permission to string wires across these properties might be tough. And keeping a relay operation profitable once it had been launched relied on continuously updating this kind of knowledge. Relay managers must "*know* every subscriber," they insisted. They should call on some at home every week, and interview those who withdrew to find out why. Some called this the "sick visitor" principle: a relay manager must act like a physician and make routine house calls.[25]

The knowledge relay operators gained of their communities took effect in the editorial effort that they called "programme building." This was the development of regular, predictable, and popular schedules by combining the output of different sources into one stream. It could be prepared for in advance by keeping tabs on published timetables, but the actual management had to be done on the fly. Control rooms must be kept clear of distractions, so that the operator could achieve the seamless effect it demanded. Moment by moment, the relay officer took what the broadcasters transmitted and applied his social knowledge to it, "taking the raw material out of the ether and moulding it into a harmonious entity."[26] Needless to say, to conceive of the operator's role in this way—as refining the "raw material" put out by the BBC and the likes of Radio Normandy into a single processed product—was radically incompatible with the BBC's mission. But the relay managers were proud of their skill in performing it. They even claimed to be able to measure, in real time, the responses of their listeners as they carried it out—a claim with major consequences, as we shall see in the next chapter.

The significance of relay was therefore that it allied Continental commercial broadcasters to very local knowledge about practices of listening among mass audiences. As a result, the relay companies trod on very delicate ground in defending their right to exist. If they openly professed embracing commercial programs, or if they acknowledged *creating* "programmes" (that is, schedules) themselves, then they ran the risk of being refused licenses by the Post Office. So their own trade association exhorted them "not to relay any large percentage of foreign programmes, and in particular to restrict to the minimum those containing advertisements." Yet even the more cautious among them insisted on one point: that the BBC must learn the lesson of their success. That lesson was to know one's listeners.[27]

THE RISE OF relay created a fashion for utopian visions of a future with wired broadcasting. Some of them rather resembled schemes that had been advanced in the early days of the telephone system during the nineteenth century—or, more hauntingly for modern readers, ambitions for the early Internet. Take this one, for example:

I have a dream about the future. I see the interior of a living-room. The wide windows are formed from double panes of glass, fixed and immovable. The conditioned air is fresh and warm. Old-fashioned people would feel uncomfortable without the fire and fireplace, others might miss the raucous brown box we used to call "the wireless." But flush against the wall there is a translucent screen with numbered strips of lettering running across it. The lettering spells out titles which read like newspaper headlines. These are the titles describing the many different "broadcasting" programmes [including television]

which can be heard by just pressing the corresponding button.
. . . So I lower myself into a chair and press the proper numbered button on a remote control panel placed conveniently
beside me. The voices are suddenly in the room, startling in
their naturalness. . . . [I miss the tennis, but] I shall get the
result in my house newspaper to-morrow. This will be printed,
while I sleep, by a machine in the lobby. Wonderful service
the Wire Broadcasting Company gives me for half a crown a
week; only a shilling if I cut out television and the newspaper.
I'd rather cut out cigarettes—perhaps.

This prophecy was conceived in the mid-1930s, and published in
1941, by the most important proponent of "wired wireless" by far: the
ex–chief engineer of the BBC, Peter Eckersley. It was, as he himself
admitted, "a whale of a dream."[28]

Heroic myth focuses on John Reith, but Peter Pendleton Eckersley
(1892–1963) was as pivotal a figure in British and international broadcasting prior to World War II. He came from a family of Unitarian
and reform-minded railway engineers in Manchester, and was one
of three brothers who all did pioneering work in radio. Peter was
born in Mexico while his father was engaged in building the national
rail system. His schooling took place at Bedales, a progressive, non-
denominational private school in Hampshire that set itself against the
strict regime adopted by most boarding schools of the time (not least,
Bedales was unusual in being co-educational—a situation of which
Eckersley took full advantage). It was as a teenager that he discovered wireless from his elder brother, then a scientist at Cambridge's
Cavendish Laboratory. Eckersley swiftly established a transmitter in
the school grounds. When war broke out he enlisted as a wireless officer in the Royal Flying Corps, only to be banned from flying because
his technical skills were deemed too valuable to risk. He ignored the
order, repeatedly taking to the skies in his unit's slow and vulnerable
B.E.2 biplanes to test new gizmos. In Egypt he almost killed himself
and a pilot when a wind-powered generator disintegrated in midair,
and in 1917, on the western front, he was shot down by the Germans.

By the time he had recovered from that experience, the war was winding down.

Eckersley took a position with Marconi.[29] As we saw in chapter 1, he pioneered the use of the new technology for broadcasting at the company's Writtle site, taking to the microphone himself to do so and proving that he was a gifted performer in the medium. When the BBC came into existence, he was Reith's natural choice as its first chief engineer. In that position he guided the construction of the first generation of broadcasting systems. He also took a vanguard role in urging the establishment of international wavelength allocations, supporting Reith's early efforts to get a European agreement among broadcasters.[30] But from this point on, Eckersley and Reith parted ways.

In the late 1920s, the BBC planned to centralize program making and broadcasting in London. Eckersley disagreed. He preferred that broadcasting be "federalized." But to make this possible he would need a way to multiply stations, and for this he seized upon an idea that he called "wired wireless." This was a way of transmitting programs over the wires used to carry domestic electricity supplies. Wired wireless could overcome the problem of spectrum scarcity and permit several different channels to operate at once, without interference. Eckersley himself envisaged having four to six channels, devoted to discrete kinds of fare, such as chamber music, variety, news, and so on. In 1928, he wrote a memorandum envisaging a Britain of 1950 in which wired communications had extended across the nation, making wireless virtually obsolete. It failed to persuade Reith, however, and a year later his disillusionment came to a head when Eckersley's marriage collapsed and his character became a topic for heated debate within the corporation's hierarchy.[31] The archbishop of Canterbury having been consulted on the matter, Eckersley was jettisoned. Reith's BBC was no place for adulterers.

After his departure from the BBC, Eckersley spent a couple of years drifting between various radio-related jobs. He even speculated about outfitting a ship to broadcast from offshore.[32] But he remained convinced of his vision about wired networking, and in

1931 he participated in the launch of Rediffusion, a company formed to franchise out wired broadcasting in local areas across the country. Rediffusion soon became the nation's largest relay company. But for Eckersley this was a misapprehension of its real purpose. He wanted to use its profits from conventional relay to develop his wired wireless system. Since it would use mains cables to transmit information, he pointed out, it would avoid the need for massive investment in new wiring, and it would make "piracy"—that is, the old practice of listener piracy—very difficult indeed. Rediffusion chose not to pursue an unproven technology, however, and Eckersley was forced to resort to independent experimenting. His own company, Wire Broadcasting Ltd., made ready to begin field tests in Liverpool.[33] Meanwhile he traveled far and wide to publicize his scheme, even confronting his successor as BBC chief engineer at a public meeting. Only a wired system, Eckersley lectured the BBC man, could both eliminate interference and end the corporation's "international difficulties."[34]

In 1935–36, Eckersley's project got caught up with Plugge's IBC in a potentially mortal crisis for the BBC. Commercial rivals and relay companies alike were challenging the corporation's rationale, and the highly public resentments of ex-employees like Eckersley himself had drawn critical attention to its internal culture. Parliament had to renew the BBC's charter by the end of 1936, and suddenly it seemed conceivable that the MPs would weaken the monopoly. But the Ullswater Committee, appointed to recommend a policy, blasted the hopes of the critics. It reaffirmed faith in the BBC and its role, and recommended that the relay industry be nationalized under the aegis of the Post Office, with program control ceded to the corporation. The industry scrambled to avert the threat, and won a reprieve of sorts. The government extended relay companies' licenses after all. But it did so for only three years, and at the same time urged the Post Office to experiment with its own high-frequency wired system using telephone lines, which might give rise to a national network. If that happened, it warned, the relay companies might be subsumed without compensation. The prospect killed investment overnight. Eckersley's wired wireless research was abruptly halted as its money ran out.

Yet Eckersley managed to find a new backer. Bill Allen, head of the W. E. D. Allen advertising agency and acolyte of the British Fascist Sir Oswald Mosley, stepped in with new financing. Allen helped Eckersley push his scheme to the government once more. But as Eckersley now described it, it was no longer a tool for a utopian future; it was an imperative for national security. Unlike wireless, he told the mandarins, wired wireless could not be jammed, and it involved no transmitters that incoming bombers might use to navigate to their targets. It could carry on throughout a war, giving the government a vital direct link to the people. The BBC, in contrast, would surely have to shut down during air attacks, which would give the enemy an opportunity to substitute its own programs pretending to be BBC ones. (The suggestion may sound far-fetched, but in fact the British would do exactly this to German broadcasters in World War II, using a secret high-powered transmitter code-named "Aspidistra.")[35] For the nation to remain united and committed in the coming air war, communications must be removed from the ether. Wired wireless was a vital element in national defense.

It was partly in response to Eckersley's lobbying that the government instructed the Post Office to experiment with wired wireless technology. But opposition by relay and wireless interests delayed the trial. Only in mid-1939 was ground finally broken, after the prospect of war had focused minds. The trial would take place in Southampton, the city where wired systems had begun almost fifteen years earlier. It looked like the Post Office was going to create its own multi-channel system, which might be ramped up to a national network.

But it was too late. War was imminent. There was no time to produce the Luftwaffe-proof network that Eckersley had wanted, even on a trial basis. In September the conflict began, and all development of new wired systems ceased.

THE WIRED WIRELESS idea was only one element in an extraordinary project that could have revolutionized the media of the mid-twentieth century—and perhaps done much more besides, if Eckersley's more extravagant visions for its impact had borne fruit. One reason why it foundered, perhaps, is that its progenitor was overstretched. As the fortunes of his scheme waxed and waned, Eckersley was dashing back and forth across Europe on an odyssey—his wife Dorothy called it a "mad career"—to find a location for a major new transmitter and found an international broadcasting empire.[36]

Eckersley and his partners (Allen being the most conspicuous) gave their plan a code name. They called it "Gemona." It was similar in nature to Radios Normandy and Luxembourg, but immeasurably more ambitious. In his bid to launch it, Eckersley went first to Berlin. There he had high-level meetings with Nazi officials in a hotel suite arranged by Allen. He also visited Copenhagen, Dublin, Ljubljana, Nice, Toulouse, Vienna, Rome, Brussels, and Encamp in Andorra. At one point it looked like Toulouse might be the chosen venue, and in 1937 an opening address was actually read on air by Winston Churchill (who chafed throughout the thirties at BBC limits on his access to the microphone to address what he saw as major issues like India, the Navy, and Nazism). But that venture folded, and Eckersley found himself on the move again. A contract was signed for a station on the Channel Island of Sark, only for Eckersley to pour cold water on the idea because the Post Office would surely forbid such an enterprise. Another possibility was scotched when threats from the German government caused the local authorities to withdraw support. In the end, he returned to his starting point. The most realistic prospect seemed to be the nation with the best technical facilities and the greatest political need for a broadcaster to target the British: Germany.

Eckersley's credentials to set up a pro-German station beaming into Britain were good. After his ouster from the BBC, his new wife, Dorothy Carrington, an actress and already a divorcée, had made their London flat a venue for fashionable dinner-party conversations with the likes of Wyndham Lewis. It was a moment when political allegiances were in flux, and Lewis was an exemplary case; he was writing a book, *Hitler*, that would be sympathetic to the Nazi leader. They also met Sir Oswald Mosley, then on the verge of abandoning the Labour Party to found his New Party, with a platform advocating state control of industry to combat mass unemployment. Mosley's venture appealed to Eckersley and his circle, promising as it did government by expertise. John Strachey—once Mosley's parliamentary private secretary, now a follower, later a Communist—introduced them, and Eckersley proceeded to chair the New Party's London Central Committee. After it crashed to an ignominious defeat in the General Election of 1931, and Mosley wound up the party to form the British Union of Fascists, the Eckersleys stayed in contact.[37] And Mosley himself began to see an opportunity for his movement in Eckersley's media schemes.

In the mid- to late 1930s, Mosley's Fascist movement struggled. It was poorly funded, and new laws restricted its activities. Mosley himself was not permitted to broadcast on the BBC. So with Allen and Eckersley's help he hit on a scheme to create a broadcast medium of his own, be it a wireless station on the Continent or—more ambitious still—Eckersley's wired wireless system. Profits from a commercial station modeled on Luxembourg would finance the British Union amply, allowing Mosley to buy up newspapers to add even further to its exposure. "One thing is certain," he would insist at his interrogation in 1940: "but for the accident of war we should have made an immense fortune."[38] So during his travels across Europe and his lobbying for wired wireless, Eckersley was in fact being paid by a front company for the British Union of Fascists, Air Time Ltd., that Mosley had set up for this purpose. It was Mosley himself who signed the contract envisaging a station on Sark. The active involvement of his organization was kept strictly secret, however. He did not wish to alert Whitehall to the real purpose of the new commercial broadcaster.

It seems that Eckersley himself was an inconstant Fascist. But that could not be said of his wife (unless to note that fascism represented her more moderate mood). She became an ideological partisan, outdoing even Mosley in enthusiasm. The couple went to Germany on holiday in 1935, and she returned a convinced Hitler acolyte. She joined the Imperial Fascist League, and then the National Socialist League that William Joyce formed after Mosley expelled him for being too anti-Semitic. At one point she even bailed Joyce out of prison.

Meanwhile, her son by a previous marriage, James, changed his name to Richard to sound less Jewish and more Wagnerian. As the prospect of war loomed in mid-1939, mother and son left for Berlin; and they stayed there when the conflict started. In Berlin they drifted into the role of propaganda broadcasters for the Reich. Eventually, they would both go silent—they later claimed to have feigned illness—and at length they would suffer internment by the Gestapo. They survived, however, to be tried in England for their activities. Unlike Joyce—the man popularly identified as Lord Haw Haw—who was hanged for treason, they were treated leniently. Dorothy got a token prison sentence, while James was released on bond.[39]

Eckersley therefore had realistic hopes of patronage from Berlin. But at first it did not arise. The German postal authorities were interested in his schemes, and economic officials appreciated the prospect of foreign specie coming into the embargoed country. But Propaganda Minister Joseph Goebbels refused to permit a station that would not be under his control. Stalemate ensued, and Eckersley went back to his wanderings.

What allowed the stalemate to be broken was the Nazi takeover of Austria. One of the lesser consequences of the *Anschluss* in March 1938 was that a wavelength allocated under the Lucerne protocol to Austria was now made available to Berlin. Hitler—persuaded, it seems, by Diana Mitford, who had secretly married Mosley in the Führer's presence and nagged Hitler relentlessly about the matter—consented to allot it to Eckersley's project over Goebbels's objections. An official called Von Kaufmann helped the collaborators form a company, Gemona AG. Fifty-five percent of its equity was held by the German Post Office, 45 percent by Air Time Ltd. In Britain, Eckersley's Wire Broadcasting would handle the enterprise. Allen, determined that his advertising company not be linked to the Fascists, handed over his share of the starting capital in the form of a suitcase full of used pound notes. The deal was that Mosley's company would pay the Germans royalties for a decade, in precious sterling, and Eckersley would be a consultant. All involved were sworn to secrecy about the Fascist role.[40]

Builders quickly began to construct the transmitter. It would stand in Osterloog, a bleak promontory on Germany's North Sea coast. Berlin projected a date of November 1939 for broadcasting to begin.

To tell the story this far is to give the impression that Eckersley was at best a foolish Fascist fellow traveler, and at worst a traitor. But there is another side. The BBC was not the only institution anxious about cross-border broadcasting. In fact, the German government had complained to the IBU about incoming transmissions from Poland as early as 1930, and after the Nazis came to power they pursued more disputes about international broadcasting in their characteristically direct way. Opposition groups, ruthlessly expelled from Germany itself, had put radio to use to combat the Nazi regime from outside the country. Their ventures were precarious in a sense never felt by Plugge or Williams. Pirate listening was difficult and perilous in a totalitarian state. Informers could turn you in. And it took more than merely turning a dial to find an unapproved signal. Goebbels had overseen the design of a "people's set" (*Volksempfänger*) that sold in huge numbers to German citizens; it received the nearest regional station and the national long-wave broadcaster, but no others. By early 1938, there were over 9 million of these sets in use, one for every two German households.[41] Beyond the borders, the broadcasting ventures themselves were not safe either. In early 1935, a Gestapo squad killed a broadcaster named Rudolf Formis in Czechoslovakia. Another assassinated the ex-Nazi Heinrich Grunow in France.

British efforts to ostracize all international broadcasting take on a distinctly unattractive appearance in this context. But in fact the British government was about to turn pirate itself. Whitehall was looking for ways to transmit broadcasts into Nazi Germany. The first of its concerted efforts was masterminded by the Secret Intelligence Service (SIS), which arranged for a speech by the prime minister, Neville Chamberlain, to be broadcast to the German people. The SIS did not utilize the BBC for this—how could it, when the corporation had set its face so publicly against international broadcasts? Instead, it bought time on Europe's wireless pirate, Radio Luxembourg. The deal was kept secret, even—perhaps especially—from the BBC itself. But from then on, Luxembourg became Chamberlain's vehicle for speaking to the Germans. Techniques that had become standard in the commercial broadcasting of the IBC and its counterparts—recording in London onto disc, flying the disc to Luxembourg, sending other speeches by land line, and so on—now became tools of propaganda. A hint from Whitehall was the real reason why the BBC, after its near success at Lucerne, suddenly stopped pressing home its attacks on Luxembourg for its "pirated wavelength."[42]

Before long the British had created a standard route for making broadcasts into Germany. The operation was run from a Whitehall office called the Joint Broadcasting Committee (JBC), which was formed in 1937 under an ex-BBC figure, Hilda Mattheson, who had been a pioneer of listener research in the UK. The practical details were arranged through a front operation for SIS's Section D, situated in Paris and called the Travel and Industrial Development Association of Great Britain and Ireland. The JBC and the Travel Association did not restrict their efforts to Radio Luxembourg. They tried to establish other vehicles—a permanent station within Germany itself being one possibility. The JBC even reportedly assisted in setting up a shipboard transmitter in the North Sea. Certainly, in mid-1938 the Postmaster General, in a secret memo on "unprincipled" broadcasting, suggested using a vessel chartered in Paraguay or Panama to "discharge wireless salvoes of advertising matter" into Germany; and apparently such a vessel was later raided by the Germans. The Travel Association thus became the focal point of a determined effort to create some kind of broadcaster into the Reich.

By the late 1930s the British were therefore searching avidly for a way of sending radio programs into Nazi Germany. The JBC's agents approached several Continental stations. They would offer a relaxation of the BBC campaign to shut the station down in return for cooperation in beaming propaganda into the Reich. Even after the SIS had begun using Luxembourg, it continued to negotiate in this fashion with other operations. But local authorities tended to be nervous of Nazi retaliation. For example, Robert Boothby (another Mosley fellow traveler) at one point mooted broadcasting from Neuchâtel—an old center of European information piracy, dating back at least to the eighteenth century—only for German threats to quash the possibility. Progress was slow to nonexistent.

The JBC's principal agent in this effort was none other than W. E. D. Allen—the same Bill Allen who was partnering Eckersley in his own project for an international broadcasting station. The two projects naturally merged.[43] Even as Eckersley was receiving his instructions and money secretly from Mosley, he was also working, just as secretly, for this effort. He and Allen traveled to Paris ten times in the space of a year, and the shows he was hoping to broadcast from his planned station were in fact concocted by the JBC. (At the same time, however, Mosley's negotiations with high Nazi officials for a German transmitter were taking place in Paris hotels, and it is likely that Allen and Eckersley killed two birds with one stone.) It is not hard to see why his gambit would appeal to the British. Gemona would give the British a station that they ran themselves, and therefore free them from reliance on independent stations that might be intimidated by threats from Berlin. So Whitehall approved of Eckersley's missions from Paris to Austria to Czechoslovakia. It even endorsed his agreement to build the Gemona transmitter in Germany itself. It did so because the Foreign Office was convinced it would be used for transmissions into the Reich.

Eckersley himself knew by 1938, if no earlier, that his and Allen's project for a commercial station was being helped along as part of the SIS project for a broadcaster into Germany. The most successful manifestation of the collaboration was a station in Vaduz, the capital of Liechtenstein. Peter Hope, once a stalwart of Radio Normandy but now an agent for the British Secret Service, worked with Eckersley on the scheme; the BBC's Guy Burgess, the Soviet agent, was sent to Vaduz to help with it. Whitehall took care to quieten the BBC's campaign against international commercial transmissions in order to secure a wavelength for Vaduz at the ITU's Montreux conference in March 1939. After an inauspicious start—the team rather insouciantly ordered major components from Germany itself—Eckersley's Vaduz station did become operational, and seems to have been accepted as a legitimately commercial operation.[44] In the event, it transmitted successfully from February 1939 until the outbreak of war.

But Eckersley's juggling of different interests and different masters could not continue for long. During those hectic and ominous months of 1939, his projects accelerated toward a common climax. In Britain, the wired wireless venture in Southampton finally broke ground in July. The same month, Dorothy and James (or Richard) took ship for Germany. Vaduz was on the air. A Scottish accountant named James Herd, whom Eckersley had hired, had put the finishing touches to a cloud of companies, many empty shells designed solely to hide the German venture from association with Mosley. Wire Broadcasting was one of them; Eckersley also became a director of another, Radio Variety, slated to provide the programs for Gemona.[45] Allen, charging Mosley with having stolen the money he had put into Gemona, had stormed out, severing the prospective station's crucial link to the advertising world. But Gemona itself was fast approaching completion.

It was the last of these that was truly perilous. When it did start operating, the moment of truth was sure to come. What, in the end, was Eckersley doing with the Gemona project? Was he working for Mosley, to make a commercial station to fund the British Fascists? Or was it to transmit propaganda from Berlin? Or, on the other side, would the Gemona transmitter broadcast British programming in the opposite direction, into the Reich, as Whitehall seems to have planned? Similar uncertainty attended his grand wired wireless scheme for Britain itself. Was that another Mosleyite vehicle, designed to pipe the leader's words into every household, or was it genuinely a measure for national defense? Perhaps it even had the visionary potential that Eckersley himself publicized, to liberate broadcasting from problems of interference and open up a utopian future of access to information. Up to this point, Eckersley had been able to keep all of these prospects in the air at once. The moment was fast approaching when that would become impossible. As he tramped across Europe trying to keep all his projects (and his many love affairs) alive at once, Eckersley began to suffer intense stomach cramps and headaches. It is hard not to see them as symptoms of the encroaching crisis. The Gestapo had already killed radio men for less than he had done.

The most plausible explanation for Eckersley's actions, I think, is one of simple human weakness. He himself never faced up to the need to resolve what his allegiances or purposes were. He told friends that the point of his projects was to become "filthy rich," and Plugge had certainly shown that it was possible to do that from international radio. But in the late 1930s it was impossible to venture into this domain without becoming involved in international conspiracy as well as grand capitalism. Eckersley certainly did both. He was genuinely devoted to fascism, but that devotion was not exclusive. He kept postponing the decision to take one side or the other, hoping that the decision need never be made. He did the same in his personal life during these years. Dorothy stayed at home in Britain, where her imposition on him of vegetarianism and celibacy he found harder to take than her ardent Nazism. Meanwhile, in his mad career he sustained passionate affairs with Jutta Szabo, a "Slav" whom he had met at a brothel in Berlin, and a married woman named Betty Poulsen, who lived in Cornwall but moved to Paris for their rendezvous. Just as he could not decide on Gemona, so he could not bring himself to commit to one consort—and in this too he took after Mosley. The strains told on him. The result was that by mid-1939 Eckersley had trapped himself into playing a fantastically dangerous game that he could not possibly win. But by now he could not abandon the field either. He was trapped. When Gemona began transmissions in November, the game would be up. He would have betrayed either the Nazis or the SIS. And one side or the other would surely have exacted retribution.

Then, on August 15, a way out offered itself. An associate of Eckersley's was called to Dover. He went down to the port, where he met a German agent disembarking from the Continent. The agent traveled under the name of Von Kaufmann, and was presumably the same man who had handled the German side of the Gemona project. They took the train back to London. There Von Kaufmann told Eckersley that Gemona was being canceled. Berlin was abrogating his plan with immediate effect, and would take over the nearly finished station for its own purposes. Mosley would be compensated, but Eckersley himself was being cast adrift.

Although the cancellation may well have saved his life, Eckersley was distraught. He pleaded futilely for the decision to be rescinded. That same night he accompanied the German to Plymouth, where the visitor took ship again.[46]

Two weeks later, the reason behind the cancellation became clear. Germany invaded Poland, and Britain and France declared war on the Reich. In the event, the Gemona transmitter at Osterloog did begin broadcasting that November, right on schedule. Operating as Bremen I, it was used for propaganda broadcasts into Britain, as part of a Nazi network that soon reached all of Europe. It became the main relay point for Lord Haw Haw's regular harangues to the British people.[47]

3

POLTERGEISTS AND POLITICS

By the early 1930s it had become standard to hail the BBC as the harbinger of a quantum change in British institutions, and indeed in Britain itself. It was the classic instance, and the most evidently successful one, of that new institutional species, the public corporation. The model's success—in stark contrast to the everywhere evident failures of laissez-faire capitalism—seemed singular and self-evident. Enthusiasm for it was almost universal, and increasing all the time. "Not even the typical Tory," proclaimed the future Labour chancellor of the exchequer Hugh Dalton, would "disestablish" the BBC now. Writing in the BBC magazine *The Listener* in 1934, the economist Sir Arthur Salter proclaimed that "vast spheres" of the economy—insurance, transport, munitions, food, and more—should and would be reorganized on the model it represented. "We should certainly, I think, be able to bring more than half the country's economic life under public ownership and management," he explained, adding that "almost all of us really know that we cannot if we would restore the old *laissez-faire* system." A year later, a multi-party group convened to discuss *The Next Five Years* concurred. On into the postwar era, many proposals to "plan" the British economy—including schemes for the Bank of England, coal mining, and New Towns—were premised not on crude nationalization but on the model of the public corporation that the BBC had pioneered.[1]

As war approached, and even more during the war itself, calls multiplied for a thoroughgoing overhaul to take place in the nation's political and economic life. The broad 1930s consensus on the need to plan economic affairs gave way to more ambitious and concrete proposals to take major sectors of the economy into public hands. The very experience of total war tended to reinforce this conviction. If Britain could manage to mobilize and beat back the totalitarian menace by coordinated planning, could it not defeat poverty, inequality, and injustice at home by similar means?

The symbol for this aspiration became the report on *Social Insurance and Allied Policies* issued by Sir William Beveridge in 1942. Beveridge, then in his mid-sixties, was a veteran of Fabian socialism who had directed the London School of Economics from 1919 until 1937. His report identified "five giants" named Want, Disease, Ignorance, Squalor, and Idleness, which together stood athwart "the road of reconstruction" along which Britain must travel after the war. To get past them would require not piecemeal reforms but "a comprehensive policy of social progress." Central to that policy would be a national system of social insurance, creating what amounted to a new contract between state and individual. "A revolutionary moment in the world's history," Beveridge proclaimed, "is a time for revolutions, not for patching."[2]

When the Conservatives were soundly defeated in the 1945 general election, Clement Attlee's incoming Labour government committed itself to realizing Beveridge's proposals. The next few years saw the creation of the National Health Service and a national insurance scheme, the nationalization of the Bank of England and many strategic industries, and the dedication of the state to the preservation of full employment. Attlee created a political and economic consensus around the so-called welfare state that would endure until the election of Margaret Thatcher in 1979.

A prolonged and intense debate took place in midcentury, not just about these initiatives but about the destiny of liberal democracy itself in the face of rising totalitarianism. What were the appropriate places of laissez-faire, planning, and intervention in a free society?

How could liberal values and practices be sustained in a world of scientific and technological transformation and mass media? The scope of these exchanges extended from mundane politics to the nature of knowledge itself. As both the public corporation par excellence and the overseer of a responsible mass medium, the BBC could not help but be central to them.

THE ANTAGONISTS OF the BBC believed that its Achilles' heel was its ignorance of listeners. They often complained that the corporation simply ignored its audience, or at best that it treated citizens' preferences with high-handed disdain. Neither charge was entirely true. But it *was* true that the knowledge that the corporation cultivated about listening was knowledge of a certain kind. The BBC wanted individual, critical, and qualitative reactions to its offerings—the kind of reactions, that is, that would be useful in developing more improving programs. To get them, it approached listening through reading. It emulated the higher newspapers, especially *The Times*, and solicited the equivalent of letters to the editor.[3] It did not look for different kinds of information because it did not need them. Until the late 1930s, that is, when suddenly it did.

The impetus for a transformation in the BBC's approach to listeners came from the challenge posed by Continental commercial broadcasters in alliance with the relay industry. In particular, it originated because of the Continental stations' need to make credible claims about their own audiences. And that need derived in turn from the rivalry between the commercial stations and the newspaper industry. Companies like the IBC competed with Britain's press for major advertisers such as Cadbury's, Rizla cigarette papers, and Stork Margarine.[4] Fleet Street was at the height of its power at this point, however, and newspapers had a major advantage in that they could trumpet circulation figures to confirm their impact. When they did so, they fed data into what protagonists hailed as a new "science" of mass persuasion. Introduced by American companies, this "science" of advertising depended not on the "hunch" beloved of old British advertising hands, but on research. Sales figures were major resources for this research, as, indeed, were letters to the editor. The one told *how many* people read a paper, the other *how* they read it. But companies also sent researchers into the field to examine householders and their homes. The alliance between newspapers and advertising agencies thus organized some of the earliest systematic social science surveys. They created a sociology of reading.

They did this because their business was plausibility. Advertising agencies sought to persuade clients that they could predict accurately which audiences would perceive a given advertisement, when, and to what effect. That knowledge, they claimed, allowed them to target clients' money most effectively. At first, the credibility of this claim was by no means clear. Early research into readership was often denounced for sloppy or even fraudulent methods: researchers were said to sit in pubs and make up data. But by the 1930s that had changed. Researchers were trained and experienced; sampling techniques were more reliable. What was now being called "market research" enjoyed more credibility, and the advertising agencies' claims for a science of readership were carrying conviction.

What was significant about radio in this context was that its reception could *not* be tracked straightforwardly. Market researchers could claim plausibly to know who read newspapers, and (to some extent) how they read them; they found it much harder to claim that they knew who listened to the wireless, let alone how they listened. Relay companies, for their part, did have an answer to this demand. Every exchange had a load meter that provided the operator with an account of how many subscribers had their machines turned on at any moment. Companies recorded graphs of these readings over days, months, and even years, and by correlating them with their schedules could deduce the popularity of different programs and program types.[5] But the wireless companies themselves had no equivalent to such data. They especially lacked information for areas without relay, where audiences listened through their own wireless receivers—this typically meant the most prosperous and therefore, from the advertiser's perspective, desirable areas of the country. Yet if the IBC and

Radio Luxembourg were to tempt advertisers away from Fleet Street, they had to claim an equivalent degree of knowledge to that possessed by any press baron.

The scope of the knowledge that companies like the IBC needed was quite broad. Stations had to know about more than raw numbers of listeners. Advertisers were used to being told how effective newspaper advertisements were; they would expect a similar assessment of radio spots. Moreover, the rationale for commercial radio was that it gave people not what the BBC thought they should want but what they in fact wanted. Broadcasters therefore had to make assertions about listeners' preferences, and about the effects that their listening had on them after they stopped listening. If the commercial stations and the relay companies could not plausibly claim to know *how* listeners listened, then their excuse for existing meant little.

In practice, the IBC did claim to know something about this. It even purported to discern what listeners retained in memory from their listening. But its problem lay in making good on such claims. It needed ways of getting this knowledge and of making it believable. In effect, the company needed to invent a social science of listening, to rival the social science of reading that the newspapers had invented.

THE IBC'S CHOICE to run this operation fell on a professor at the London School of Economics. The choice was momentous. The LSE had been founded in the late nineteenth century by Sidney and Beatrice Webb in a spirit of Fabian socialism, and in the thirties its director, Sir William Beveridge, continued that tradition. But the School had also become the redoubt of a small group of economists radically antagonistic to the emerging orthodoxy of social democratic interventionism that would come to be called Keynesian. This opposition was led by a triumvirate who lived cheek by jowl in Hampstead. The first of them was Lionel Robbins, the second Friedrich von Hayek. The third—and the man chosen for the IBC's task—was Arnold Plant.

Their initial leader was Robbins. Himself an LSE graduate of the mid-twenties, he had been appointed to a chair in 1929 at the young age of thirty. Hugh Dalton had sponsored him, partly with the conscious intent of throwing a cat among the pigeons. He had led a revival of the economics unit, and been instrumental in the hiring of Hayek. It was originally at his invitation that the Austrian economist, then thirty-two, came to give a set of lectures on monetary theory. Hayek was then asked to stay, and shortly afterwards given a permanent chair. He and Robbins immediately charged into two battles, one public, the other private, that would be highly consequential for the future of political economics. One they lost, but in the other they tasted victory.

The first struggle was a highly public contest between Hayek and John Maynard Keynes. Robbins may well have been planning it when he urged Hayek's appointment in the first place, as he and Keynes had just clashed violently in their role as government advisers. Keynes himself was now finishing the grand synthesis of interventionist economics that would become *The General Theory of Employment, Interest and Money*. Their conflict climaxed publicly in 1937 with Hayek's apparent defeat. At the same time, however, the group also conducted a second, private but harsher campaign within the precincts of the LSE itself. Their target here was Beveridge and all that he stood for. Robbins, Hayek, and Plant collaborated on a seminar about the problems of "collectivism," while Robbins himself ran a longer-term seminar addressing economic issues like monopolies. A roster of participants including Plant, Hayek, and (among students) Ronald Coase dissected collectivist policies for weeks on end. And the three took full advantage of the LSE's house journal, *Economica*, to publish the resulting arguments and analyses. Under Robbins's direction, *Economica* became the public home of an emerging anti-Keynesian party. As they assailed Keynes, therefore, at the same time they engaged in an internal war with Beveridge over the fate of economics at the School. This feud, which also culminated in 1937, they won. The director departed for Oxford amid celebrations by the triumvirate. They had made the LSE a bastion of "liberal" convictions to stand against Keynes's Cambridge.[6]

Arnold Plant was the same age as Robbins, and a year older than Hayek.[7] Having started life as an engineer, he had matriculated as a student at LSE in 1920. There he had participated in the same earnest student conversations as Robbins. After graduating with degrees in both economics and commerce, he had worked for seven years at the University of Cape Town, before returning to London to take up a new chair of commerce. He lost no time in setting out his opposition to the rise of public corporations. In his inaugural address, in October 1931, he insisted that the ultimate controller of the business world was not the capitalist boss, as fans of public corporations liked to think, but "that relentless controller and employer, the community of consumers." The businessman was merely an "organising agent" for this public. He therefore warned against the temptation to replace communal control by "some other ill-defined criterion." What Plant had in mind was the extension of rationalization through public corporations. Monopolies had not been a major concern, he affirmed, until state intervention entrenched them. When it did, it prevented the public from benefiting from new inventions that inevitably challenged existing interests. State monopolies were therefore not only a "menace to individual liberty" but a debilitating one. Plant also noted a similar trend *inside* businesses. As they grew, their "expert management" came to enjoy substantial autonomy equivalent in some ways to the position of managers in a public corporation. A company ought to tell its shareholders periodically the worth of their shares, for example, but in practice it tended to avoid doing so, ostensibly to avoid revealing strategic information. As this "business secrecy" increased, it impeded the operation of a market. It therefore made managers partly responsible for accentuating the kind of slump that had happened in 1929. And it was but one among many practices that obstructed commerce. They were nothing new, Plant remarked: there was a history to such techniques extending back to the East India Company's military responses to "interloping" ships (which the company termed "pirates") in the seventeenth and eighteenth centuries.

Plant therefore embarked on his years at the LSE by identifying the problem of public corporations central to a broader set of concerns about knowledge in the economy. He recommended that along with studying business secrecy, the School should research advertising—a subject that he believed to be "of sociological and philosophical as well as business interest."[8] In the next few years he pursued those themes himself, most notably in the fields of patenting and copyright. He published strong attacks on both in successive issues of *Economica* in 1934. He also drew up hundreds of pages of statistical notes for a broader historical analysis of intellectual property, which still survive among his papers at the LSE. That broader study was never published, as Plant found himself consumed by commitments to teaching and administration, including working for the government in World War II. But for decades he was a regular contributor to government inquiries into what he called the "new commerce in ideas and intellectual property." In each domain of that commerce he mounted a libertarian case for the prerogatives of the recipient. He assailed the BBC as a monopolist for neglecting listeners (and later viewers); he criticized copyright law for protecting publishers and authors against readers; and he assailed patents for serving monopolies against users. He devoted an enormous amount of time and attention to calculating the consequences of favoring producers at the expense of receivers in each of these arenas. Plant quietly became Britain's most important critic of such monopolies before the rise of the open source software movement.

When the IBC asked him to investigate listening, Plant therefore seized the opportunity. His study would adopt a new approach, he declared. It would not rely, as the few previous attempts had, on listeners' own accounts of what they "regularly" did. Instead, Plant had an army of researchers knock on doors and record what they observed at the moment they entered each home. This approach, adopted from the advertising industry, would yield statistically reliable numbers—what Plant called "facts beyond question or uncertainty." (Or at least, it would for those times when British politeness did not make it inconceivable to knock, such as Sunday lunchtimes.) His staff would record the results in terms of average numbers of listeners over short intervals—again, something so different from earlier efforts as to be incommensurable with them. Overall, Plant aimed for a fine-grained account of the temporality, forms, and geography of listening. The geography mattered because the IBC's transmitter was only one tenth as powerful as Luxembourg's; whereas Luxembourg was audible across the UK, Normandy had to sell itself as reaching the best (that is, wealthiest) part of the country.

The survey was duly done in February and March 1938, with a large follow-up later in the year. Plant sent staff to over 25,000 households in 34 of Britain's major urban centers. What they found was that citizens were listening to four principal commercial stations—Luxembourg, Normandy, Paris, and Toulouse—as well as to the BBC. And there were major geographical variations in listening. Overall, the BBC retained a dominant share of the audience, but in the south, Normandy sometimes pushed it close. And on Sundays Reith's austere policy left the BBC an also-ran. The corporation would remain off air until 10:30 am, and then offer only a sober schedule of services, Bible stories, and religious and chamber music, falling silent again at times when the population should be in church. In stark contrast, a typical Radio Normandy Sunday of the late 1930s began at 7 am and continued until after midnight. In fifteen-minute chunks it offered children's serials, dance and other popular music, sport, astrology, variety, and drama.[9] Plant demonstrated the popular victory of this schedule in innovative graphical displays, of the kind fashionable in the period.

The implications of Plant's research extended far beyond the mundane commercial needs that had instigated it. In the first place, the study (along with another carried out independently at the same time) marked the dissociation of reading and listening. Earlier attempts by the BBC to know about listening practices had relied on writings—in particular, they had adopted the model of letters to the editor. Now they were to derive from observations and inquiries, ideally taken in real time. In the second place, Plant showed definitively that the BBC monopoly was a myth. In other words, the whole debate about broadcasting in midcentury Britain was based on false premises. And in the third place, the inquiry implied a new and different vision of the listener, as consumer rather than citizen. It helped create a media analogue to the economic liberals' concept of individualism.

———

THE BBC TOOK notice. It had to: the IBC's inquiry into listening appeared at a moment of unexpected crisis for the corporation, that saw it facing the serious prospect of dissolution. This was the same crisis into which Eckersley had stumbled. Its catalyst was an invisible poltergeist mongoose.

The poltergeist mongoose went by the name of Gef. He appeared in a remote farmhouse on the Isle of Man, and starting in 1931 the British press took pleasure in telling of his jokes at the expense of the resident Irving family. Gef claimed to hail from India, where he had been born in 1852, and he had a rich repertoire of knowledge and interests. But the renowned paranormal investigator Harry Price failed to find him on a visit in 1935, as a result of which the case became the occasion of an embarrassing slander prosecution.[10] Richard ("Rex") Lambert, the editor of the BBC's flagship magazine, *The Listener*, had gone along with Price as a witness. Lambert then ran an article on the mongoose during the summer months when the usual rule that the magazine print BBC talks was relaxed. There was nothing intrinsically remarkable in this. The corporation had several times broadcast programs sympathetic to psychical research, and *The Listener* itself had previously published Price's exposés of fake performers. Indeed, nowadays it is hard to read the report that Lambert and Price published as *The Haunting of Cashen's Gap*, despite its studiously neutral tone, without concluding that Gef was a rather transparent fraud. But it landed Lambert in trouble. He had long been an advocate of using films in adult education, and was prominent in the new British Film Institute. Over lunch, Sir Cecil Levita, the husband of another BFI governor, suggested to Lambert's superior at the BBC, Director of Information and Publications Gladstone Murray, that Lambert was clearly unfit and that the BBC should compel him to withdraw. The BBC man showed his notes to Lambert, who sued for slander. The Chairman of the BBC, a friend of the Levitas, then hinted that he should drop the case. But Lambert refused, and in the event went on to win substantial damages. The incident caused a crisis for the BBC because of the Chairman's intervention. It prompted a flood of expressions of discontent from within the corporation. Before long, it had emerged that some BBC employees even believed the corporation to keep secret dossiers on their private lives.

Strange as the mongoose incident was, the question to which it had now given rise was entirely serious: whether the BBC was essentially a corporatist body, akin to those established by the Fascists in Italy. A series of public statements by ex-employees, even very senior ones, implied so, and contemporaries were not slow to recall its conduct toward Eckersley and others (Eckersley's departure after his divorce had received wide attention in the press).[11] Lambert himself declared that a demand that individuals subsume themselves to the interest of the corporate body "lies at the root of the Fascist theory of life."[12] Such contentions revived what had long been anxieties lurking semi-dormant behind all the utopian rhetoric about public corporations. Critics now voiced the fear explicitly: the corporation was on a road to totalitarian managerialism. The laissez-faire advocate Sir Ernest Benn was not alone in assailing the "microphone monopoly" as "the child of the modern determination to govern everything."[13] But it was Lambert himself who leveled the charge with particular venom:

In spite of its lively youth, the BBC has chiefly succeeded in fitting itself to be an instrument of government—for intellectual and cultural purposes—in the totalitarian state of the future. There has never been any Ministry of Fine Arts in Britain; and now one will never be needed, for the BBC is supplying its place. That active individualism which used to be the basis of culture, entertainment, literature, and sport in old England is withering away, under the steady concentration of cultural "patronage" in the hands of great corporate bodies—commercial, governmental and "public utility"—of which the BBC, with its possession of a monopoly of broadcasting, is far the most powerful. . . . It has become the main indirect organ of Government, all the more potent because its influence *is* indirect. . . . No doubt the tendency is inevitable—and we are doomed, in this twentieth century, to see individualism in art, music, drama, literature and journalism disappear and in its place rise a kind of corporative system, within which the formerly independent thinker, writer, performer will have to seek absorption. If some new Dark Age, brought about by war, is to settle on the earth, such organizations as the BBC must supply the place of the old-time monasteries—enclaves of learning within a new feudal system. Yet it is not a pleasant prospect, this realisation of the "Servile State" long ago foretold by Belloc and Chesterton![14]

Every element was here—the association of the BBC with totalitarianism, the lament for a decline in individual liberty, even the invocation of those liberal icons, Belloc and Chesterton. Most significant was the identification of the corporation as a "public utility," which made Lambert's indictment as broad in its implications as the BBC's supporters held it to be. Friedrich von Hayek would soon represent public corporations as steps on a road to totalitarianism; Lambert thought that the BBC was already almost at the destination. Strange, then—and revealing—to find that in 1936, while the slander case was wending its way to the courtroom and the BBC had placed him on administrative leave, Lambert should choose to spend his enforced leisure visiting Nuremberg to take in that year's Nazi rally as a guest of Adolf Hitler.

For all that writers like Dalton supposed its destruction to be unthinkable, the possibility suddenly loomed that the BBC might face disaster. The charter would expire at the close of 1936, making the sudden controversy about its nature untimely indeed.[15] In April, everyone expected Sir Stafford Cripps, opening the parliamentary debate on renewal for the opposition, to focus on the IBC and the relay companies. Instead, he seized on Lambert's "scandal" and denounced the corporation as fascistic. Other members joined in. One charged that the BBC would establish "cultural dictatorship." Another was heard to describe it as "the nearest thing to Nazi government that can be shown." The BBC's future was suddenly in the balance.

The IBC/Plant science of listening had cropped up at just the wrong moment for the BBC. It seemed to prove that the corporation's position was not nearly as unassailable as it implied. BBC officials took care to pore over Plant's report. They decided that they finally had to stop putting their faith in listener correspondence. For the first time, the BBC instituted its own listener research.

The initial result of the corporation's new strategy was a remarkable social document. Hilda Jennings and Winifred Gill's *Broadcasting in Everyday Life* (1939) went beyond listeners' letters, but it also departed from Plant's statistical emphasis and identification of listening with consumption. Instead, Jennings and Gill used intensive interviews, in a bid to answer more profound and qualitative questions than had been conceivable in Plant's project. Was radio decreasing parochialism? Was it tending to produce "a docile, receptive listener," or was it "increasing critical faculties and releasing creative energies"? How was it affecting listeners' sense of nationhood and their performance of citizenship? Did it erode class barriers? With these questions and more, the study posed problems and articulated theses that would become central to studies of media and culture for the rest of the century. And its conclusions were strikingly auspicious for the BBC. Most notably, Jennings and Gill emphasized that in the working-class district of Bristol that they studied, listeners did not in fact regard radio merely as a medium of entertainment. Critical and discriminating practices were strikingly—and, for the BBC, hearteningly—prevalent. "Broadcasting," they discovered, was becoming "an educational service in the homes of the people." Their view of the listener—far from either the critical reader of the earlier BBC or the liberal consumer of Plant—was that of a creative learner. They called for a deliberate policy to encourage this practice. Such a policy, they urged, could make "the desire to learn and to create" into an "inherent" virtue of citizens.[16]

This call to elevate the BBC's original mission by aligning it with education would reverberate for decades. In the meantime, however, the BBC responded to its rivals' claims to science in more enduring fashion by setting up its own "listener research" operation. To run the unit, it hired (amid a certain amount of hush-hush) Robert Silvey, a veteran of a major advertising agency called the London Press Exchange. Silvey came to the corporation already familiar with Plant's survey, which he had compared to a mammoth "Reader Interest Survey" on the popular reception of press advertisements and headlines. That conjunction captured much of its implicit point, of course, and Silvey, impressed by Plant's report, had actually suggested to Lambert that the same methods be applied to the BBC's audience. Lambert had replied morosely that "no one would ever be allowed to do it."[17] But now Silvey was asked to pursue just such research in the interest of the public monopoly. The departure for the BBC was quiet but fundamental. *The Listener* hailed it as "really a new form of scientific investigation"—one made necessary, it noted, by the impossibility of tracking reception directly.[18] "Listener research" would from now on be an indispensable element in media planning. It would also become a major source of change in social science methods.

Meanwhile, the government announced a public inquiry to appraise broadcasting ahead of the decision on whether to renew the BBC's charter. The chairman was the seventy-nine-year-old ex–Speaker of the House, Lord Ullswater. Ullswater's panel called dozens of witnesses in the second half of 1935, including representatives of the relay industry and the IBC (much to Reith's disgust) as well as of the BBC itself. The BBC forthrightly defended itself as a "monopoly," dedicated, in memorably Reithian terms, to providing "a service somewhat ahead of what the public would demand were it possible for such demand to be made articulate and intelligible." At that moment, it almost seemed that the corporation's case depended on there *not* being an objective knowledge of listener tastes. But the BBC focused its hostile attention on the claims of the relay industry, which believed that it had such knowledge. By incorporating Continental commercial broadcasting, it said, relay managers would upset the all-important principle of "balance." They might, for example, relay only one side of a political debate of which the BBC had broadcast both. The warning may seem implausible; but, given that Sir Oswald Mosley was secretly one of the biggest backers of wired broadcasting, it was not beyond

possibility. Already relay services filtered out the corporation's challenging material and replaced it with programs from the IBC and its
peers. Effectively, the BBC representatives contended, relay managers
were fast becoming program makers. The BBC had long warned of
this, charging in 1933 that "each exchange may increase to the stat-
ure of a BBC in miniature." If exchanges merged into larger units—
and were perhaps bought up by some press baron—then the alliance
between relay and the Continental stations would truly become a
national media enterprise. It would then be capable of skewing public
knowledge and culture in the interests of corporations and political
extremists.[19]

The Ullswater Committee was convinced. It recommended that the
relay industry's programming should be put under BBC control, and
its technical facilities appropriated by the Post Office. Essentially, it
should be nationalized. Only one Ullswater participant, Lord Selsdon,
sounded a discordant note. Selsdon defended relay, insisting that subscribers should have the same freedom to receive the IBC as wireless
users did. He also pointed out that load meters provided relay companies with a more accurate insight into listener tastes than anything
the BBC had. Prominent among the proponents of nationalization, on
the other hand, was Beveridge, placing himself in opposition to Plant
just as their confrontation within the LSE approached its climax.[20]

The BBC still faced the House of Commons. In a bid to head off
the most hostile criticism, it requested a public inquiry into Lambert's
allegations.[21] The inquiry took place that autumn. Trying to steer
a middle course, it suggested that the corporation adopt civil service protocols. As a defusing exercise it was at best a partial success.
Parliament's debates still echoed with denunciations of the BBC as
high-handed and imperious. Even if such rhetoric is discounted as
hyperbolic—the charter was eventually renewed, and Eckersley, who
was present, reported that the consensus among MPs was generally
favorable—its articulation nevertheless amounted to a warning.[22]
Accurate or not, the charge that the BBC was a state in miniature
could not be permitted to rise again.

The crisis therefore triggered a change in the BBC's internal character. Its nature as an institution resembling the civil service dates from this moment, when its survival might depend on repudiating any impression of being a fiefdom. The personal symbol of the old order was, as he had to be, the prime public casualty of the change. After the review had been completed, John Reith was quietly eased out. At the instigation of Neville Chamberlain, now prime minister, he left the BBC for the last time in June 1938.

And Gef? The Irvings moved house, and Gef was never heard from again.

AS THE SOCIAL science of listening took shape, and as the scale of the crisis facing the BBC in the wake of the Gef scandal became clear, at the London School of Economics another struggle was consuming attention. Hayek was on the attack against Keynes. Their struggles culminated with his speech *Economics and Knowledge*, delivered to the London Economic Club, an LSE group of which he was president, in late 1936. In context, Hayek's presentation embraced and extended much of what Plant was arguing in more limited fashion (and Robbins more sweepingly). It also presaged Hayek's own later and much better known book, *The Road to Serfdom*. But Hayek himself nominated the speech as a turning point in his thinking and as his most original work. The talk laid out concisely what would become his most characteristic claim: that the problem of economic governance was at root a problem of social knowledge. Not only would state "planning" intrude on individual freedoms—many conservative writers already believed that. Effective and successful state intervention was impossible in principle, Hayek maintained, because it would require a kind and a degree of knowledge about the complex system of the economy that no person or institution could possibly achieve. By contrast, Keynes's "great conceit," as Hayek elsewhere intimated, was his idea that "he could play public opinion like an instrument."[23]

To represent the greatest controversy of modern political economy in this way was to assert that economic policy and theory hung on questions of knowledge and information. And that is indeed what

Hayek thought. He believed that the hopes for government "planning" voiced so ubiquitously in the 1930s were dangerously hubristic. Indeed, he believed that the European crisis of the time reflected the futility of such ambitions. At the height of the LSE triumvirate's campaign against Beveridge, Hayek composed a memorandum to the LSE director about Nazism to explain why.[24] Beveridge—and most contemporary opinion—took it for granted that Hitler was a conservative figure, perhaps conjured up by capitalists who feared Socialist advances. That made Nazism, in their eyes, a peculiar phenomenon fated to fail. Hayek deplored this notion as complacent and false. He insisted that Hitler's ideology not only had deeper historical roots but also, far from being conservative, had originated in socialism. There was nothing in principle to prevent Britain ending up with a similar regime, and, given what he called the "inherent logic" of collectivism, that outcome might even be likely if thirties policies persisted. Hayek edited a volume called *Collectivist Economic Planning* to reinforce the point. And he taught classes on the problems of such planning, often in the face of colleagues who advocated it. Then, in 1938, he returned to his Beveridge memo and published a developed version of it in *Contemporary Review* as "Freedom and the Economic System." By now his attention was focused far more explicitly on the problem of knowledge that he perceived to be central to planning, and which entailed the use of propaganda and coercion. A year later he expanded this paper once more, making it into a pamphlet.[25] And Hayek made plans to elaborate it into a historical synthesis tracing the "abuse of reason" from the Industrial Revolution to the Nazis. He never completed that project. Instead, spurred by what seemed the overwhelming enthusiasm in Britain for moving to a planned economy devoted to full employment—enthusiasm that focused on his old *bête noire* Beveridge's report on social insurance—Hayek recycled its later sections into a more accessible and polemical form. It appeared in March 1944 as *The Road to Serfdom*.

Hayek's polemic soon found an audience, notably in America. There it met with rejection from several major publishers before landing at the University of Chicago Press. At Chicago, Aaron Director,

the Russian émigré economist who would play a key role in creating
the field of Law and Economics, urged the Press to publish Hayek's
book, and it agreed. *The Road to Serfdom* rapidly proved a success. Much
of its fame, however, came from secondary versions. Max Eastman
arranged for a twenty-page condensation to be published by *Reader's
Digest* in April 1945. The Book-of-the-Month Club offered reprints of
this abridgment for 5¢ each—even less for bulk orders—and more
than a million were circulated. A magazine called *Look* even issued
a cartoon version, reducing Hayek's sometimes nuanced positions
to crude moral absolutes. Hayek himself was startled to find he was
the center of media attention when he came to the United States. He
found himself having to denounce crudely ideological caricatures
of his positions, insisting, for example, that he was not absolutely
opposed to all "government activity as such."[26]

Where Keynes advocated what he saw as a "middle way" between
the extremes of communism and Nazism—and figures like Dalton,
soon to be Attlee's chancellor of the exchequer, saw the public corporation, exemplified by the BBC, as embodying that middle way—
Hayek retorted that those extremes were in truth variants of a single
ideology. The root of this ideology was the contention that a nation's
economy (and its culture) could be planned centrally according to
scientific knowledge, and that such planning would yield common
benefits not forthcoming from competitive markets. This belief was
what Hayek termed "socialism"; whether its manifestation be *national*
socialism or communism was relatively unimportant. By his lights, any
attempt to construct a middle way on Keynes's terms could not lead to
an equilibrium between two extremes. It could only be a step toward
the central principle underlying both.

Hayek's alternative was what he called "individualism." It was
not quite absolute laissez-faire, since it entailed that the state act to
secure a clear and stable legal framework to maximize competition.
That might well justify quite an active role, for example to prevent
entrenched monopolies. And its scope extended beyond economics
and politics per se, into questions of creativity, discovery, and epis-
temology. Like his interlocutor Michael Polanyi (then a chemist at

the University of Manchester), Hayek wanted to insist on the irreducible role of individual and ineffable skills in the practice of science. Polanyi's point was that true research was intrinsically unpredictable, and therefore could not be subjected to state planning—an argument with similarities to the old radio amateurs' claims, but directed now against the Marxist crystallographer J. D. Bernal and others who wanted concerns about the public good to determine research priorities.[27] For Hayek, the implications were a little different. He argued that an elevated estimation of the certainty and objectivity of physical science had been transferred to the social sciences, with the result that the facts and forecasts on which state planners based their strategies assumed an unwarranted credibility. "Scientism" was therefore at the heart of the problem of planning. But as the state expanded, so, he warned, scientism would be reflected back onto the sciences themselves, so that "facts and theories must thus become no less the object of an official doctrine than views about values." Pure science would be anathematized. In the end, "the whole apparatus for spreading knowledge"—educational institutions, as well as cinema, the press, and radio—would have to be controlled. Only approved knowledge would circulate. This would be the terminus of the road to serfdom.[28]

Hayek's claim therefore involved—indeed, depended on—a view of creativity, centering on its premier organized form, science. Central planning rested on a false view of science, and in practice would destroy the foundations on which science itself rested. And to cast the principal problem of mid-twentieth-century politics and economics in this way likewise had severe implications for communications policies. Indeed, Hayek's work was a contribution to what we are beginning to recognize as an international debate about the relations between politics, creativity, and information. The pioneer sociologist of science Robert Merton (who cut his teeth in research on radio listening) and Polanyi were among the most influential contributors. So was Karl Popper. Hayek was in close communication with Popper in 1944–45 as *The Road to Serfdom* approached publication. Theirs were "parallel actions on different frontiers," Popper told him at the time. "You are fighting 'scientism'; I fight rather 'philosophism.' But we both fight collectivism." At that stage Popper's projected book was called *The Flight from Freedom*—on the other lane, presumably, of the road *to* serfdom. Hayek found it a publisher as well as obtaining for its author a position at the LSE.[29] The book eventually appeared as *The Open Society and Its Enemies.*

The large and diverse readership that encountered *The Road to Serfdom* in one of its forms found itself presented with a stark warning —the same warning that Hayek had spent the thirties refining at the LSE. (Harold Laski, the most prominent Socialist at the LSE, believed that the book was targeted specifically at him.) Thanks to the problem of knowledge intrinsic to economic planning, a long-term trend of increasing state intervention threatened to take Britain—and by extension the United States—down the path to totalitarianism that had already been trodden by Germany. "To anyone who is familiar with the history of the major Continental countries of the last twenty-five years," Hayek concluded pointedly, "the study of the recent program of the Labour party in England, now committed to the creation of a 'planned society,' is a most depressing experience." The prospect of an Attlee administration presented "mortal danger to everything a liberal must value."[30]

Hayek's point was not really that Attlee himself was about to create a totalitarian state. His target was ostensibly not a political party so much as a political culture. All parties, he claimed, had collaborated in building a consensus that would lead inexorably to a centralized, all-powerful state. Yet coupling Labour with Nazism (and to a lesser degree Stalinism) made for notoriety. And in fact Hayek's connections with party politics were stronger than he gave out. When his British publisher, Routledge, ran out of paper—which was still rationed—the Conservative Party diverted supplies from its election campaign so that an abridged version coordinated by party headquarters (and prefaced by a quotation from Winston Churchill) could be published.[31] And the book inspired what became one of the most notorious uses of radio in British history.

On June 4, 1945, Churchill came to the BBC to pitch for votes. He was preoccupied by the descent of an "iron curtain" across Europe, having telegraphed Truman about the danger that very morning. Now he spoke forcefully, in bald, uncompromising terms. He denounced "socialism" as incompatible with British traditions of liberty, remarking that any Socialist government, however moderate or well-intentioned at the outset, would inevitably "have to fall back on some form of Gestapo." "There can be no doubt," Churchill added, "that Socialism is inseparably interwoven with Totalitarianism and the abject worship of the State." It would threaten not only property but "liberty, in all its forms."

Portraying the mild-mannered Attlee in this fashion was a serious misstep, of which Churchill's own family had tried to warn him, and the next day Attlee made the most of it with a carefully poised response before the microphone. "I shall not waste time on this theoretical stuff," he declared, "which is merely a secondhand version of the academic views of an Austrian—Professor Friedrich August von Hayek—who is very popular just now with the Conservative Party. Any system can be reduced to absurdity by this kind of theoretical reasoning, just as German professors showed theoretically that British democracy must be beaten by German dictatorship." Then Attlee proceeded to define the distinction between Conservative and Labour plans for the postwar future. Churchill's men would leave all to self-interest—which he called "a pathetic faith resting on no foundation of evidence." His plan held that the public interest must come first, and that in peace, as in war, only by planning to improve it could the victory be won. Labour would not move to a wholesale socialization of the economy, Attlee pointed out. But some "great basic industries"— transportation, coal, gas and electricity, iron and steel—were "ripe for conversion into public services." And then he added a critically important point: "in every case there must be a suitable organisation which, while protecting the public interest, will give scope for business organisation and the application of scientific methods." That was almost an exact description of the public corporation model pioneered by the BBC, and through which he was speaking to the voters.

Churchill had spoken extravagantly about individual freedoms, Attlee added; but he himself could recall when companies had been "free" to employ children and women in sweatshops, and to neglect sanitation so egregiously that thousands died. "It was in fact freedom for the rich and slavery for the poor." Individual freedoms were valuable, but "wherever there is the danger of monopolies and cartels, there must be public supervision to prevent exploitation." The power of the state, conferred by Parliament, was essential to protect the public. And with Labour in power, the government would continue to protect the public from "profiteers and monopolists," limiting inflation and ensuring that housing remained affordable. In the wake of the war, with much of the housing stock destroyed or dilapidated, there was no more urgent issue. Indeed, in his second broadcast a few weeks later Churchill himself tacitly admitted as much. Abandoning the Hayekian high ground, he devoted most of his time to outlining the Conservatives' own policies for "food, work, and homes." It revealed much about the preoccupations of the time that the answer to the fundamental threat posed by state planning was . . . a Four Year Plan.[32]

The whole exchange was, by common consent, a disaster for Churchill and the Conservatives. His attack seemed extravagant, hyperbolic, and not least, given the recent history of shared effort and sacrifice, in poor taste. The notably temperate tone of Attlee's response, by contrast, played well. When the Labour Party inflicted a crushing defeat on the Tories at the polls, many believed that Churchill's Hayekian moment had decided the fate of the realm for the foreseeable future.

DURING THE WAR, the BBC's national and international position improved dramatically. It endured while the commercial broadcasters expired, and its relatively responsible programming helped it regain both respect and listeners. It emerged from the conflict with no Radio Normandy to face, and with Radio Luxembourg weak and dependent. When Sir Arthur Salter (the same Salter who had advocated controlling much of the economy on a BBC model) edited a celebration of "the impact of broadcasting on Great Britain's life and outlook," the tone was resolutely sanguine and optimistic. And a year

later, in 1949, the head of the Third Programme—the uncompromisingly highbrow channel created in 1946 and devoted to serious music,
drama, poetry, and intellectual talks—produced what was probably
the definitive statement of the BBC's ideal of listening as critical, civic
work. "Response itself must be responsible," the veteran announcer
and corporation executive Harman Grisewood intoned. Unlike a
commercial network, the BBC could shield listeners from "mere fad
or capricious unpopularity," but it could not succeed alone. British
broadcasting was a form of "organic life" and depended intimately on
the "atmosphere" in which it lived. For example, the BBC's "impartial-
ity and tolerance" could hardly survive in a society that did not itself
cultivate those virtues. Listeners therefore bore a threefold responsibility: for the material broadcast, for the system itself, and, most of
all, for their own engagement. This last Grisewood likened to the old
Roman ideal of *pietas*, which had connoted the exercise of responsibility to both oneself and the external world. A listener who did not
uphold wireless *pietas*, he warned, might "degenerate into a mind-
less machine." To evaluate critically meant more than being a good,
assiduous citizen (of the kind familiar from Milton's *Areopagitica*). It
meant being properly human in a technological age.[33]

Yet the demise of Radio Normandy and its peers did not mean that
a broadcasting paradise had been regained. British listeners could
still tune in to American stations, and advertisers in the United States
could sell to them through those stations. Unless the government proposed to jam broadcasts from its strongest ally, the editor of *Advertiser's
Weekly* pointed out in *The Times*, it would have to accept that "sponsored radio projected to overseas markets" was here to stay.[34] And
some advertising agencies planned to do more. Before the war they
had already considered recruiting European and American transmitters if the British ether remained closed to them, and after VE Day this
kind of speculation hardened into real planning. In June 1946, some
of this planning was leaked to the magazine *John Bull*. Apparently as
many as seven U.S. corporations were planning to start broadcasting
into Britain. *The People* added that the ventures would include at least
three stations based on Danish-owned ships. The BBC was likely to

face commercial competition "on an unprecedented scale" from these "radio pirates."[35] As it transpired, the alarm was a false one. The ships did not set sail—yet.

More important in the short term was the criticism of the BBC itself that continued in the war years. It intensified as the prospect of radical reforms in the postwar era became clearer and more immediate. Tellingly, several assaults came from former BBC employees, including Lambert and Eckersley. Another arrived from Arthur Turner, later a founder of the University of California at Riverside. And the veteran economic liberal Sir Ernest Benn devoted the sixth of his "post-war questions," published for his revived Society of Individualists in 1941 and reissued three years later, to broadcasting.[36] A long-standing opponent of the BBC, Benn warned that Britain was risking its citizens' "power to reason" by persisting with the "slavery of monopoly." It encouraged citizens to neglect their civic duty of active selection and engagement. Worse still, the BBC itself recruited its staff from "the new class, the product of the new education machine, the intelligentsia"—and that class "naturally" supported "modern theories of economics." So the BBC tended to favor interventionist ideals of the kind proposed by Beveridge, Keynes, and Attlee. Benn therefore accused the broadcasting regime of facilitating state expansion, favoring the Soviet Union and the League of Nations, and discounting the benefits of free trade. He even hinted that "this evil monopoly" was largely responsible for World War II. The distinction between Britain's broadcasting regime and a totalitarian one was, he concluded, a difference "of degree rather than of principle." The issue was "the gravest of the questions with which the advocates of freedom are now faced." He suggested that the government restore "the freedom of the air" by turning the BBC's own stations into autonomous companies. Finally, shortly after the war the BBC's own *Quarterly* recalled nostalgically that it was not long since the press had "tended to represent the B.B.C. as a body of men and women cringing under a dictatorship, whose private lives were spied upon and whose careers were dependent on a single whim." Yet while this "myth" might have been exploded, it cautioned that another already held sway. The BBC was now seen as "a vast bureaucracy" in which "originality and enterprise" were stifled.[37]

Concerns about the managerial character of the BBC and the political implications of its monopoly drew powerful, although largely implicit, support from the writings of George Orwell. Orwell's own attitude to the corporation was ambivalent. He defended its news broadcasts during the war, and indeed he worked for it himself in 1941–43. Moreover, he hopefully identified radio engineers as exemplifying a "new kind of man" who might inaugurate a postwar English nation of "classless beings." But his experiences in the Spanish Civil War had exposed him to the real propensity of newspapers or broadcasters to manipulate facts or even invent them, and to the likelihood that readers or listeners would follow along. His resolute insistence that his experiences in Spain revealed the real danger of totalitarianism—which lay in its denial of objective truth and its demand that one submit wholly to an "artificial universe" projected by the state—became common ground after 1945 for many who were concerned about the broadcasting monopoly. *Nineteen Eighty-Four* dramatized that experience in a Swiftian satire, central to which was the party official O'Brien's systematic undoing of the Scientific Revolution itself in his torture of Winston Smith. The novel was not about the BBC per se, but it was not hard for those so inclined to infer relevance. Already in 1947 Orwell had declared it "certain" that Britain's major newspapers would at length be nationalized, and had warned that all media—books, journalism, broadcasting, cinema, and theater—might be combined under a government ministry. That kind of vision would often lurk in the background as skepticism about the corporation revived, especially among antagonists holding political views very different from Orwell's own.[38]

From the dark days of British isolation to the late 1940s, a swell of criticism against the BBC thus slowly grew. It gave rise to a number of more or less plausible proposals for change. Most of them envisaged splitting up the corporation, as Benn advocated, or launching local stations, public or private, using the new FM technology. In 1944, for instance, *The Economist* published a series of editorials advocating three broadcasters.[39] All of these arguments were, and were seen as being, about more than the BBC itself. They were elements in the very wide public discussion then taking place about the kind of national culture that should be re-created after the defeat of the Nazis. In the short term they could be defied successfully. But economics and the science of listening would soon give them a new force, such that they could no longer be beaten back.

In early 1946, however, Prime Minister Clement Attlee announced that the BBC's charter would be renewed, as it must be every decade, without delay. There would be no public reflection. The government claimed that the issues had been adequately aired and resolved in the 1920s and 1930s. The decision satisfied no one, sparking incredulity from some experts and indignation from the corporation's critics. The most prominent objection among many came in the form of a letter in *The Times* from Lord Reith's successor as Director General, Sir Frederick Ogilvie. It appeared on the morning of the Commons debate on the charter. Ogilvie decried the "automatic nationalization of the infinitely precious things of the mind," and trumpeted the issue as "not a matter of politics, but of freedom."[40] In the end the Cabinet gave ground, appointing a new investigation. But it was chaired by none other than William Beveridge, and it duly produced an endorsement of the BBC's privileged position. Parliament renewed its charter with no more fuss.

By the late 1940s, the BBC seemed secure once again. The projected pirate ships had not been heard from, and it could face expanding FM and television services with confidence. That security was about to be shattered.

IF THE PURPOSE of nominating the architect of the welfare state to appraise the BBC had been to garner another unqualified endorsement, it was not entirely met. Beveridge's report contained a hundred recommendations—most of which were quietly ignored—for broadcasting to proceed on less monopolistic lines. And one of the panel's members, the backbench Conservative MP Selwyn Lloyd, insisted on including a short, uncharacteristically incisive statement of his own. Lloyd's dissent proved to be a time bomb in the midst of Beveridge's otherwise staid report. Little noticed at first, it would become the rallying point for a campaign in favor of commercial broadcasting that would break the BBC's quasi-monopoly.

Among those prominent in this campaign was Arnold Plant. Plant returned to the arguments about information monopolies that he had been making before the war. Ever-lengthening periods of copyright did nothing to stimulate better quality or more quantity in creative works, he repeated. He also deplored the quasi-monopolistic powers of the Performing Right Society and Phonographic Performances Ltd.—the rights agency partly responsible for a so-called needle-time rule that severely limited the BBC's use of recorded music. And he attacked the BBC itself for claiming what he called "property in programmes." Such monopolies, Plant warned, could stifle what he labeled a "new commerce" of intellectual property. He endorsed commercial television and even pay TV. The controversy he helped fuel would be a major stimulus to the establishment of the Pilkington Committee in 1960, which, in restating the BBC's radio monopoly, set the stage for the pirate radio boom.[41]

But it was a young acolyte of Plant's who blew open the simmering controversy over broadcasting and politics, with consequences that were to last for decades. Ronald Coase had arrived at the LSE a budding student Socialist. The child of two Post Office telegraphers, he had overcome an early assessment of physical disability—as a young child he wore iron casts on his legs—to win a scholarship at a grammar school. By the time he left, he was already enrolled in extramural courses at the University of London. He was set on pursuing a degree in the LSE's commerce program, and his early convictions did not survive the encounter with Plant and his group. He heard Hayek too, and found his explanation for the economic slump of 1929 "magical."[42] Plant encouraged him to examine the key question of the day: the nature of public corporations. Coase began with the Post Office, and in particular the broadcasting monopoly. He then spent about a decade researching the BBC. He focused squarely on the monopoly, investigating how it had come about, its effects on rivals (relay and commercial stations), and its public reputation. The project was entirely a product of the intellectual culture of the London School of Economics: it was undertaken there, funded by the School, and initially published in parts in *Economica*. In 1950, the School was also responsible for publishing the resulting book, *British Broadcasting: A Study in Monopoly*.

British Broadcasting was the first authoritative account of its subject, the origin of the monopoly broadcaster. Coase looked not just at published records but at the minutes of crucial meetings in the 1920s. He also interviewed major players from the BBC (including Reith), the relay companies, and the commercial broadcasters. No other discussion had anything like the same empirical grounding. But Coase used his evidence to mount a sharp critique. He contended that there was a void at the center of British broadcasting policy. The question of the monopoly had never been addressed. In the 1920s, successive inquiries had explicitly left the question open; yet in the 1930s it was always assumed that those inquiries had settled the matter. The monopoly had come about, not quite in a fit of absence of mind, but by complacency and opportunism.

Coase began with a history of the monopoly's emergence, recounting those early controversies over the experimenter's license. He argued that a consensus on monopoly had crystallized somehow between 1923 and late 1925—that is, between the Sykes Committee, which tackled the experimenters issue, and the Crawford Committee, which recommended the formation of the British Broadcasting Corporation. He further contended that nothing technical or economic had dictated that this must occur. In fact, it emerged largely for *cultural* reasons. And it was mainly the achievement of John Reith. It was Reith who articulated the ideal of a public corporation for broadcasting, identifying its virtues as independence, even-handedness, and the upholding of standards. In this period the highbrow press began to refer in Reithian terms to the cultural necessity of a monopoly, even denouncing the potential use of the ether for vulgar commerce as "a blasphemy." Coase then revealed how this conviction had crippled the alternatives of wired and commercial broadcasting. The BBC had been able to call upon its identification with standards to pressure the government to constrain these services. But again, it was not clear exactly what drove it to exert this pressure, or what made the pressure effective. BBC officers had said that they were "bound" by the charter to defend its monopoly on the creation of programs—but no such monopoly existed in any BBC charter. Nor was it clear exactly what policy or rule was contravened by sponsored programming: the BBC itself had been permitted to broadcast sponsored programs until 1936, although in fact it did not do so after the mid-1920s. Again, it seemed that practices had been driven by cultural perception rather than statute or rule.

Coase therefore argued that the case for a monopoly on technical or economic grounds had never really been made. Yet the central fact about British broadcasting policy was that it was widely assumed not only to have been made, but to have been decisive. The problem of interference, for example, was still adduced after World War II, yet Coase believed that it was technically false, and in any case it had never been sufficient to necessitate a monopoly in the creation of programs. The British Establishment typically asserted the BBC's monopoly to be essential for British broadcasting to be "the best in the world"—and in particular better than the American system—but nowhere could a coherent account be found of why. After the early days, when a few classical liberals had opposed the BBC's formation, the monopoly had faced remarkably little criticism until World War II. What criticism there was rested on concerns that it infringed freedom of speech, by analogy to having the newspaper press controlled by one body. But even the controversy stirred by the Gef case had not led to overt attacks on the monopoly, Coase pointed out, although the monopoly was in large to blame for Lambert's predicament because it left unhappy employees with nowhere else to go.

This peculiar situation was a problem for more than just the system of broadcasting. As Coase put it in complaining of Attlee's decision to renew the monopoly without a second glance, the greater issue was that in the interwar period a "legend" had arisen that public corporations were "the answer to all problems of the administration of new public services." The issue was thus a very general one, "of the greatest importance" to the future of Britain. The support for the BBC monopoly in the 1920s–1930s might have lacked a logical basis, but it certainly reflected "the spirit of the age." Britons had come to welcome, or at least accept, expansions of "central planning" in all spheres, even that of information. "Virtue" was taken to reside in the maintenance of high standards, and only public service bodies freed from the constraints of competition could make high standards their raison d'être. The BBC's prized notion of "balance" exemplified that ideal. In the end, when all the arguments for a program monopoly were examined, this was the only one that remained in play. On its own terms, it was a powerful argument. But it had special ramifications, because broadcasting, unlike other industries, affected "the very existence and nature of public discussion." This argument for the monopoly implied a claim "to determine on behalf of the listener which broadcast material he should hear." Accepting it as valid—or even as properly posed—therefore required one to adopt what Coase called "a totalitarian philosophy." Totalitarianism: that, in the end, was the veiled reality that for Coase lay behind Britain's complacent embrace of the BBC.[43]

Coase had by now eviscerated every argument for the broadcasting monopoly based on physics, technology, or economics. He had insisted that the real reasons for the monopoly's creation had been cultural and moral, not to say moralistic. The Continental broadcasters (obliterated by the war) and the relay industry (still enduring, but without Eckersley's visionary ambitions) proved in his portrayal a diverse, dynamic, and unpredictable economy of listeners. And he drew much the same message as Hayek, that central planning was a step to totalitarian rule. His analysis rapidly became second nature to economic liberals. Selwyn Lloyd's dissent from the Beveridge Report, in particular, certainly echoed Coase in both argument and language.

Few could have predicted that Lloyd would be the author of dramatic change in British media. He had only recently entered Parliament, having been an unremarkable lawyer and a mid-ranking Army officer in the war. He had little by way of an ideological track record, the only exception being that he had resigned from the Liberal Party in 1931 over its abandonment of free trade. But on being appointed to the Beveridge Committee Lloyd visited the United States to experience broadcasting there, and came back impressed. The experience proved to him that a cultural counterpart to Gresham's Law was not nearly the threat that the BBC's supporters suggested. This being so, he became determined that Parliament should end "at any reasonable cost" what he accounted a "perpetual monopoly" in the provision of information, education, and entertainment. He denounced in rather eloquent, if conventional, terms the "terrifying" dangers implicit in the notion of a public corporation with a mandate to elevate the general culture. After all, nobody would advocate a single "British Publishing Corporation" to control the production of books. Lloyd proposed commercial television and radio channels to run alongside the BBC's surviving stations, with a counterpart to America's FCC (Federal Communications Commission) to oversee them all.[44]

At first, few took note of Lloyd's dissent. But its plausibility waxed as the vitality of the Labour government wilted under Austerity. With the fear of interference receding in the face of new VHF and television technologies, and with Coase's pointed analysis finding readers, questions of principle now came to the fore. By the time the Conservatives returned to power in October 1951, Lloyd's position had acquired a reputation among Tory backbenchers as a powerful and principled statement—one "firmly based upon the very foundations of Conservative philosophy," as MP Gilbert Longden put it.[45] Lloyd found himself with supporters both at Westminster and, quietly but powerfully, in the advertising industry. They launched an intense lobbying effort—one of the first in modern British politics. Its strength unsettled even Churchill's Cabinet, which was filled with older grandees who liked the BBC and had not recognized the potency of the issue for the party's Young Turks. The Turks' initial target was not radio, however, the regime for which was entrenched. Their target was television.

After much parliamentary infighting, the bill permitting com-

mercial television passed at the end of July 1954. The first actual broadcasts went out just over a year later. In the meantime, Lloyd's position
had exposed him to attack, not least from his own constituents. They
regularly wrote to him to threaten that they would vote "socialist" if
he masterminded the introduction of commercial media. The correspondence (relatively little of which supported his stance) reveals
much about attitudes to the public service at this critical juncture.
A Professor Hearnshaw, for example, calling himself "an educator
who is much concerned with the evil effects of commercial influ-
ences on growing minds," and who claimed to have lived in a country
where commercial broadcasting reigned, declared himself "absolutely
opposed to allowing commercial interests to control any form of
broadcasting." A headmaster from Anglesey urged that there could
be no real choice when "the sole criterion of content is the breadth of
popular appeal," and contrasted the "delicate subtleties of humour" of
the BBC with the "ranting roaring commercialism" of American stations. Another constituent added that slogans about freedom on the
air were sure to prove "illusory" when it came to television, because the
large capital required to establish a TV station meant that in practice
access would be limited to the few. And a fruit merchant in Liverpool
lamented that Lloyd's proposal for commercial broadcasting—
or, as he put it, his plan to "prostitute television"—would "lower still
further the general standard of intelligence and of selectivity."[46] Lloyd
was civil to these citizens, and occasionally conceded that a correspon-
dent had a point. But he held his ground, robustly declaring that he
meant to vote against the monopoly just as he would against a single
institution to publish all newspapers, or to run all theaters, or to publish all books. To leave broadcasting in the hands of a single institution
would "endanger the freedom of our whole society." In what seems to
have been an unsent draft, he added that "many millions" had already
listened for years to Radio Luxembourg with no ill effects, exposing
themselves to commercial broadcasting over which the British state
had no control at all.[47]

By the mid-1950s, then, Coase's argument had become pivotal to
creating a commercial television service in rivalry to the BBC. It also

provided what would remain the principal foundation—typically quoted verbatim but without acknowledgment—for defenses of pirate radio into the 1960s. The clash over broadcasting set in train at the LSE in the 1930s extended in this way through the forties and fifties, and on into the sixties. It was seen by all sides now as a conflict about culture itself—its definition, character, quality, and future. Indeed, it became a central battleground in the conflicts over high and low—or elite and mass—culture inaugurated by the Leavises before the war and given new force a generation later by Richard Hoggart and others. We shall encounter some of the consequences later. Meanwhile Coase himself left for the United States in 1951, eventually to end up at Chicago and win a Nobel Prize. But back in the UK his *British Broadcasting* had already become the *Road to Serfdom* of the modern media.

THE ROAD TO SERFDOM itself may have had the appeal, for some, of emphatic clarity, but if anything its starkness was counterproductive, as Churchill found to his cost. Yet immediate impact was not Hayek's aim. He recognized the strength of the Keynesian consensus, and was given to telling friends (rather accurately, as it turned out) that another generation would pass before that consensus shifted. In the meantime, he urged them to avoid the fray of day-to-day political causes and instead seek to effect that larger, more momentous change. Doing that meant seeking to influence not so much active politicians as the intelligentsia: academics, respected journalists, and cultural critics. The real battle would be on this ground. Practical politics would follow, not lead.

Heeding his own advice, Hayek began to propose establishing some forum at which allies might confer. Within Britain, organizations like the Society of Individualists had long existed, but they had proved both parochial and ineffective. There was nothing more cosmopolitan. When a Swiss entrepreneur volunteered to finance an exploratory meeting, Hayek therefore jumped at the chance. He invited Popper and Polanyi, among others, to participate. The meeting took place at Mont Pelerin in Switzerland in 1947. Others attending included Milton Friedman and George Stigler (among a cohort of Chicago economists), Henry Hazlitt, and Hayek's mentor, Ludwig von Mises. The point, Hayek told them, was to reexamine "the whole relation between governmental coercion and individual freedom," in order to boost "the chances of preserving a free civilization." The effort would be a long-term one, because the journey to a "new kind of serfdom" was itself long. "We must raise and train an army of fighters for freedom," Hayek continued, in much the same way that the Fabians had raised an army of collectivists in the years around 1900.[48]

This 1947 occasion became the launching point for a more or less regular series of meetings at different centers around the world. The Mont Pelerin Society attracted more members—including Plant and Coase—and grew into the leading international forum for economic liberalism. Within Britain, politicians as well as academics and economists attended its regional meetings: Geoffrey Howe, John Biffen, and Keith Joseph, representing a new generation of Tory politicians, all participated at events in the 1960s. The spirit was very much that which would animate the first Thatcher government in 1979, in which these figures would hold commanding roles: Howe as chancellor of the exchequer, Biffen as chief secretary to the Treasury, and Joseph as secretary of state for industry. Another participant was at the time perhaps even more promising than these, but Enoch Powell's career as a Conservative politician would be destroyed by his notorious "Rivers of Blood" speech against immigration in 1968.

The triumph of Thatcherism created its own mythology. One part of it was that Hayek and his society represented lonely voices of resistance throughout a generation of Keynesian ascendancy. Hayek himself remarked that his views were out of favor, and sympathetic writers have portrayed him and his group in heroic terms ever since. This is misleading. Economic liberalism may not have been in power, but it was never in eclipse either. Nor was it as united as retrospective mythology has tended to imply. For example, members of the Mont Pelerin Society constantly grated against the self-denying ordinance prohibiting involvement in quotidian politics. In Britain, especially,

4

THE ABOMINABLE NO-MAN

I n northern France during the summer of 1944, debates about public broadcasting and democracy seemed arcane and luxurious. Europe's immediate future was being decided on the battlefield. Advancing slowly after D-Day, the Allies pushed back German forces, fighting for every yard of territory. By early July, Britain's 69th Infantry Brigade had reached the town of Audrieu. There they halted in the face of intense heavy-machine-gun fire from the 12th SS Division. An artillery strike was ordered on the German position, but the gunners hesitated to fire for fear of hitting their own side. A tall, heavy-built lieutenant came forward to break the deadlock. Head down to avoid incoming rounds, he ran forward, lugging a wireless transmitter to within sight of the German lines. From there he was able to guide the artillery shells onto their targets. The British infantry were soon freed to advance again; Canadian forces further along the line with no such luck were captured and massacred. The lieutenant won a Military Cross for his exploit. His name was Oliver Smedley.[1]

The man who would try to build a broadcasting revolution on the foundations laid by Coase and Hayek was by then thirty-three. Born in Surrey, he had been raised in the west country by his grandfather, William Thomas Smedley, an accountant, amateur astronomer, and chairman of the largest film enterprise of Edwardian Britain. As boss of British Mutoscope and Biograph, the elder Smedley had displayed a notable skill in financial legerdemain. But he was not only a capitalist, for William Smedley dedicated much of the fortune he accrued to one of the most notorious lost causes of the age. Convinced that the works of Shakespeare should be ascribed to Francis Bacon, he accumulated a valuable collection of Renaissance books that he believed Bacon had annotated. (They now reside at the Folger Library in Washington, D.C.) The combination of financial creativity and focused dedication to an apparently quixotic "search for truth" seems to have rubbed off. Certainly, Oliver Smedley would display both traits.[2]

Smedley attended Monkton Combe, a prestigious private school, in the 1920s. Rather than going on to university, however, he left at sixteen and went to work for the office documentation company Roneo. Mutoscope had bought the company decades before, and his grandfather remained chairman. Roneo sent him to Paris for a year, where he lived in a working-class *arrondissement*. Back in London, he took a position at an accountants' firm and rapidly rose in the ranks, making partner at an early age. But in 1939 Smedley joined the Territorial Army, and less than a year later he was serving in the Royal Artillery. By the time of that battle at Audrieu he would have seen service in India, the Middle East, Africa, Aden, and Sicily. Trained as a parachutist, only a bout of malaria had prevented his being dropped over Caen during the invasion. He had crossed the Channel on a landing craft: it was blown up under him.

Smedley seems to have loved the military, and he emerged from the war a decorated and twice-wounded veteran. Toward the end of the conflict he married Eileen Faulkner. Known as "Mike," she was the daughter of a British newspaperman living in China and a Latvian/Russian émigrée who had endured a long odyssey to escape the Russian Revolution. She was working for the British consulate in Shanghai when the Japanese invaded. Both her parents were interned, but she returned to Britain via an exchange in Mozambique for Japanese personnel held by the British. Smedley met her while she was serving in the Women's Royal Naval Service (the "Wrens"). After demobilization the pair moved to Essex, renting an old stable block in the grand old estate of Audley End. They lived there from

1948 to 1956, and then moved to a cottage in nearby Wendens Ambo. Meanwhile Smedley embarked on what became a remarkable career of political and economic adventurism.

At first Smedley took up his old position in the City. But like so many returning from the war, he had been profoundly affected by the experience of the battlefield. Most hoped for the kinds of changes that had been so widely advocated at home while they were in uniform: full employment, social security, greater access to education, and universal health care, all to be overseen by state ministries like those that had managed the war effort. They were the ones who voted in huge numbers for Attlee. But Smedley was among the minority who demurred. His convictions were very much those of Hayek's *Road to Serfdom*, of Arnold Plant, and of Ernest Benn's Individualists. But unlike Hayek and Plant he was no academic, and he had little time for Hayek's gradualism. Already he had become a member of Benn's group, making common cause with economic liberals like the erstwhile Beaverbrook journalist and ardent free trader S. W. Alexander. Smedley now began to write actively for Alexander's polemical *City Press*, and before long had become deputy editor. In that capacity he found himself making contact with what would become a generation of conservative activists, notable among them Keith Joseph, John Biffen, and Enoch Powell.

Among the survivors of Benn's Individualists, Smedley soon stood out as the most doctrinaire and uncompromising of all. He believed that the country had taken a wrong turn long before the war. At the worst point of the slump, Whitehall had abandoned free trade in favor of an "empire preference" policy championed by the supreme press baron of the age, Lord Beaverbrook. According to Smedley, the tariffs then erected around the empire had set the country on a road, not merely to serfdom, but to mass starvation. In innocuous-sounding bodies like the Milk Marketing Board he saw foreshadowed a future of humiliation, tyranny, and death. As memories of war faded, as Britain retreated from its world role, and as (in the late fifties) Austerity retreated, such rhetoric came to seem increasingly extreme. But he stuck with it. As late as the 1970s, he could be found telling his neighbors to stockpile dried "rainy day foods" in preparation for catastrophe.

In 1952, Smedley issued his own declaration of faith: a statement that he entitled *The Abominable No-Men*. Alexander, who published the tract, forecast that it would surpass even Hayek's *Road to Serfdom* in its impact, making Smedley "world renowned."[3] It was devoted to the character, creed, and commitments of "Radicals," whom Smedley described as society's "original thinkers in the truest sense." These were his eponymous no-men. They had a long lineage. It had been a Radical who refused to pay Ship Money in the days of Charles I, and they might even be thought of as remnants of the ancient Britons themselves. Their major characteristic was defiance. They stood against collectivism, state planning, protection, monopoly, and military conscription. They decried Marx, Beaverbrook, and Beveridge alike. Nowadays, that meant defying an almost uniform consensus. Smedley vowed to renew the tradition of passionate dissent. "It is time," he proclaimed, "to frighten a few babies."

Yet Smedley's no-men would say yes to some things. In particular, they revered "sound money." That is, Smedley wanted exchange controls abolished, taxes reduced, and public spending slashed. With inflation defeated, he sought an eventual return to the gold standard. And above all, radicals advocated free trade. Here, indeed, was radicalism's "Ark of the Covenant"—its only absolute.[4] "Free Trade is morally and economically right for every country in the world," Smedley proclaimed, "whatever the state of its civilisation or the nature of its industries. There is no exception to the rule whatsoever." Smedley urged that the UK withdraw from GATT—the world trade referee—in order to race ahead and eliminate its own tariffs unilaterally. Claims of unfair competition were no reason to hold back. In truth, they were simply claims of *effective* competition. The Japanese, already looming as challengers to some British industries, merely recognized realities. They "prefer to trade than to die."

Thus far, Smedley's views seemed merely a rather one-dimensional counterpart to Hayek's. But unlike Hayek, he was a devotee of action, not ideas. So Oliver Smedley set out to foment a counterrevolution.

FIRST SMEDLEY BECAME a politician. He became active in the Liberal
Party immediately the war ended, and by the 1950s was fast rising in
the ranks. He hoped to revive the once-great party on the basis of a
renewed commitment to its traditional principles of free trade and a
stable currency. That meant adamantly opposing not only agricultural
subsidies but also the emerging Continental trade zone—what would
later become the European Union. He similarly saw the European
Free Trade Area as a counterpart to the despised empire preference
policy, leading to "an international bureaucracy which would hamper
individual liberty."[5] In those years, before the Liberals tilted decisively
in favor of Europe and a more social democratic vision of liberalism,
his was a potentially viable platform. Indeed, the party's older grandees tended to endorse the free trade credo. Smedley duly stood for
Parliament in Saffron Walden, against R. A. ("Rab") Butler—a major
Tory figure, but one whose majority at the start of the fifties was only
about 1,000. Failing in that bid, he later stood again at Walthamstow,
Attlee's old seat. Again he fell short. Smedley never did become an
MP. But he served on the party's executive committee from 1953 and
became a vice president three years later. By now he was a major force
in Liberal politics.

Yet beneath the surface Smedley's position was becoming impossible. A new Liberal generation found his free trade absolutism dated
and intellectually exhausted. He was accused of trying to revive
the long-dead figure of *Homo economicus*, who lived by bread alone.
Younger activists argued that true liberalism had to take account of
other, more complex and collective kinds of freedom, extending to
issues of health, education, and civic rights. (It was at this moment that
Isaiah Berlin gave his famous lecture at Oxford on "Two Concepts of
Liberty," which highlighted the rival notions even as it gave grounds
for preferring Smedley's.) And they embraced the idea of Britain joining the Common Market, which for Smedley was anathema. At the
1958 party conference he "uncorked a volcano" by advocating "unilat-
eral" free trade, not least with China and the USSR. By 1960 he was

being described as a "rebel" for his refusal to compromise. The next year, the crisis came to a head. Smedley had recently launched the latest of his many advocacy groups, the Keep Britain Out campaign, only for Jeremy Thorpe (later the Liberals' ill-fated leader) to propose a policy for joining the Common Market. At the party conference in Edinburgh, Smedley was finally left the leader of a small sect of irreconcilables. He lamented the vote for Thorpe's motion in extravagant terms—hinting that it would destroy the party, and if enacted would lead Latin American countries to fall to communism. He would never again be able to stand as a party candidate.

Possible futures for Liberalism diverged at that moment. The Liberal Party went in one direction. Smedley, along with Alexander and a rump of free traders, took a radically different path.[6]

SMEDLEY'S SECOND STRATEGY was to create his own politics. This he did from the early 1950s onward, using his expertise in financial management to launch a dizzying number of associations, clubs, leagues, and institutes. Most were short-lived. Those that endured, however, would have profound and even revolutionary consequences.

In 1952, Smedley had heard murmuring about his political activities being incompatible with the duties of a City accountant. Resigning his job, he resolved to strike out on his own. He now established his own company instead in an office in Austin Friars, deep in the City of London. He named it Investment and General Management Services Ltd. For the next quarter century, IGMS would be the hub of an almost endless series of enterprises devoted to an array of conservative political, financial, and entrepreneurial causes. Some seem to have taken a rather entrepreneurial approach to prevailing norms of financial ethics. One example was the Austin Friars Investment Service, which offered "counselling" to savers wishing to invest in the stock market. It was not registered with the Stock Exchange (although IGMS was). Austin Friars never made much of a profit, and when questioned, Smedley tended to portray it less as a business than as a vehicle for his ideological commitment to a capitalism for everyman, not just the magnate. In due course he twinned this service with something he called the Reliance School of Investment, which purported to educate would-be investors in appropriate strategies. The "School" gave out diplomas, which Smedley openly admitted were universally unaccredited. It lasted into the 1970s. IGMS itself endured for some two decades, never making more than a tiny annual profit, before eventually being liquidated in 1977 with debts of about £500,000.

As the number of ventures emerging from IGMS multiplied, Smedley hired a personal assistant to help with financial management. His choice fell on one Aubrey Boutwood—a bankrupt as recently as 1956, who had earlier served prison time for a check fraud serious enough that the bank manager he conned committed suicide. With Boutwood to handle financial matters, Smedley could concentrate on ideological concerns. And most of the operations that he launched from IGMS were not companies but advocacy and pressure groups. He and Alexander proposed one in honor of Benn on their erstwhile patron's death.[7] Another was the Cheap Food League, which advocated for the abolition of agricultural subsidies and protections. Others included the Council for the Reduction of Taxation, and the Keep Britain Out group already mentioned. And where he did not inaugurate groups himself, he took over existing ones. Smedley thus commandeered the venerable but moribund Cobden Club and the Free Trade League. From 1959 he ran the latter's *Free Trader* magazine, which began to include advertisements for his Austin Friars investment company. Later still—at the very peak of the pirate radio crisis—he would find time to launch an organization for Sound Money Research, designed, as he modestly put it, "to stop inflation in this country."[8] In 1957, Smedley also founded the National Benevolent Fund for the Aged—a charity, but one that remained unregistered while he ran it; its assets were managed by Austin Friars.[9]

Most of Smedley's ventures left little trace: they either wilted rapidly or preached only to the already convinced. But in 1955 he joined with another ex-Individualist to form one that had a far more lasting impact. A straitlaced Christian Scientist, Antony Fisher was an old

Etonian who had piloted Hurricanes in the war and, after being shot down, pioneered the use of simulators in training. He and Smedley had met at Benn's society. After the armistice Fisher joined Smedley and Alexander at the *City Press*, authoring a series of anti-Socialist screeds. He also became a farmer in Sussex, leaving the City in 1950 to manage his farm full time. But he continued to collaborate with Smedley in opposing agricultural subsidies, which he too saw as presaging starvation. Fisher became joint treasurer of another of Smedley's advocacy groups, the Farmers' and Smallholders' Association.

Fisher was an admirer of *Reader's Digest* for its strict anti-communism. In 1947 he therefore found himself reading its condensed version of Hayek's *Road to Serfdom*. He was apparently impressed enough to seek out Hayek in person at the LSE. Immersed in planning the first Mont Pelerin meeting, Hayek gave his acolyte much the same advice he would take to Switzerland: to eschew political engagement and concentrate instead on shifting the cultural consensus. At the time, Fisher was neither able nor disposed to do this, although he did join the Mont Pelerin Society and attend its meetings. Like Smedley, he wanted action. He too stood for Parliament, in his case for the Conservative Party, but with no greater success. And he also published a manifesto, *The Case for Freedom*. Developed from his *City Press* articles, Fisher's tract laced a rough-and-ready version of Hayek's philosophy with calls for a return to the gold standard and an illiberal dose of ersatz McCarthyism. Fisher, unlike Hayek—or even Smedley—contended that Britain's progress along the road to serfdom was a result not of well-meaning planners but of clandestine Communist conspiracy. He wanted decisive action to root out infiltrators. Significantly, in evidence he cited the BBC. Such "'impartial' sources of information," Fisher remarked, could be devastating, because they were "vulnerable to infiltration." He gave no evidence that infiltration had in fact occurred (although in the shape of Guy Burgess it had), but moved immediately to his conclusion that the BBC must be made to face competition. The one intervention Fisher allowed a government to undertake—that to prevent monopolies—must be used to end the BBC's.[10]

Fisher and Smedley's chance to act came fortuitously, when Fisher suddenly found himself independent. His cattle had been wiped out in a foot-and-mouth epidemic. Thanks (it is worth noting) to a government subsidy, he was able to parlay the loss into a windfall. While visiting like-minded associates in the United States, he saw an experimental battery farm in operation at Cornell University. He returned to Britain determined to launch his own counterpart, quietly smuggling enough eggs through Customs to start a flock of White Rock chickens. He soon had tens of thousands of birds, and their numbers continued to grow rapidly. Fisher's Buxted Chicken Company inaugurated factory farming in the UK. It made poultry into a mass-market food, bought at the huge supermarket chain of Sainsbury's by the millions.[11] And it gave him and Smedley the resources they needed.

The two men decided to create another organization, similar to those Smedley had become used to launching. But it would have grander, Hayekian ambitions, and a better strategy to achieve them. It would be a force for economic liberalism. Unlike the Mont Pelerin Society, however, this operation would concentrate on topics of relatively immediate consequence. It would garner research from respected authors, and publish it in forms compelling for a general audience. Smedley undertook to provide it with premises, and began to ponder a name. It must define its mission, he noted, in "cagey" terms, lest it be accused of toeing an ideological line and risk losing the charitable status that would allow it to reap donations tax-free. With this in mind, Smedley settled on his name for the new body. He called it the Institute of Economic Affairs.

THE IEA BEGAN operations in an office at IGMS in late 1955. There Smedley gave a desk to Ralph Harris. Fisher had met Harris back in 1949 when he gave a talk against food rationing; he had regaled the young Conservative Party researcher, fresh from a first-class degree in economics from Cambridge, with his dream of a conservative counterpart to the old Fabian Society. He now made a point of tracking Harris down to run the new body. He was soon joined by Arthur Seldon, an ex-student of Arnold Plant at the LSE. But recruitment stopped at two. The counterrevolution would have to start small.

At first the IEA survived on infusions of money from Smedley and Fisher. But Smedley soon told his collaborator that he could "do no more," and from then on it leant heavily on Fisher's farming fortune. He provided £1,000 a year, that sum rising sharply to a peak of £12,000; he also actively solicited donations from rich businessmen. In essence, loans and income from Fisher and his business, industrialist societies, corporations, and merchant banks kept the operation afloat. The income from publications, by contrast, was tiny, when it existed at all. Meanwhile Smedley retreated into the background, consumed as he was by his other ventures and the crisis in the Liberal Party. The Institute moved to new premises at Hobart Place, in Westminster. Subsequent memories have tended to remove Smedley all but entirely from the story, so it is all the more important to note that he continued to give the IEA as his address in letters to the Mont Pelerin Society for years, and that IGMS continued to provide administrative services. Well into the 1960s, Smedley's personal assistant, the unsavory Boutwood, was doing the Institute's accounting.[12]

Not only was the IEA financially fragile—a state it shared with all of Smedley's ventures—but during the Macmillan years of the late fifties and early sixties its mission was also seen as distinctly quixotic. What press attention it did attract was usually in tones reserved for deluded utopians. Yet as time went on it began to make an impact. Seldon, as manager of its publication program, was immediately responsible for this. At first Fisher and Smedley had considered using the IEA to train public speakers, or perhaps to launch a journal. But Seldon discarded these ideas and instead produced provocative but substantial research tracts. The first tended to be by Seldon and Harris themselves, but over time more authors signed up. Given the straitened finances, the hope was to attract interest through Fleet Street columnists, and thus to multiply each tract's impact. As it began to work, Fisher's funding provided for an expanding body of arguments addressing every realm of policy, from pensions, through the impact of advertising, to the welfare state.

The IEA survived. And at length, after the Tory defeats of 1964 and 1966, it began to flourish, gaining a reputation as the most influential source of "new right" ideology. It became the prototype for the array of think tanks launched in the 1970s and 1980s. Sir Keith Joseph and Margaret Thatcher alike hailed the IEA as the incubator of their radicalism.[13] Milton Friedman too would call Fisher the "single most important person in the development of Thatcherism." Such memories were selective and full of hindsight. But they were not false.

IT IS NOT clear precisely when or why Smedley and the IEA parted ways. But by the early 1960s they were both set to embark on separate ventures focusing on the nature and role of information. The IEA's would lead to detailed analyses of intellectual property systems, commercial television, and pirate radio. Smedley's would make pirate radio a practical reality.

Harris and Seldon introduced the IEA's project at the Mont Pelerin Society's Oxford meeting in September 1959. The moment was a delicate one. The IEA had organized the conference, and would end up meeting its arrears; but the society's secretary, Albert Hunold, vehemently denounced Harris for treating it as an opportunity to recruit supporters for the IEA itself. He represented this as "infiltration" and complained that Harris "did not behave like a gentleman."[14] The charge presaged an internal rift destined to culminate in Hunold's expulsion. But it made for an electric atmosphere as Hunold—along with Smedley—came to hear Harris and Seldon speak on "The tactics and strategy of the advance to a free economy."[15]

Harris and Seldon began by telling the story of early IEA productions, which had focused on topics in the news and been targeted at "retailers and wholesalers of ideas" like students, teachers, journalists, and broadcasters. They were also often written by authors from very different ideological backgrounds—a strategy that Seldon and Harris called "infiltration in reverse." They especially singled out their own treatment of advertising. It had appeared at a time of widespread agitation for government action against purported abuses. The IEA tract took the opposite tack, of course, and on provocative grounds. It denounced the perception, common at that time to all sides, of a distinction between "informative" and "persuasive" advertisements. All advertising was beneficial: it enabled that massive Hayekian knowledge system, the economy, to operate.[16] The story, like that of the IEA in general, was "an object lesson in the role of ideas," not because the ideas themselves were powerful or even new, but because there had been a change in the cultural "climate" that made them so. Austerity had brought home to "the national mind" the consequences of a planned economy. A vital opportunity therefore existed. Any economic system had to command broad "moral allegiance" in order to function—something that the laissez-faire camp of the 1930s had forgotten, presuming to assail government interventions that were often undertaken to avert real catastrophes. Now, the chance existed to gain that allegiance once again. The case of advertising showed how to do so, at the same time as exemplifying the commercial information system that should be the objective.

It made sense, therefore, that Harris and Seldon immediately pointed to commercial broadcasting as marking a fundamental turning point. "Conviction that broadcasting is too important to be left as a State monopoly has now firmly taken root," they claimed—and this despite persisting criticism of broadcast advertising. Their point was partly that the campaign for commercial television and radio must not be seen in isolation. The early 1960s were about to witness a combined interrogation of the entire information system: broadcasting, press, and advertising in general.[17] With such a massive reexamination in train, for the first time since the 1920s the trajectory of culture might be changed. So, as Harris revealed three years later (again with Smedley in the audience), the IEA would focus its attentions on "the role of information in a market economy." In the campaign to revive laissez-faire, information was going to be the principal battleground.

The opportunity had to be seized, and the IEA existed to do that. But here Harris and Seldon made an important and, for the Mont Pelerin audience, challenging point. Their "battle," they said, was not only against outright deniers of laissez-faire. Almost equally

dangerous were business people who claimed to endorse the free market. Managers often sought to avoid its disciplines in their own cases,
by monopolizing and concealing information. Indeed, IEA researchers had already found themselves confronting corporate secrecy—not
least in the advertising profession, which had been happy to cooperate
until it realized that Harris meant to denounce its restrictive practices.
In the end, experience had revealed the existence of two kinds of businessmen. Traditional managers entrenched in older companies were
skeptical of IEA efforts. But "more vigorous and less conformist entrepreneurs" were enthused. One of the principal findings of the IEA
overall was the vital role the latter played in breaking down traditional
customs and restrictive practices. The market system itself would be
crippled without them. Harris and Seldon called them "privateers."[18]

AUSTIN CHURTON FAIRMAN was thirty-six and at a loose end. Born
into a theater family—the son of actress Hilda Moore, he liked to claim
that after Moore's death his father had sold him to his aunts—he had
drifted between various dramatic and artistic careers since leaving
Oxford. He danced for a while with the Ballet Rambert, published photographs, played flamenco music, performed magic, and wrote a book
about the Spanish landscape. He helped out in several of Peter Brook's
productions, sometimes acting in minor roles, and also did some television work. A visually arresting presence—he liked to dress in what he
thought of as Renaissance garb, which gave him an appearance somewhere between Zorro and Dracula—Fairman's current employer was
the long-dominant West End theater agency, H. M. Tennent. Binkie
Beaumont, Tennent's flamboyant manager, had decided in 1957 to
expand into TV, in alliance with the mogul Lew Grade. They had put
together an experienced team, with the old IBC man who had organized Radio Normandy before the war, Richard Meyer, playing a central role. But Grade had feared that concerns about monopoly power
would get in the way, and indeed his initial Independent Television
Company was rejected on that basis. Grade was more successful with
Associated TeleVision (ATV). To keep the enterprise at arm's length,

Beaumont had told his production manager, Ian Dow, to establish the studio. And Dow had hired Fairman.

Now, however, after years of lugging sets from the workshop at Lambeth to the studios, where plays were performed live before the cameras, Fairman had had enough. He had decided to try recycling his theatrical experience into a new career in interior design. All he needed was someone to set up the company, which he wanted to call *Mise en Scène*. So Fairman went to see his cousin, who was a financial expert. Over a series of lunches in a London chophouse they agreed on the outlines of the new venture.

The cousin was Oliver Smedley. And it was there that Smedley one day showed Fairman the prospectus for a new idea of his own. He called it "Project Atlanta."[19]

Project Atlanta arose from conversations begun in the late fifties and consolidated in the early sixties, at first between two figures from the theatrical and music worlds. First and probably foremost was Dorothy "Kitty" Black. Born in South Africa to British parents in 1914, Kitty Black had been educated there and in the UK, before moving to Paris with the intent of becoming a concert pianist. Before the war she had returned to London and begun work in Binkie Beaumont's office at H. M. Tennent, where eventually she would come to know Fairman. From a secretarial position she had soon risen to exercise real aesthetic authority, scouting out plays for Beaumont and effectively deciding their fates. Black had a penetrating critical judgment and a decisive approach that stood her in good stead. She became a behind-the-scenes impresario. Fairman hoped she would even consider staging his own work.

Since 1945, Black had played an especially instrumental role in introducing new and avant-garde drama. She was a key participant in an offshoot of Tennent's operations based at the Lyric, Hammersmith, and devoted specifically to new and experimental work. The group called itself "the Company of Four," because it would rehearse a production for four weeks, present it outside London for another four, and then give it four weeks at the Lyric. There Black played a pivotal role in bringing to Britain plays by Jean Cocteau, Arthur Miller,

Tennessee Williams, and others. She also worked on the first UK production of Beckett's *Waiting for Godot* in 1956. A fluent francophone,
she herself translated pieces by Cocteau, Anouilh, and Stravinsky, and
it was as the leading translator of Jean-Paul Sartre that she was known
in France. She had helped John Gielgud write his first autobiography,
while in her own right authoring several radio dramas and TV scripts.
Her clients and acquaintances amounted to a roster of the greatest
names in British theater.

As the older West End gave way before the wave heralded by John
Osborne's *Look Back in Anger* (a play, as it happens, that she disliked),
Kitty Black became a principal shaper of what would come next. That
shift bore marked similarities to the pressures building up in broadcasting—pressures to abandon stilted, formal conventions for spon-
taneity and integrity. Ronan O'Rahilly, founder of Radio Caroline,
started out at just this time by running a drama school specializing in
Method acting, and it seems plausible that the ostentatiously sponta-
neous style of some pirate DJs did hark back to this training.[20] Black
herself was contemptuous of government intervention in the arts,
especially when it was defended as emancipating artists from commercial pressures in the name of creative integrity. Such protections,
she thought, upheld mediocrity. So she was intrigued when, on a
business trip to the Continent, she came across a radio station that
trumpeted the same virtues. It was called Radio Mercur. Mercur was
transmitting pop music into Denmark from a ship in the North Sea.
It was the first modern pirate station.

Although we tend to identify pirate radio with ships off the British
coast, the British ventures in fact took their inspiration from northern Europe. There, several ships were already rigged up as offshore
broadcasters. By late 1962, at least five stations were up and running.
The first of them was Mercur, which used an ex-fishing boat called
the *Cheeta*. Since August 1958 Mercur had transmitted sponsored programs into Denmark and Sweden. Registered in Panama, the *Cheeta*
was owned in Switzerland and leased to a Liechtenstein company;
Mercur sold airtime from an office in Copenhagen. After a rocky
start, the station was successful enough to move to a larger ship, the

Cheeta II. It also inspired Radio Nord, launched in March 1961 to broadcast into Sweden. Nord used an old German cargo ship, registered at first in Nicaragua and then in Panama as the *Magda Maria.* As with Mercur, a Liechtenstein company held the ship's lease but a Swedish office sold airtime.

Guided by its Texan backers, Nord avoided the old custom of sponsored programs and instead issued a continuous stream of chart hits. From April 1962 another station, Radio Syd, competed for its Swedish listeners, using the old *Cheeta.* That October, Radio Antwerpen appeared off Belgium, created by a veteran named Georges de Caluwe who had obtained his first license back in 1922. And from rather earlier, Radio Veronica broadcast into the Netherlands from a converted lightship. Again, the ship's registration shifted around—from Panama to Guatemala, and then to East Germany—but a Liechtenstein company held the lease and sales were organized locally. In early 1961, Veronica even briefly experimented with broadcasting into Britain under the name CNBC, with an office in Dean Street, London. It thus became the first of a new generation of pirate broadcasters to transmit into the UK.

Curious, Black asked about Mercur's commercial structure. She returned to Britain impressed enough to entertain thoughts of imitating it. Here might be a way of setting a cat among the pigeons in broadcasting, much as the new playwrights were doing in the theater: with naturalistic voices and an empathy for the predicaments of everyday people. There was nothing like it in Britain. Someone with experience in attracting audiences to exciting new work could make money.

Black found an ally in an Australian music publisher, Allan Crawford, whom she seems to have met while organizing the production of a musical in Oxford. Crawford had been a manager for a major American house, Southern Music, first in Sydney and then in London. But he had resigned to set out on his own. His new company was named Merit, and was devoted to new acts often doing cover versions of American pop songs. He was convinced he had the material to succeed, but needed a way of reaching a large audience. But the only popular commercial station, Luxembourg, had become the preserve of other, better-established labels. The BBC was clearly not an option, although Crawford later claimed to have made a sarcastic suggestion to Broadcasting House around the time of the Pilkington Committee that the BBC and Merit should join forces—an idea that its credulous managers seemed to entertain as a serious proposition.[21] Whether acknowledging reality or, as he later claimed, repelled by the BBC's willingness to go along with his spoof plan, Crawford resolved to forge a new outlet of his own. Like Black, he seems to have come across the solution by happenstance. He rented offices in London that had recently been vacated by the defunct CNBC. There he found intriguing documents that the Veronica staff had left behind. Crawford was impressed enough that he decided to form an alliance with Black and launch the first British pirate station.

Crawford and Black knew broadly what they wanted to do. What they lacked were two things: capital, and the financial acumen to set up the kind of elaborate corporate structure an offshore radio station required. For these they turned to Oliver Smedley as someone likely to be both willing and able to create the kind of international consortium needed for a semi-licit broadcaster. It was the moment when Smedley's relations with the Liberal Party were at a breaking point, and they intrigued him with their talk of anti-BBC broadcasting. By 1960 he had joined them in forming a company, CBC (Plays) Ltd. Despite its name, CBC was intended from the start as a vehicle for a commercial radio project. And as that project took shape, they gave it a name. They called it "Atlanta."[22]

Black, Crawford, and Smedley were not the only people in Britain to see an opportunity. At least two other projects were in the offing. The first of them was called, splendidly, the Voice of Slough—Slough, for those unfamiliar with the place, being a notoriously dull town west of London made memorable only by Poet Laureate John Betjeman's poem beginning "Come friendly bombs and fall on Slough!" (in the 2000s, the hit BBC series *The Office* was set there and captured its atmosphere very well). Voice of Slough was announced to the press in October 1961, with quite elaborate plans including a studio in Aylesbury and a boat called the *Ellen* from which to broadcast. At least one announcer who would later work with Atlanta, Keith Martin, was involved. The other was GBOK, created by one of the Voice of Slough's original backers, Arnold Swanson, at the end of 1961. Swanson set up a studio in the grounds of his magnificent Tudor mansion, where he installed Ed Moreno (later a Radio City DJ) to record programs. He planned to broadcast from an aged lightship registered in Liberia. Both projects had convincing publicity machines, and both continued to sound plausible well into 1962. But neither ever got on air. Voice of Slough reportedly ran into opposition from record companies, which would not permit the taping of discs on shore. In GBOK's case the problem was that the ship—which had been built in 1878—was simply too decrepit to be seaworthy. By late 1962, Atlanta was the only game in town.

AS A BUSINESS, Project Atlanta originated as another of Smedley's myriad initiatives forged in IGMS. He himself became chairman, and the press publicly identified it with him, although Crawford too was a director (along with Arthur Mathers, another Australian with experience of radio).[23] In general, pirate radio concerns were not exactly clandestine enterprises—they depended on advertising, after all—but their financial operations were often, and to varying extents, intentionally obscure. It certainly helped if one's financial expert held a conviction that offshore financial havens were not only prudent in general but morally necessary. Smedley fit that bill.

Smedley was extraordinarily optimistic in his forecasts. He estimated start-up costs as barely over £30,000, not including docking and legal fees—£15,000 to buy a ship, £10,500 for station equipment, £1,250 for an aerial, and £4,250 for installation. Against this, he forecast that profits could well amount to £1–£2 million a year.[24] To forestall legal problems, he obtained a letter from the Bank of England confirming that CBC could send money abroad to a Liechtenstein company to sell airtime for an offshore station—a necessary move in an era of currency controls. And he secured an opinion from F. E. Skone-James, QC, editor of the standard work on copyright, that broadcasting from a foreign ship outside territorial waters would not require a Post Office license, and that programs could be taped ashore for transmission provided performance and copyright fees were paid. These were critically important documents. They provided the fundamental financial and legal credit that potential investors would demand.

Revealingly, Smedley does not seem to have sought a legal opinion about the international conventions that supposedly governed wavelength allocations. Presumably this was because the conventions had never become directly enforceable at law. Yet they did exist, and as ventures like his got going, they would get stronger. The gamble he and his allies were taking was that they could entrench their stations before the international regime caught up with them. But here experience suggested that the odds were good. The old agreements that the BBC had done so much to foster between the wars in opposition to Radio Luxembourg had desperately needed revising after 1945. World War II left countless transmitters operating on unapproved frequencies, often impinging on neighboring countries' claims. In 1947 a massive conference at Atlantic City, New Jersey, involving some six hundred representatives from almost eighty countries, convened to sort out the mess. The result was the creation of a new, formal "right to international protection from harmful interference," guarded, like all respectable rights, by a branch of the United Nations. The International Telecommunication Union was now brought under UN auspices, and administered an International Frequency Registration Board with a Master Frequency Register. Through the 1950s this register grew. By the early 1960s, with the advent of satellite communications, there were proposals to extend its remit even further: the ITU published a discussion of the question, "Will space be open to piracy?" And it was also now, at a meeting in Geneva, that the Union finally moved to outlaw "pirate broadcasts"—that is, "broadcasting stations . . . on board ships, aircraft or any other floating or airborne objects outside national territories." This was the basis for government contentions that Atlanta and the other pirates were illegitimate. But the ITU asked national regimes to act against these pirate stations, and not until 1965 would they conclude an agreement to take concerted action. In the meantime the Cabinet did nothing. The pirates' gamble remained a gamble, but it paid off.[25]

By February 1963, Smedley was deep in planning his "commercial radio ship project." He hoped to get the operation running "at short notice," he told Fairman. Smedley asked his cousin to take the documents from the Bank and Skone-James to show to potential investors. This Fairman did, approaching an East End funeral home entrepreneur named John Delaney. Delaney said he would fund the venture, but only if Fairman himself were on the board to look after his interests. Crawford turned him down—he and Fairman seem not to have got along well—and insisted that they look instead for small investors. Fairman now asked a number of acquaintances from the theater scene, including his old boss, Ian Dow. He eventually signed up a handful, the writer Francis Wyndham among them. *Mise en Scène*, its original purpose now forgotten, became an intermediary for these shareholders. Also among the investors were a group of sea pilots, who might be called upon for expertise. But when Project Atlanta Ltd. was incorporated on August 2, 1963, it was the initiators themselves who took the overwhelming majority of shares. Black invested. CBC (that is, Black, Crawford, and Smedley) took a 24 percent holding in consideration for an exclusive license it granted to Atlanta. And the second largest shareholder after CBC was Smedley's IGMS, with 20 percent.[26] When share certificates went out in November, investors were told that transmissions should begin by February 1, 1964.

The operation had to be complex and transnational to avoid national laws, and it was. This kind of elaborate system had been established by Radios Mercur and Nord—and at one remove, 1930s pioneers like Eckersley had invented it. But Smedley's financial acumen perfected it. Project Atlanta became one end of a long corporate chain. It acquired the right to sell airtime on a forthcoming Radio Atlanta from CBC (that is, from Smedley, Crawford, and Black), paying a lump sum of £48,000 and giving CBC 36,000 (24 percent) of its shares. Project Atlanta also undertook to pay monthly sums to cover CBC's costs in maintaining and supplying the station, and to reimburse CBC for Crawford's services. But that was just the start. CBC got the right to the airtime from a different company, Atlantic Services Anstalt, based in Liechtenstein. CBC would pay the running costs of the station to this company, which would formally run operations. It seems to have been Atlantic Services that paid the DJs, too, via another British company, Hengown Ltd. Hengown was headquartered alongside Project Atlanta in Dean Street. Meanwhile, Atlantic Services had leased the ship from a fifth company, also based in Liechtenstein, called Rajah Anstalt. And Rajah Anstalt had chartered the vessel from yet another company, this time based in Panama. In what seems to have been a piece of laconic humor on Crawford and Smedley's part, they named this last company Rosebud.

The organization that was going to become Radio Atlanta thus spanned two continents, three countries, and at least half a dozen companies. It may well have been more complex still; it is difficult now to reconstruct its intricacies. With this complicated arrangement in place, Crawford, Smedley, and Black hoped to broadcast to an area extending from the Wash in the northeast to Southampton in the southwest—an area that included the most prosperous, and therefore prized, parts of the country. And thanks to the government of Sweden, they even had a ship. Or so they thought.

They hoped to take advantage of a coordinated move by several European governments to silence their pirates. In 1962, the Nordic states agreed to pass national legislation in concert to outlaw the stations. The laws were slated to come into effect at the end of July, with Belgium following suit at the end of the year. Mercur had little choice but to close down (the Danish state broadcaster hired its presenters to launch its own pop-orientated schedule shortly after). Radio Antwerpen did likewise, and its ship was wrecked almost immediately. Veronica survived because the Dutch authorities were not party to the move. Only Syd tried to hold out. Nord, seeing the writing on the wall, capitulated before all the others. It had decided to sell up to Atlanta.

Nord's ship, the *Magda Maria*, was an aged vessel, much modified since its original launching in 1921, but it housed a fully operational broadcasting station. Realizing that their station was unlikely

to survive, and seizing the chance to sell the boat to British entrepreneurs with all its equipment on board, Nord's owners capitulated in
June 1962. After a voyage to Spain for maintenance, by September the
ship was in the Thames estuary. But at the last moment Atlanta's plans
were stymied. The Danish authorities had moved against the pirate
station that had initially piqued Kitty Black's interest, Radio Mercur.
Suddenly, some of Smedley's backers got cold feet. The partners found
themselves without the cash to buy the ship. The existing owners
refused to consider a lease, and sent the vessel—now renamed the
Mi Amigo—to America to be refitted as a leisure fishing vessel. Only
after the mast had been removed did Crawford and Smedley finally
get together the money to purchase it under the Rosebud company.
She set sail again from Texas in the last days of 1963. Heavy weather
now slowed the crossing. Only in March 1964 was the *Mi Amigo* ready
for a new mast to be fitted. By that point a crucial year had been lost.
The delay would prove disastrous in more than one way.

In their search for small investors, one possible backer Atlanta had
approached was a young music entrepreneur named Ronan O'Rahilly.
O'Rahilly was a twenty-three-year-old from Ireland who was then
making a fortune from London's burgeoning music scene. He was
involved in the management of new R&B bands, especially through
the Scene Club in Soho, which hosted acts like the Rolling Stones
and the Animals. Like Crawford, O'Rahilly needed some way of raising the public's awareness of his bands. He had already considered
re-creating the practice of the old prewar Continental stations by
renting time on European transmitters, but had found that this was
no longer feasible. So when Crawford approached him with talk of
Project Atlanta, O'Rahilly realized immediately the potential for the
idea. He hesitated to venture financing, but did introduce Crawford
to his father, a businessman who owned a port in Ireland. Greenore
was a tiny town, situated in the remote northeast of Eire, but it had a
deepwater dock. Originally built to serve a ferry crossing to Britain,
it had fallen into neglect after the rail connection was abandoned in
the 1950s. It looked like an ideal location in which to fit a radio mast
on a ship without attracting notice.

During their conversations Crawford handed O'Rahilly the letters Atlanta had obtained to confirm the viability of an offshore station. Realizing immediately the value of what he had been given, O'Rahilly resolved to use them as a foundation to launch his own station. Atlanta could still use Greenore, he said, but his men would be there too, fitting out an offshore station of his own. Yet he reassured Crawford that he did not intend to compete with Atlanta. O'Rahilly intended his ship to broadcast from the Irish Sea, he said, not the Channel or the North Sea. This was not necessarily implausible, given the vitality of the northeast in contemporary music, and Crawford believed it, offering engineering and studio facilities to help O'Rahilly's station along. But it did not in fact happen, and it seems likely that Crawford was unwise to accept the reassurance in the first place. At any rate, O'Rahilly moved fast. He secured £250,000 of capital for his gambit, under the hastily appropriated name of Planet Productions, and set up an office in the Chelsea premises of Jocelyn Stevens's *Queen* magazine. He then had a Swiss holding company buy a defunct ferry named the *Frederica*, which was sitting in Rotterdam. He let the existing owners believe that he meant to use it for carrying livestock. But Planet immediately leased the ship and had it sailed to Greenore. By the time the *Mi Amigo* arrived, O'Rahilly's vessel was already there. He had renamed his the *Caroline*.[27]

The *Mi Amigo* needed far less work than the *Caroline*, so the Atlanta vessel should still have been ready first. But delays strangely accumulated. Amid an operation that was carried out in considerable secrecy (although word of it did reach the British government), suspicions and mistrust pervaded both sides. It soon became evident to the Atlanta crew that Greenore's workers were agents for a competitor, not a friendly counterpart. Equipment went missing, only to turn up on the *Caroline*; progress was markedly slower on the *Mi Amigo*. But only in late March, when the *Caroline* sailed out of Greenore, did Crawford realize the extent of Atlanta's failure. Instead of dropping anchor in the Irish Sea, the ship sailed south. It passed through the Channel and dropped anchor off the Essex coast. After a day of test transmissions, it began broadcasting in earnest on Saturday, March

28, 1964. "Radio Caroline," as the first announcer, Simon Dee, called it, had become Britain's first "all day music station."

The *Mi Amigo* was not ready to leave Greenore until almost three weeks later. On April 17, the ship sailed out into the Irish Sea. But it soon developed problems with its aerial, which, like those on all the radio ships, was tall—168 feet—and liable to be unstable. It had to put in to Falmouth in Cornwall for shelter and repairs. Only after ten days at sea did the *Mi Amigo* finally arrive at its anchorage off Essex, within line of sight of the *Caroline*. And it was another ten days after that before test transmissions could start. When they did, Atlanta pointedly broadcast on the same frequency as Caroline (1520kHz), picking up at the end of its rival's daily programming in hopes of alerting listeners to the new station's existence. On May 12, Atlanta's real broadcasting began on a slightly different frequency. Smedley was cock-a-hoop: he blazoned the front cover of *Free Trader* magazine with a photograph of Radio Atlanta, "the new voice of freedom."

But making up for lost time would be critical. During the six weeks that it had had the airwaves to itself, Caroline had demonstrated its ability to draw listeners, and had used that demonstration to attract advertising. Atlanta was not only second on the scene, but its programming was distinct and in some ways more conservative. Neither broadcast solely "pop" music, despite the pirates' reputations. Caroline mixed pop records with jazz, light orchestral music, country and western, rhythm and blues, ballads, folk music, and songs from West End musicals. Between the Searchers and the Beatles listeners could hear Etta James, Leonard Bernstein, Ella Fitzgerald, Mantovani's orchestra, Nat King Cole, and Tony Bennett. Atlanta, meanwhile, favored Crawford's record labels, which meant that it frequently broadcast cover versions by little known groups rather than original Beatles or Stones discs. Unlike Caroline, moreover, Atlanta also cleaved to the norm of dividing its schedule into discrete programs, which it devoted to specific musical genres. Fairman's R&B show, *All Systems Go*, which he presented under the alias of Mike Raven, was the most important of these, but others focused on Latin American, ballad, and country and western styles. These programs were recorded professionally in

London to be relayed from the ship, and they came across as less spon-taneous than Caroline's more impromptu efforts. At times they could even sound distinctly similar to BBC fare.[28] The relative staidness of Crawford's programming became a problem that would persistently dog the *Mi Amigo*.

In the event, the new voice of freedom was silenced rather quickly. Within weeks O'Rahilly and the Atlanta directors were talking of joining forces, and on July 2 they ratified a merger. The next day, Atlanta began taking in a proportion of the advertising revenue that would from now on be collected by O'Rahilly's Mayfair office, Caroline Sales, for both ships. Crawford and O'Rahilly became joint managing directors. The *Caroline* sailed north to an anchorage off the Isle of Man and began broadcasting as Radio Caroline North, thus taking on the role that O'Rahilly had initially ascribed to it. The *Mi Amigo* meanwhile stayed put, broadcasting into London and the southeast as Radio Caroline South, with two of the five DJs who until now had lived on the other ship. Broadcasting continued without an audible hitch. But the merger was in fact less than total, and proved quietly acrimonious. For many in the Atlanta operation, including Smedley and Black, to see what they thought of as the more profes-sional operation—and the true pioneer of the pair—being subsumed was galling in the extreme. The *Mi Amigo*'s captain resisted the deal, and several Atlanta staff—including Fairman, and the company's gen-eral manager—resigned rather than continue in the new regime. And relations between Atlanta and Caroline remained fractious, with each side suspecting the other of scheming for control. The two ships meanwhile retained distinct program policies. Caroline North took full advantage of the vibrancy of the music scene in Liverpool, but Caroline South remained dominated by Crawford, who continued to favor records produced by his own label. Caroline North would play Beatles singles, while Caroline South would play cover versions of the same songs by Crawford's bands. It was as though Radio Atlanta had continued.

Yet the original pirate rivals had now created what they significantly called a "network." It was a remarkable moment. For the first time since the prewar days of Normandy and Luxembourg, a pirate commercial broadcaster could claim to offer a national service.

THE GOVERNMENT WAS in a quandary. The offshore stations were clearly popular, and they were anchored outside territorial waters. It was unclear what could be done against them that would be legal and politically acceptable. "To stop them we will have to send a torpedo," mused a Post Office official. "But that's a bit drastic, isn't it?"[29]

The Cabinet ducked the issue, deferring it until a European consensus could be reached. Meanwhile, however, other opposition began to manifest itself. It tended to concentrate on three major themes: wavelength scarcity; intellectual property theft; and the commercialization of culture.

The first of these rested on the fact that the pirates helped themselves to wavelengths allocated to others by international agreement. This might provide a legal basis for action against them, but the fact was that the old Copenhagen accord was hopelessly out of date. Most AM broadcasters across the continent—including stations like Voice of America—were not operating on allocated wavelengths. They were licensed by local governments on the understanding that they would not, in practice, interfere. British advocates of commercial broadcasting wanted Whitehall to adopt a similarly relaxed posture. But the pirate stations *did* cause interference, their antagonists charged. The BBC even affected to fear that piracy might lead to "the end of all intelligible sound broadcasting." This clearly played to fears of ether chaos that had survived from the earliest days of wireless.[30] But it was not entirely groundless. Contrary to what is often asserted, the British government received dozens of complaints of interference caused by the pirate stations, some from as far away as Yugoslavia.[31]

A second charge that returned time and again was that of intellectual property theft. The offshore stations were said to be copyright pirates as well as wavelength pirates. With the government reluctant to act, it was Sir Alan Herbert, the author and chairman of the British Copyright Council, who kept insisting that they be shut down, if necessary by force. Long used to the BBC's acquiescence in restrictions, and to Radio Luxembourg's willingness to be bought, the record companies denounced the pirates for simply making free with their music. Pirate stations played records almost continuously, playing fast and loose with performing rights, and often taped them ashore for broadcast at sea, thus treating copyright just as insouciantly. Phonographic Performance Ltd. (PPL), the record industry's agent in matters of broadcasting, announced that it would seek an injunction against Caroline even before the station began operations, and the Performing Right Society (PRS) likewise accused it of skirting payments. John Stanley of the radio and television firm Pye, a major advocate for commercial radio, warned that there might soon be sixty stations, all ignoring copyright.[32] The Postmaster General, Anthony Wedgwood Benn—nephew of the old Individualist Sir Ernest, but of very different political views—told MPs in late 1965 that "listening to a 'pirate'" would lose its pleasure if the listener "contemplated—as he should—the fact that this is stolen copyright." And in October 1966, his successor Edward Short would once again insist that "pirate stations ignore copyright laws and play records all day long." No licensed station could do that. Told that the pirates wanted a legal system of commercial broadcasting on land, Short replied in words borrowed directly from Herbert: "every burglar, too, would like legalizing."[33]

Of course, such loud complaints about intellectual property violations were largely disingenuous. The record companies always made sure that the pirate stations obtained and aired their latest releases. But copyright law did lie at the heart of the clash between the pirates and the BBC in another sense. It was the 1956 Copyright Act that prevented the BBC from doing what the pirates did and broadcasting records all day. It enshrined the corporation's obligation to obey a so-called needle-time restriction. This was an accord that the BBC had originally reached during World War II with PPL, and indirectly with the powerful Musicians' Union. The union, fearing for its members' jobs, had pressured PPL, which itself feared for the retail sales of records. They had combined to limit the BBC to broadcasting records for only twenty-two hours per week, rising to twenty-eight by the time

culture itself. Even a Conservative government shied away from association with "a candy-floss, bread-and-circuses image." The BBC's view, mirrored by much of the quality press and by successive governments, was that capitalistic activity was in itself incompatible with public service. The most insistent advocate of this line throughout the sixties was to be Richard Hoggart. Hoggart was newly famous for his book *The Uses of Literacy* (1957), written while he was teaching extramural classes at Hull University. Hoggart insisted on the richness of working-class culture and its legitimacy as an object of study, paving the way for a future generation of researches. But he also warned of its erosion at the hands of mass media, comprising newspapers, magazines, pulp novels, cinema, and the commercial broadcasting at that time available only from Radio Luxembourg. Hoggart continued to insist on the imperative to uphold critical practices of reading and listening in order to counter such pressures. As a member of the Pilkington Committee on broadcasting in 1960–62, he was instrumental in creating a report that wholeheartedly endorsed the BBC's radio monopoly. For Hoggart, therefore, the advent of commercial radio in the wake of that success posed a familiar threat: the cheapening—and in the end the eradication—of critical public culture itself. He warned that the pirates' sheer longevity would lend de facto legitimacy to whatever "the sharpest operator has managed to get away with." To license unbridled commercialism would be even worse: it would constitute "an act against democratic growth roughly comparable to reinstituting the taxes on knowledge."[38]

On this view—as, again, on that of the economic liberals—public knowledge was fundamentally at issue. It would soon give rise to a conviction that the true antithesis to pirate radio was not the BBC at all. What should replace piracy was a *more* responsible institution. In contrast to the "freedom of the air" proclaimed by the pirates and their backers, it came to be called the "university of the air."

IN APRIL 1965, Smedley could report to Project Atlanta's shareholders that things were looking up.[39] Establishing the intricate web of companies needed for an offshore broadcaster had required "imagi-nation, originality, courage and hard-work," he conceded, and "frus-trations" had severely damaged Atlanta's financial state. The company had had to take out both an overdraft (which Smedley and the other directors guaranteed) and a long-term loan from a finance company, Elysian Investments. By November 1964, shortly after the deal with Elysian, it had accrued a deficit of almost £150,000, and had had to issue 50,000 more shares to gain capital. Rumors of government action to close down the pirates had not helped. All those early hopes for "lush profits and fat dividends" had not been realized. Yet "good sense" had prevailed, and Caroline and Atlanta had undertaken to share net sales revenue on a schedule that would trend toward fifty-fifty. This was now working satisfactorily, Smedley declared: "coopera-tion between the two groups is increasingly cordial." As a result, Project Atlanta was turning a daily profit. It was not large—total advertising revenue from this and from its short period of independence came to about £31,000—but it seemed set to increase, "provided we are not prevented from continuing in business." Smedley cautioned that if Caroline were indeed silenced, Project Atlanta would be ruined. But for now, the company was in business. "And in all the circumstances that may be considered miracle enough for one year."

Two threats loomed against the Caroline network. The more dras-tic, but also the more remote, was that of state action. The govern-ment had signed a new European Agreement for the Prevention of Broadcasts Transmitted from Stations outside National Territories, which was directed against the offshore broadcasters. But nobody knew when Parliament might act to implement it. Even if that hap-pened, Smedley suggested, the situation need not become impos-sible. It would probably stop British companies from advertising on Caroline; so be it. In that event, Smedley declared, he would not allow "an overdose of false sentimentality or chauvinism" to stop him finding replacements in Europe. The other threat, less severe but more proxi-mate, was of competition from other stations. Several rival outfits had already launched initiatives. The one that Smedley feared was Radio London. With reason: it was set to be a well-funded and professional operation. But he confidently affirmed that Caroline could see off even this threat. Indeed, its existence would enhance the credibility of commercial radio itself, and hence bring benefits in the longer run.

But that prospect betrayed the greater threat that the state posed. As an enterprise dependent on advertising revenue, a pirate station depended on reputation and credibility. The perception of real out-lawry might kill it without any law ever being passed. Revenues had increased every month, Smedley pointed out, until the European agreement was announced—but advertisers had then reasoned that Caroline was doomed and had refused to make more commitments. With the government's power resting on a slim parliamentary major-ity, it had preferred not to act, and the rumors had died down. Profits then rose again. But the lesson was clear: the viability of the enterprise depended entirely on confidence, and confidence was fragile. Atlanta and Caroline must take care to remain above reproach, and they must do their best to ensure that smaller, less predictable stations toed the line too. Nothing must be allowed to happen that might make state action politically possible, for the very possibility might be fatal.

Smedley had one thing to add. "We have no wish to enter the politi-cal arena," he remarked, "otherwise than in our own defence." But he forthwith did precisely that. "I sincerely believe," he proclaimed, "that together we have succeeded in striking a blow for freedom and against rule by monopoly." Atlanta had demonstrated a demand for pop music that the BBC could not meet. "In modern Britain, where it is fashionable to believe that bigness is all, we may have helped to light a torch for the spirit of true private enterprise." This was the real reason, he concluded, why Project Atlanta continued to deserve support and would be destined for success.

To drive home his point Smedley circulated a printed tract, saying that it laid out the "philosophical and political" stakes of commercial radio "more objectively and independently than I might do." The tract was entitled *Competition in Radio*. It originated from the Institute of Economic Affairs. In creating and sustaining Project Atlanta, Smedley was clearly still aligning himself with the Institute that he had founded almost a decade earlier.

COMPETITION IN RADIO was one of a sequence of papers to emerge from the IEA in the mid-1960s. All were products of the Institute's project on information. They addressed in turn intellectual property, commercial television, and pirate radio. A critic and ex-manager at Independent Television News named Denis Thomas substantially authored all of them. They appeared in the critical window between the reinforcement of the radio monopoly in 1962 and the climax of the pirate radio boom in 1966–67. Their centerpiece was to be a new study of the pirate radio phenomenon, produced in association with the ITV franchise Granada TV and Radio Caroline—by now amalgamated with Smedley's Project Atlanta. It defended pirate radio as a key element in a long-term strategy to do away with the BBC and hence, eventually, overturn the whole model of the public service corporation that it represented. The struggle to end Keynesianism had returned to the original battleground of the 1920s.

TV: From Monopoly to Competition—and Back? was issued twice in 1962, before and after the Pilkington Report. It placed commercial television in the context of a radically revisionist history based explicitly on the theories of Ronald Coase. Commercial TV was on this account merely the latest (and not necessarily the most successful) in a series of alternatives to monopoly, commencing with the amateurs of the 1920s and proceeding through the relay operators and continental broadcasters of the thirties. Now, however, with Pilkington's reaffirmation of the monopoly, that sequence seemed to have hit a dead end. For the IEA—as for Arnold Plant—the way to revive it was by licensing subscription television. But with the government wedded to the monopoly, and the ITV companies apparently agglomerating into a monopoly of their own, the prospects were not good.[40]

Those in radio were far more auspicious. Published in 1965, *Competition in Radio* took the IEA's case much further than *TV* had. It commenced with the same Coasian argument, sometimes reprising whole phrases verbatim from the *TV* tract. But the period between *TV* and *Competition in Radio* had seen the sensational rise of pirate radio, so now this history proved a new point: that pirate stations had a critical role to play in bringing about a new age of commercial communication. And, it added, this fact bore a lesson about the role of so-called pirates in general.

The IEA, again following Coase, denied point-blank any claim that there was a shortage of wavelengths. It cited the Pye company—a stalwart of the original campaign for commercial television, and now a supplier of equipment to the pirates—to the effect that Britain had produced a "false shortage." Applying the Copenhagen agreement in a needlessly stringent fashion, it had produced a broadcasting monopoly. Significantly, the IEA portrayed this as akin to the intellectual property monopolies created artificially by copyright laws. Alternatives certainly existed. Several other countries licensed stations on the practical condition that they did not in fact cause interference. Were Britain to follow suit—which might mean withdrawing from the Copenhagen accord—then it would create room for a hundred daytime local radio stations. The pirates had proved that this was perfectly possible. They had claimed squatters' rights on just a few wavelengths, and after a lot of huffing and puffing even the Postmaster General had had to admit that there had been no interference to speak of. "The surprising thing about this," the IEA tract argued, "is not that it should have happened but that it should have been so long in coming."[41] After all, more than half Europe's long- and medium-wave stations paid no attention to the 1948 wavelength allocations.

If the pirates were not unusual in flouting Copenhagen allocations, and the state had no recourse against them, why were they the subject of so much hostile rhetoric? Because, the IEA argued, they represented a form of commercial life that the state and existing businesses alike regarded as *immoral*. A major aspect of this was that they flouted copyright and performing rights restrictions. The rights agencies and record companies denounced them bitterly and at length for this, and occasionally even urged military action to suppress them. But the pirates did pay courtesy sums, much as nineteenth-century American publishers had to writers like Dickens. And, as the IEA did not fail mischievously to point out, the record companies were not slow to provide them with their new releases. For the IEA, it was clearly the prevailing moral economy—copyright itself, and its scion, needle time—that was at fault.

This was why the IEA's tract on pirate radio concluded with a section entitled " 'Piracy' as a Business Force." The argument in favor of pirate radio stations here became a general point about economics— the same point, in fact, that Harris and Seldon had made before the Mont Pelerin Society about "privateers." "Hostility to commercial 'piracy' is neither new nor unfamiliar," Thomas charged. It was in truth a "reflex reaction" on the part of established interests when faced with "adventurous competition." Newcomers to any existing industry violated "tacit rules" by which such an industry operated, so opinion inevitably cast them as acting against the "public interest." One John Bloom was a good example. Bloom had tried to revolutionize the trade in domestic appliances, and for a while achieved spectacular success; his subsequent fall had become an equally sensational morality play in the British press, which associated it with the tawdry commercial ethos of an end-of-term Conservative regime.[42] Another was Logie Baird, the inventor of television, who had been given short shrift by the BBC. A third was Allen Lane, whose Penguin Books had initially been repudiated by a tradition-bound publishing industry (and who, incidentally, had supported Plant in his skepticism about copyright). In each case the "pirate" had been portrayed as an immoral *arriviste*. But in each case the pirate had been an innovator who transformed tacit rules and revolutionized an industry.

Competition in Radio commanded a wide readership, with the IEA filing responses from across the world. But in some ways its most significant readers were those handed the tract by the IEA's forgotten founder. Project Atlanta, they read, was putting the principles of the IEA into practice. The IEA had come to recognize three things: the importance of information; the pivotal status of advertising; and the essential role of "privateering" for transforming capitalism itself. Commercial radio tackled all three at once. Smedley's shareholders were fomenting a transformation in public communications, and, in the end, a revolution in Britain's politics.

THESE DEBATES TOOK on increased urgency in the months after Atlanta and Caroline merged. Now that the viability of offshore radio had apparently been proved, other entrepreneurs had quickly moved to take advantage. Fears—or hopes—of an unstoppable "armada" of pirates suddenly seemed all too realistic.

The most professional of the new pirates was Radio London. Operated from a converted U.S. minesweeper, the *Galaxy*, London was the creation of a Texas car dealer named Don Pierson. Pierson had been attracted by rumors of large profits to be made, and hoped to replicate the success of a Dallas station devoted to endless Top 40 records. With the aid of wealthy Texan associates he put together capital of some £300,000—double what Atlanta had accrued—and set to work.

The structure of the enterprise adhered quite closely to what was becoming the pirate norm. The ship was owned by a company registered in Panama, which leased it to a second company based in the Bahamas. This then delegated the sale of advertising time to Radlon (Sales) Ltd., housed in Mayfair, close by Caroline Sales. Here Pierson shrewdly installed as managing director a veteran of the advertising agency J. Walter Thompson, Philip Birch. Far more than Crawford, Smedley, or even O'Rahilly, Birch saw immediately how to make a pirate station work. He recruited an experienced cadre of colleagues, familiar with the workings of British advertising and with good contacts in Fleet Street and the magazine world, and by the time Radio London began broadcasting just before Christmas 1964 he had already secured an impressive roster of advertisers. No other station had such a start.

It was soon clear that Radio London was winning the competition with Caroline. The *Galaxy* had the more powerful transmitter, and its programming exhibited a calculated professionalism that Caroline South could not match. Crawford saw advertising revenue from the *Mi Amigo* shrink drastically. By late spring 1965, he had been forced to abandon his programming policy. Previously, he had signed contracts with advertising agencies to produce fifteen- or thirty-minute sponsored segments for major companies. This was the old convention inherited from the IBC and its peers. It had resulted in lucrative but rather staid programs, fronted by the likes of the wartime stalwart Vera Lynn. Now Crawford had to change tack radically. Caroline South adopted London's Top 40 format, introduced a news announcement section, and extended broadcasting hours into the evening. It also took cues from New York, with its evening program recorded at music station WMCA's American studio. Several DJs were replaced. The shift proved effective in the sense that advertising income stopped falling. But listeners continued to drain away to Radio London. By the end of 1965, London had 15 percent of the audience, the BBC's Light Programme over 30 percent. Caroline South's share was down to 0.9 percent. The implication was clear. Project Atlanta had been in a fragile state a year earlier; now it faced collapse.

ATLANTA APPROACHED DECEMBER 1965 with a new loss of over £3,500. It was not a large sum in itself, but it meant an accrued deficit of more than £150,000. For an enterprise reliant on credibility, it was enough to be fatal. Atlanta's creditors presented an ultimatum on December 17, and Smedley and Crawford saw no alternative but to capitulate. They transferred Atlanta's remaining assets to O'Rahilly's Planet Productions, in return for £53,000, which they hoped would be enough to meet the creditors' demands. Atlanta retained only a paltry £3,000 that happened to be in its bank account, and a claim on new sales in excess of £40,000 per month—an implausibly high level, and one never to be reached. It looked like Smedley's adventure in pirate radio was over.

What had gone wrong was a combination of three things: fear of government intervention, internal acrimony, and commercial competition. The company might have reduced its deficit, Smedley said, but for "constant threats of political action which destroyed the confidence of advertisers." In the event, the income from advertising had been barely enough to meet the station's servicing costs, which had been rising inexorably. In 1965 they had totaled almost £120,000; net advertising revenue had been only £5,000 more. And even that income had been hard to secure, because of mysterious delays in transferring funds out of the Caroline office. Finally—although Smedley did not dwell on this—Radio London had provided much more formidable competition than he and Crawford had anticipated. Project Atlanta had been left falling further behind every month. Surrender was the only option.

A year later, after the dust had settled, Smedley would claim that he had warned at the outset that Project Atlanta was not a suitable investment for widows and orphans. "So, unfortunately, it has proved." But he would also insist that the venture had been partly a victim of its own principles. Determined to "make the case for commercial radio," Atlanta had adhered to "the very highest traditions of the best commercial practice." It had never taken "short cuts" or descended to illegal or unethical practices. Although he did not say so, such self-denying propriety was hardly what the IEA had in mind when it hailed pirates as the renewers of capitalism. Nor was it what Harris and Seldon had seen fit to praise in privateers. Atlanta was apparently that rarest of pirates, a paragon of respectability.[43]

But that was after it was all over. Earlier, at the end of 1965, as he signed over Atlanta's assets, Smedley was not prepared to be so philosophical. He could not yet bring himself to concede that Project Atlanta was lost irrevocably. He still saw a slim chance to revive his scheme. But it would take the kind of determination and creativity that could reverse an apparently hopeless situation. He decided to try. Before long, the decision would lead to Smedley's undertaking a "short cut" more radical than any he had envisaged before.

5

THE TWO TOWERS

muggy Saturday evening in the nondescript Midlands town of
Nuneaton, late in the spring of 1964. It is dance night upstairs at
the huge old Art Deco Co-operative Hall that squats at the corner of the Queen's Road. Every week, hundreds of teenagers from
the town and its surrounding villages converge on this hall to hear
the latest bands. Last year the Rolling Stones played here; the year
before, the Beatles. Tonight's act is nothing special, but the steady
throb that can be felt from the car park behind the hall indicates
that all is going well. The two men sitting there in a big sedan can
hear it as they talk. One is a northerner in his mid-thirties, enthusiastic and energized. He is the organizer of the event. He has left
his young daughter in charge for the moment, but he is not unduly
worried; she has handled these affairs before, and both of them
know how to deal with trouble. The other is ten years younger, with
a London accent. Initially taciturn, he has perked up and is now
talking almost as excitedly as his boss. Their talk is by turns technical and rhapsodic—details of aerials, transmitters, and frequencies
intersperse with visions of popularity and profit. But the real subject
is the big news of the day. Two "pirate" stations, Caroline and Atlanta,
have just come on air. Everyone is talking about them. For these two
men, they suggest an exhilarating possibility. What if they set up a
pirate station of their own?

Reginald Calvert and David Sutch were not the only people inspired that weekend to dream of becoming pirates. Atlanta and Caroline sparked off an extraordinary period for British broadcasting. For months, commercial stations multiplied rapidly. Announcements of new ventures appeared regularly in the press, some spurious, others optimistic, a few hardheadedly plausible. At least ten stations would come into lasting operation in the next two years. For the first time since the 1930s, the BBC's radio supremacy came under serious challenge. But the pirate station that resulted from the conversation that night in Nuneaton was the most unusual of all. It would trigger the biggest transformation in British radio broadcasting in its history.

The new pirates helped themselves to insights from the earlier commercial broadcasters. They emulated their convoluted international structures, and in Atlanta's case, at least, adopted a similar programming format. One new station (not technically a pirate because it was legal in its home of the Isle of Man) was even run by a veteran of Leonard Plugge's IBC—the same Richard Meyer who had been active in ATV. And their rhetoric was often quite similar, too. But the context had changed profoundly, and that made all the difference. The rise of independent television in the late 1950s had already fractured the BBC's supremacy. At the same time, what might be called the ideological environment had altered profoundly. If the economy was an information system, and if, as Coase had argued, the familiar justifications for a broadcasting monopoly were not only invalid but historically irrelevant, then a commercial medium took on quite different meanings. And, most important of all, a revolution had just occurred in the practice of listening. This revolution was already in effect when Atlanta and Caroline arrived, and the pirate boom could hardly have happened without it. It was based in the massive popularity of transistor radios, and it cast the most precious assumptions of the BBC once more into doubt.

The ultimate origins of the transistor radio are contested, but the first commercially available units reached the public in the mid-1950s. In the UK, sales already stood at 1.3 million by 1956; they would reach 3.5 million by 1965.[1] "Transistors," as they were called, were by no means the first portable receivers, but they were the first "miniaturized" ones that could be carried casually in a pocket. Cheap, individual, and unpretentious—and with atrocious sound quality—they changed listening practices immediately and radically. It suddenly made no sense to think in Reithian terms of the listener as actively engaged in a close, critical, and constructive relationship with the broadcaster, conducted as part of a domestic unit in a hushed household. Listening became fragmented, casual, mobile, and transient. It was also often inaudible to others, because many transistor users listened through an earphone. While television took over the living room, radio won every other space—including, importantly, the car. By virtue of this autonomy, radio now became the medium of what was recognized almost immediately as a "teenage revolution." Prior to this, young people certainly heard foreign stations, but listening routinely to them every day (and thus becoming consumers of their music) was harder; as one frustrated 1950s teen later recalled, "We had one radio, a cabinet, and my father claimed that tuning it into Radio Luxembourg would seriously distort the mechanism." But when her friend got a portable radio, she continued, "I can remember us lying on the floor in her bedroom and screaming to Radio Luxembourg."[2] Much the same euphoria now happened in a rush across the country. A generation after its first clash with commercial rivals had forced the BBC to create a science of listener research, listeners had moved out of reach once again.

This was the audience that the pirate stations hoped to win. As a result, offshore radio posed questions the likes of which had not arisen since the early days of pirate listening. With sixties piracy came a resurgence of the democratic, individualist, even libertarian ideals that the wireless experimenters had proclaimed in that early period. (The revival of earphone listening, a mainstay of that first generation, surely helped.) The amateur experimenters, it turned out, had never really gone away. But in the late 1950s and early 1960s, new technologies and novel conceptions gave them a new prominence. For an ideologue like Oliver Smedley, their world held little interest and less attraction. A very different kind of pirate radio entrepreneur, however, felt right at home in it.

REGINALD CALVERT CAME from a different generation from Smedley, and a very different culture. Born in 1928, his background lay far from high finance and politics, in that world of lay ingenuity that had spawned the wireless "amateurs" of the twenties in towns like Coventry. His parents were professional musicians, who often traveled abroad on concert tours. His father was a keen inventor as well, and his grandfather, who brought him up after the parents separated, was an engineer who spent the Depression years in the industrial city of Huddersfield, working first in the Morris car works and then in munitions. After work, he spent long hours in the cellar trying to build a perpetual motion machine. As a child, Reg (as he was always called) enjoyed working on experiments too. He attended an unprepossessing board school, but one that, unusually, had a chemical laboratory, and by the age of fourteen he was dominating chemistry lessons. Meanwhile his grandparents taught him the piano, saxophone, and clarinet. Reg began performing music publicly, and learned to compère big band events at the Huddersfield Baths on Wednesday evenings.

Calvert was not the type to relish military service, and he did his duty as an Army barber. He was still in uniform when he married at eighteen. His new wife, Dorothy, was the same age. Her father had died of tuberculosis, and her mother had done her best to bring Dorothy up in the new public housing to which the family was moved for fear of further infection. She had excelled at school, and her mother wanted her to go on to university, but marriage supplanted that prospect. In the short term the young couple faced tough times. The Calverts were typical of a generation that had great hopes for a new society, in which enlightened social policies would free people from the inequality and want of the Depression years. But for now their concerns were more pressing. Austerity was starting to bite; employment was hard to come by and even basic goods were rationed. The first and most pressing need was for a place to live. But where housing stock had not been flattened by the Luftwaffe, it was decrepit and dilapidated.[3] Dorothy Calvert decided she was determined to get out of Huddersfield. So

Reg bought an old bus, and the Calverts recruited some prisoners of war to help convert it into a trailer. Then they had it towed down to the south coast. In Southampton they rented a plot of land, parked their trailer on it, and moved into their makeshift home.[4]

Reg Calvert tried his luck at a series of enterprises in and around Southampton to make ends meet. He continued to compère dances. At one point he worked as a pianist in a hotel bar. At another, he bought Army surplus radio equipment and rented a shop to sell it from, taking time to experiment in transmitting. It is even said that he tried his hand at producing jam, encouraged by the fact that his middle name, Hartley, matched that of a major jam manufacturer; the story at least seems true to character. Certainly, when sugar rationing ended he took the opportunity to begin selling sweets. He bought a confectionary factory and began touting his produce, first at fairs and markets and then in his own store; he made all of its furnishings himself. But that too paled after a while, and he became a radio and television engineer. It would be difficult now to document all of his gambits. But he seems to have retained a keen enthusiasm for experimentation—and in particular for experimentation in communications, a field in which Southampton had a long history. Decades later, Dorothy Calvert still remembered him stringing up aerials in a field for one particularly ambitious transmission experiment.

Calvert's move into the music business began as another in this string of venturesome enthusiasms. He had organized dances back in Huddersfield and found himself good at it. Now he began booking his own singers and bands, organizing road trips to dance halls across the country. He would advertise the dances by driving around in a car with a loudspeaker strapped to the roof. Calvert had a genius for patter as well as an eye for the new and popular, and both stood him in good stead. The events flourished. Soon he was creating new bands, and, learning as he went on, managing them. The Calverts would allow the young musicians to stay in their house for free and drive them to dances in their Austin Sheerline. They found that hundreds of teenagers at a time would cram into a hall to scream at a young singer who resembled Britain's clean-cut rocker, Cliff Richard. That was one Danny Storm; Calvert cultivated "Buddy Britten" (a Buddy Holly emulator) too, and "Eddie Sex" (his version of Elvis). Before long Calvert acts like these were appearing in halls, ballrooms, cinemas, and piers all over the south of England.

Today, in a musical world dominated by slick entertainment multinationals, it would be easy to be condescending about the kind of business that the Calverts built up in the 1950s, and even about the vital musical culture that it helped create. But there was nothing routine or negligible about it at the time—and in fact it could be argued that it formed an important foundation of today's industry. Major musicians in the postwar years did not yet engage in lavish national tours, and the business of recording, although powerful and centralized, was not as dominant as it would become. In Britain the broadcasting of records was rudimentary too, especially given the BBC's constraining needle-time agreement. Radio Luxembourg, meanwhile, was by the mid-fifties closed to all except the major labels. In practice, therefore, even stars focused on live events.

These the performers undertook at a harrowing pace, and in a wide variety of venues—ballrooms, bars, clubs, pubs, and cinemas. The dance halls favored by the Calverts were a major fixture on the list. They had grown up in many areas across the country before the war, notably those with large working populations, and could accommodate hundreds at a time. As the economy revived following the Austerity years, they offered a chance to dress up and mix with other teenagers in what one historian calls a "relatively classless setting of transatlantic relaxation."[5] The Co-op at Nuneaton was a typical example: it was built in 1939, and in 1965 police estimated that nine hundred teenagers were dancing inside when four were crushed to death on the stairs. Today they are fast disappearing from view—Nuneaton's was quietly demolished in late 2008—but in the 1950s they were ubiquitous. About 3 million under-twenty-fours set foot in one of them every week.

The contrast between what was on the radio (both BBC and Luxembourg) and what teenagers could hear at these local venues was thus profound and, to them, meaningful. By the end of the

1950s, Liverpool alone had about three hundred bands. Birmingham, Manchester, Newcastle, Belfast, and other cities all had their own circuits. Each would eventually produce its own phenomenon: the Beatles, the Moody Blues from Birmingham, the Animals from Newcastle, Van Morrison from Belfast. Calvert's became the counterpart of these circuits in the non-metropolitan southeast. Even his initial stress on emulating American originals was nothing unusual. Cliff Richard built his name by doing just that, and so did the Rolling Stones, of course. When John Lennon and Paul McCartney joined the Quarrymen in 1956 they wanted to emulate Elvis and Buddy Holly. With musical performance a local tradition, there was nothing wrong or absurd about the practice. In recording and broadcasting studios, too, bands routinely covered American originals—or other bands' covers of those originals. The BBC itself relied on this practice to get around needle time. The principle was a time-honored one, deriving from Tin Pan Alley and music hall, if not further back.

For Calvert, as for impresarios on the other regional circuits, performances were more than just musical. Bands were called "acts," and the crowds who paid to hear them expected them to live up to that title. Here Calvert's skills came to the fore. His own performance was often a central part of the evening's entertainment at a dance hall. He loved every minute of it. He would run impromptu competitions, shout out instructions for dance moves, and call for interventions from the audience. He once organized a press hoopla for a drummer attempting (successfully) to break the world record for continuous drumming. Animals became a mainstay: he would award a live piglet to the winner of a contest. Later, he would bring along a pet monkey that clambered about over the heads of musicians and dancers alike. It is even said that he got hold of a python to give away at a concert. There were other exhibitions, too many to recount here. The point is that none of them was merely eccentric. Calvert's performances (often called antics, escapades, or stunts) were and remained popular. They fell within a historical trajectory that originated in Victorian music hall traditions, if not earlier, and would reach beyond the 1960s. He contributed to that distinctive thread of humor that continued to run

Oliver Smedley's cottage at Wendens Ambo on the morning after the shooting. Calvert's car stands outside the cottage. (By permission of the National Archives, Kew)

The scene of the shooting at Wendens Ambo. (By permission of the National Archives, Kew)

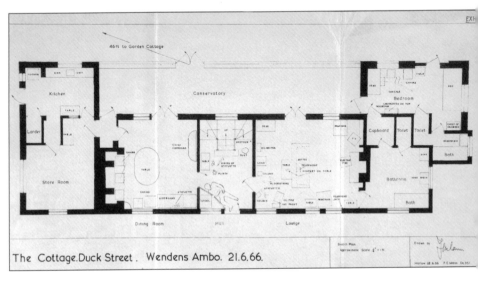

Ground plan of Oliver Smedley's cottage. (By permission of the National Arhives, Kew)

John Reith at the BBC in 1925. (National Portrait Gallery, London)

Leonard Plugge in 1927, embarking on one of his European journeys in the radio car Aether III.

P. P. Eckersley. (National Portrait Gallery, London)

Arnold Plant in 1950. (National Portrait Gallery, London)

4

Friedrich von Hayek in about 1940. (© Hulton Deutsch Collection / Corbis)

Kitty Black in 1966, shortly after Oliver Smedley's trial. (By permission of Mirrorpix)

Ronan O'Rahilly (left) and Allan Crawford in mid-1964, at the time of the merger between Radio Atlanta and Radio Caroline. (Image courtesy of Offshore Echos; reproduced by permission of Bruce Fleming)

The Free Trader *hails the arrival of Radio Atlanta.* (By permission of the Free Trade League)

SUMMER NUMBER.   PRICE 3/-

he Free Trader

—URNAL IN THE WORLD   EXCLUSIVELY DEVOTED TO FREE TRADE

Radio Atlanta—the new Voice of Freedom

Published by
THE FREE TRADE LEAGUE
80a Coleman Street London, E.C.2.

Shivering Sands. The Guardian, *June 25, 1966.* (Copyright Guardian News & Media Ltd., 1966)

David Sutch (foreground) and Reg Calvert in a publicity shot for Radio Sutch. Brian Paull stands behind Calvert. May 28, 1964. (By permission of Mirrorpix)

Alf Bullen (in cap) aboard Shivering Sands, next to DJ Tony Pine.
Daily Mail, *June 25, 1966.* (By permission. Copyright Daily Mail, 1966)

Pamela Thorburn outside the Assize court in Chelmsford, Essex, following the acquittal of Oliver Smedley, October 18, 1966. (By permission of Mirrorpix)

Oliver Smedley in Chelmsford, Essex, after his acquittal, October 18, 1966. (By permission of Mirrorpix)

The gas-pen carried by Reg Calvert. (By permission of Susan Moore)

11

Superintendent Brown aboard Shivering Sands to interview the Radio City crew and the boarders. Daily Mail, *June 23, 1966.* (By permission. Copyright Daily Mail, 1966)

Dorothy Calvert aboard the tender close to Shivering Sands, during the last days of Radio City in February 1967. (By permission of Mirrorpix)

Ronnie and Reggie Kray: the Kray Twins, 1966. (© Hulton-Deutsch Collection / Corbis)

*One of the Navy forts being towed into position during World War II.
J. A. Posford, "The Construction of Britain's Sea Forts,"* The Civil
Engineer in War *(1948).* (Courtesy of the Institution of Civil Engineers)

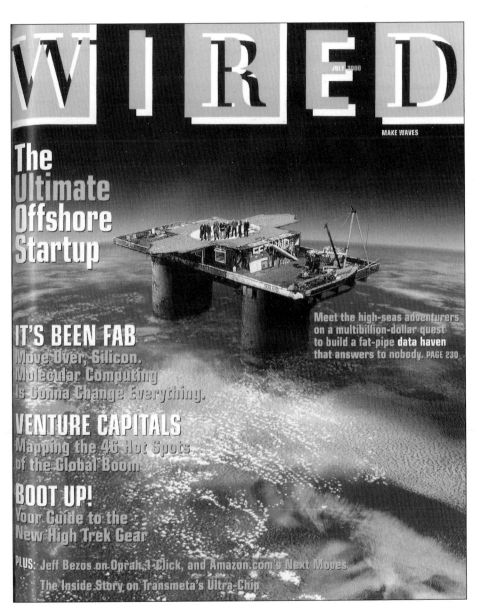

Wired *salutes the first data haven of the twenty-first century.* Wired, *July 2000.*

(Tom Meade/*Wired*; courtesy of Condé Nast Publications)

through British popular music, from the 1980s music hall–influenced lyrics of Ian Dury to the bleaker humor of Jarvis Cocker in the next decade.

Calvert made his name from the rising affluence and independence of that newly self-aware class of the 1950s, the teenagers. As Austerity began to give way to the Macmillan years, teens were gaining unprecedented autonomy, and the economic wherewithal to make their independence count. Mark Abrams's celebrated pamphlet, *The Teenage Consumer*, published in 1959 for the advertising industry, brought their powers to the fore. Transistor radios in particular promised to free teens from their families' tastes. It was a "dance-crazy era," and with *Blackboard Jungle* appearing in British cinemas in 1955, and *Rock Around the Clock* a year later, rock 'n' roll pushed skiffle aside to become the focus of the craze. *New Musical Express*, launched in 1952, left more traditional publications in its wake. A new taste offered enormous opportunities for the music industry, which moved to exploit them: for the first time, a hit record could sell millions of copies. The record companies sought to do that by monopolizing Radio Luxembourg.[6] Reg Calvert's mixture of music, performance theater, and dance was another bid—and a successful one—to seize that chance.

The enterprise was lucrative, at least in terms of its gross receipts. Yet it remained on something of a hand-to-mouth basis. None of the musicians was on a contract, and the tickets and posters were produced by a printing firm that Dorothy Calvert maintained in her own right. In fact, it seems that at times this printing business kept the music venture afloat. That was nothing unusual. She had already found herself forced several times to salvage ventures that her husband had rushed into, and this was no exception. But this business was enduring. The trouble was that even the good times brought problems. One was sheer exhaustion. The Calverts found themselves driving on longer and longer expeditions, to Winchester, Slough, Aldershot—sometimes as far as Torquay, a distance of 120 miles each way. They would not return home until late at night, if at all.

A second issue, more enervating still, was fear. Violence had been a reality of dance halls ever since the prewar years.[7] The new rock craze attracted further gang rivalries, eagerly lamented by Fleet Street. Groups of Teddy boys converged on the dances, and Calvert found himself having to recruit heavies to keep order. More worryingly, competition with a rival manager had started to turn ominous, with slashed tires a possible harbinger of worse to come. Calvert became anxious about his own safety, given that he was collecting substantial takings in cash at the end of each night's event.

His response to these signs of danger captured the attitude of the popular experimenter perfectly. While on a trip to Europe he had come across advertisements for a device about the size and shape of a pen that contained a small canister of tear gas. The gas-pen could be carried in a pocket and pulled out in an emergency. Illegal in the UK, they were readily available on the Continent from East German suppliers. Calvert bought a number of them for his bouncers, took to bearing one himself, and insisted that his wife carry one with her. As far as is known, none was ever used—although it was said that he rather hoped one would be, if only for the headlines about mass teen euphoria that it would have provoked.

FAR MORE THAN Smedley—and arguably as much as a metropolitan figure like Ronan O'Rahilly—Reg Calvert "got" the world of the teenage revolution among British youth. But the work was all too draining, physically and emotionally. The Calverts began to look for a new base, more central to their expanding circuit of halls. In 1961, they found it.

Clifton Hall was a large country house near Rugby, in England's West Midlands. It stood apart from the road in its own grounds. Big old mansions like this had languished since the war—many of them were demolished or converted into hotels—and the Calverts managed to find the resources to buy this one. The Hall was much better situated for driving to a range of venues, and its withdrawn character provided the kind of isolation needed for rehearsals. Here the Calverts expanded their Southampton enterprise into a "school" for up-and-coming pop musicians. They maintained rather a strict regimen for the young men who stayed there rent-free. No alcohol, drugs, or females were permitted. Calvert frowned on foul language—there were enough good words in the English language, he would say, not to use bad ones—and the musicians were expected not to swear. What was encouraged was extensive practice. The bands would keep in tune with current trends by listening to hit records and playing them by ear, often staying up late into the night after a dance to get their sound right. As a result, this School of Pop produced a sequence of well-drilled performers who could attract large audiences across the Midlands.

The Calverts made money from their acts, and they churned the profits from their dances back into the business, building a recording studio to produce demos for the musicians. But those profits also funded more of Calvert's experiments. He developed an enthusiasm for film, for example. He had long been keen on photography, keeping a darkroom in the Hall and taking many of the bands' publicity photos. He developed his own fireworks in a casual "laboratory." On one Guy Fawkes Day, Calvert had the musicians enact a distinctly risky form of trench warfare with his homemade bazookas. And he even mused about setting up a radio station at the Hall, which stood inspiringly close to a set of towering radio aerials that had been used since the 1920s for imperial and naval transmissions. He tried to apply for a license for his putative station, naturally without success.

Soon some of Calvert's acts began to see a prospect of cutting discs. The first of them to get a break, Danny Storm, made a single for Pye that was a middle-charting hit. But after Storm failed to make headway on television (the BBC apparently objected to what it saw as suggestive content), Calvert resolved to become sharper in his dealings with the London industry. He learned fast, and developed a reputation as a formidable negotiator. In 1963 he joined forces with a veteran of the jazz scene, Terry King, to launch an agency called Kings Agency Productions to promote the recording careers of his musicians. It was based in the concentrated musical entrepôt of Denmark Street, long regarded as Britain's Tin Pan Alley. And later that year he launched a band of academy regulars, initially called the Clifton All-Stars, but soon renamed the Fortunes, which became Calvert's

biggest success. Their hit song "Caroline" secured enormous popularity when it became the theme for Ronan O'Rahilly's pirate station.[8]

By now, Calvert had a reputation as one of the new promoter-
managers fomenting a transformation in popular music. Yet that transformation was already threatening to leave him behind. His stable,
successful as it was, did not include the most popular up-and-coming
acts of the age. Nor did it embrace the new, harder-edged fashions
of beat, R&B, and now folk rock. This may have been partly a matter
of taste—the Calverts were unsympathetic to displays of indiscipline,
which they saw as unprofessional (when they booked the Rolling
Stones, the shabby appearance of the band left them, and reportedly
the audience, unimpressed). Whatever the cause, money was soon
running short again. It did not help that Calvert had once again over-
extended himself, taking out a lease on a hall in Loughborough in
hopes of rejuvenating it as a nightclub. Largely financed, once again,
by his wife, the project was proving more expensive and troublesome
than he had anticipated.[9] This project was doomed to become a persistent and, in the end, critical drain on resources.

But the sense that an opportunity was passing Calvert by came into
focus thanks to the performer David Sutch—or, as he called himself,
"Screaming Lord" Sutch. Sutch embodied some of Calvert's fondest
assumptions about live entertainment. He would make his entrance in
a coffin, emerging to present a show of rather campish horror-themed
rock music. The act was a popular success, but the appeal seemed set
to fade. Sutch was frustrated. He wanted some new creative possibility. He was especially discouraged that he could not get his music
played on the radio. The BBC would never be interested in anything
so vulgar, and Luxembourg was the plaything of the major recording
companies.

In the short term, a recourse suggested itself in the form of the
sensational scandal over War Minister John Profumo's affair with
Christine Keeler. Profumo, a Conservative in Harold Macmillan's
government, resigned in June 1963 having admitted to lying about
the affair, and the prime minister himself followed in the autumn.
The episode revealed a spirit of casual hypocrisy on the part of what

suddenly seemed a superannuated Establishment. Calvert hit upon the lark of running Sutch as a candidate in the by-election caused by Profumo's resignation. Sutch stood as representative of the National Teenage Party. His major call was for a reduction in the voting age, apparently on Dorothy Calvert's suggestion; but his platform also included the abolition of selective education, and support for young scientists (Sutch proposed a transfer system inspired by that for soccer players, which would make U.S. universities pay hefty fees to export British researchers).[10] It also demanded the licensing of commercial pop radio. Media coverage duly provided them with a month of free publicity. On election day in mid-August the candidate lost his deposit, of course—as he would do many more times, running on the Monster Raving Loony Party ticket. But the point had been made.

When Calvert and Sutch heard about Radio Caroline, they were looking for something to keep up what they saw as the momentum from the by-election campaign. Both were captivated. Calvert lost no time in putting his long-standing experiments with radio to good use. Car batteries and other parts were hastily commandeered to rig up a trial transmitter in the Hall grounds. It worked; and before long Calvert was rooting around in the army surplus electronics shops of Tottenham Court Road to build a larger, fully functional version. Meanwhile he cast about for a boat. He did not have the money to buy one, but when he found a bedraggled old smack, ironically called the *Cornucopia*, moored in the Port of London, he hired it. The vessel was still in use for fishing, and was so tiny that even in the calm of the Thames she pitched and tossed enough to send landlubbers sliding around helplessly. Still, for the ever enthusiastic Calvert it was enough. He lugged a 500-watt transmitter on board, and strung a homemade aerial between the masts. Then he alerted the newspapers. Britain's first "teenage" station was set to go to sea—or at least, to chug ostentatiously down the Thames.

It was all done with astonishing speed. On May 24, 1964, less than two weeks after Radio Atlanta came on air, the *Cornucopia* left her mooring. Sutch and his backing group, the Savages, made a show for the press. The band was dressed in leopard skins, while Sutch bore a purple velvet cape and brandished a cutlass. The Jolly Roger fluttered from the mast—an announcement of piratical intent that neither Caroline nor, *a fortiori*, the straitlaced Atlanta would ever have embraced. At a press conference, journalists came away impressed: the newcomer's signal was strong and clear.

They fell for a trick. The signal that impressed those journalists in fact came from a portable transmitter wielded by Calvert from a hiding place only 300 yards away. It seems that Sutch never really intended to broadcast from the *Cornucopia*. At any rate, any such plan was soon jettisoned. Calvert instead found a much better platform for the station. In the sea a few miles off Whitstable in Kent he discovered a cluster of huge metal structures, looming atop sixty-foot-high steel and concrete legs. They looked like rusty quadruped versions of the Martian tripods from Wells's *War of the Worlds*. They were vast, empty, and—compared to the *Cornucopia*—stable.

The whole array went by the admirably piratical name of Shivering Sands.

CALVERT AND SUTCH had hit upon the latest—and probably the last—forts constructed by the British military during a long history of invasion fears beginning in Napoleon's era. They were something of an engineering miracle. Shivering Sands and its fellows—originally seven forts in all—were constructed in haste by the Army and Navy to replace a flotilla of ships that had been charged with stopping German aircraft and E-boats from sowing mines in the sealanes leading to London. They had also carried radar equipment to provide early warning of incoming bomber squadrons, and a battery of AA guns to disrupt the Luftwaffe's formations. The engineers charged with constructing these forts, which were designed to be self-sustaining for periods of weeks at a time, had developed innovative prefabrication techniques, which were later used to build harbors for the invading forces after D-Day.

The military built two types of fort. Four were constructed for the Admiralty and installed in a region of the North Sea then notorious as "E-boat alley"; three were Army forts stationed closer to the shore. Each of the Navy kind amounted to a 110-by-32 foot rectangular steel platform atop two massive, 24-foot-diameter cylindrical towers rising 60 feet above a reinforced concrete pontoon. The towers were hollow, containing seven decks within their foot-thick walls. They held everything from storerooms and ammunition magazines to accommodation and generators. A steel superstructure mounted atop the platform carried more weaponry and the radar equipment, which communicated with the shore by means of a submarine cable. These forts were built on the bank of the Thames in 1942 and floated out to sea, where they were sunk in position—an operation carried out with the crew already on board, so that each fort was ready for immediate action.

The fort seized by Calvert and Sutch in May 1964 was of the second kind. It was one of an original series of six, three in the Thames estuary and three in the Mersey. They were under Army control, and were intended exclusively for antiaircraft work. But that meant they had to mimic the layout of on-shore AA batteries, with six guns 100 feet apart and a searchlight, all controlled centrally. A design based on a single platform was therefore unfeasible. Instead, each Army fort was made up of seven armored towers. The support structure had to be different too, as the sea outside Liverpool was turbulent and the structure must not resist currents. The result was a set of rather sinister-looking boxes perched on steel legs. Each octagonal box contained three floors, with guns, searchlight, or radar equipment on the roof. Steel catwalks connected the boxes together, allowing the fort's complement of 120 men to move between the various units. It looked rickety, but it worked: the forts shot down more than twenty aircraft and at least as many unmanned V1s, stopped the Germans sowing mines, and successfully drove off E-boats.[11] And they proved surprisingly resilient. Some of the forts are still visible from the coast to this day.

Of the original Army forts in the Thames estuary, one had been demolished by this time. But the rest had simply been abandoned and left to decay. By the mid-sixties, they were hair-raisingly corroded. At Shivering Sands, one of the crosswalks had fallen into the sea, and a collision with a ship had put paid to one of the seven structures. Still, for Sutch and Calvert the complex seemed ideal. They clambered up, found a way in, and rigged up their homemade studio. On May 27, they began test transmissions. When Radio Sutch began broadcasting in earnest shortly after, the first record played was Sutch's own cod-horror single, "Jack the Ripper."

FLOATING DJS WERE one thing. Squatters on military installations were quite another. For the government, the brazen occupation of Shivering Sands raised questions of a new order. The War Office swiftly declared that Sutch was trespassing and dispatched a launch. But even before it could reach the fort, Whitehall had second thoughts about a confrontation and ordered it back. The squatters seemed to be relatively innocuous, after all, and would probably find life sufficiently uncomfortable that they would leave of their own accord. Better to let time take its course than risk violence.

For the government, the retreat turned into an acute embarrassment. Critics failed to understand why the authorities tolerated this "ignoble lord," as Sutch was called in the House of Lords. They would surely not have been so supine if the takeover had been by Teddy boys, Mods, or students, charged Lord Hobson. A few weeks later it got worse, when the RAF had to send a helicopter to airlift off a DJ suffering from food poisoning. "The whole thing is becoming an absolute farce."[12]

One reason for the state's indecision was a delicate issue of jurisdiction. Was the fort still the property of the British government, which had, after all, abandoned it? If not, then perhaps Sutch and Calvert could claim some kind of squatters' or salvagers' rights. And was it within territorial waters? This too was not entirely clear. Shivering Sands was 7.7 miles from the Kent coast and 8 from the Essex coast, so well outside the 3-mile limit. But the boundary could be construed differently by drawing a line across the mouth of the Thames, in which case it would lie inside what was effectively a huge bay.[13] It was also unclear which particular branch of the state should take responsibility: the police found excuses to disown it; the Army, which had originally constructed the thing, was inclined to ascribe it to the Crown Commissioners. The Port of London Authority was another possible candidate. The real obstacle, in the end, was that nobody wanted to take charge of the situation, because any conceivable strategy to deal with it would reflect badly on the agency concerned. Recapturing Shivering Sands might well produce ridiculous images of armed marines rappelling up the structure to attack a lone publicity-seeking singer, and the possibility of injury was real. The attempt might even fail: it was, after all, a *fort*.

Yet the government was on firmer ground than it knew when it assumed that the escapade would be over in a few days. The fact was that originally Radio Sutch was barely a station at all. It was an event, not an enterprise. So weak was its signal that the *Daily Telegraph* cruelly described it as broadcasting to an audience of seagulls. The abortive naval mission was therefore more than publicity gold: it transformed the entire venture. Having trumpeted their victory over the Navy, Calvert and Sutch could hardly just slink away, and they now decided that the station might be worth pursuing in earnest. They replaced the jerry-built transmitter, fired up the fort's old generators to keep a bigger machine going, and set about recruiting helpers.

Radio Sutch remained a very different kind of enterprise from Atlanta or Caroline. It had none of their modern studio equipment; at first, records could not even be properly cued. And tendering was initially a haphazard affair, organized partly by calling on air for passing fishermen to help out. The announcers were Sutch himself, Calvert, and the road manager of the Savages, Brian Poole, who broadcast as Brian Paull. They were soon joined by a few others, notably an electrical engineer named Paul Elvey, who, after working in Africa, appreciated a job closer to home. But most were friends and family, or else youngsters hired on an ad hoc basis and paid, if at all, in cash. Continuing his accustomed practice, Calvert did not use contracts for anyone. Nor did Radio Sutch have the organizational sophistication of its rivals. It had nothing like their structure of shell companies and international registrations. There was not even an on-shore sales office. The closest equivalent was the London premises of Kings Agency. What advertisements Sutch did carry were usually related to the station itself: one for a record shop in Whitstable, which provided records and where the staff went to get paid; and one for Cliff Davis Cars, a London outfit that provided vehicles for Calvert's acts. Sometimes Calvert or Paull would even play a taped reading of an advertisement from a local newspaper on air, hoping that the business concerned would pay for the spot.

Sutch made the best of all this by announcing that his station represented a radically different ethos from the raw commercialism of the existing two pirates. It would not pursue advertising or cut quiet deals with record companies. Instead, it would publicize young new musicians, and finance itself from gifts paid by the grateful stars it created.[14] Sutch issued calls for local bands to send in tapes that the station could broadcast, claiming that record company managers might be listening. In practice, it did go some way to living up to this notion, but more for Calvert's stable of bands than for outright newcomers. Sutch played demo discs from Clifton Hall and tapes made live at dance nights. It also spotlighted "Radio Sutch Dance Nights," headlined by Clifton Hall groups, in the working-class resorts of Herne Bay and Margate. In the evenings, the output became stranger still. An entire LP side might be played without interruption. Late at night, lucky listeners might even hear Calvert himself reading from *Lady Chatterley's Lover*.[15] Nothing like it could be found anywhere else on the dial.

BRITAIN'S TEENAGE STATION lasted only four months. Life around Shivering Sands quickly paled for Sutch, and he wanted to move on. Calvert, on the other hand, had lost none of his enthusiasm. The station combined his keen interest in radio experimentation with his flair for promotion and performance. He could foresee a bright future for it. Dorothy Calvert might object that it had never made money, and that the family could scarcely afford another misadventure; she later told how she had cashed out her savings and sold a couple of cars to any more. Although still known for its oyster trade, Whitstable had become a pocket of depression in an otherwise prosperous county. Narrow lanes and terraced houses accommodated an aging population, alongside youths frustrated by the dead-end character of life in what had become a backwater. Many of the station's apprentice presenters were young men from this population. When Calvert did not interview them himself, the duty fell on the man he used as local manager, Eric Martin. Martin was one of two Whitstable men on whom Radio City depended. The proprietor of the Record Center on the High Street, he had come to Calvert's attention when he helped arrange a victualling trip to the fort. Martin proved willing to supply technical equipment on easy credit, and increasingly handled local arrangements in general, including quizzing lads who wanted to be considered as DJs. Radio City's original transmitter engineer was a TV mechanic at his shop. The other local figure on whom the Calverts relied was Fred Downes, a thirty-six-year-old who owned fishing boats named *Harvesters* and *Harvesters II*. Downes would sail out to Shivering Sands twice a week with stores and relief crews, bringing back staff who were due time on shore. The Calverts came to trust him.

The equipment on Shivering Sands reflected this context, consisting largely of whatever could be found at an affordable price. The Whitstable engineer rigged up a transmitter as best he could, but radio transmission was not his specialty, and the signal tended to drift. When a real radio engineer, Philip Perkins, arrived in April 1965, he made it his business to provide a more reliable system. Perkins and his co-worker Ian West were both experienced in amateur radio experimentation. They decided to install a quartz crystal to control the frequency. Perkins painstakingly ground it himself before bringing it out to the fort. The new control brought a marked improvement. But by the time they had finished, Perkins and West had ended up creating what was virtually a custom-made transmitter, and its rough edges showed.[17] The experienced Australian broadcaster Ian MacRae, coming aboard in February 1966, found the transmitter equipment to be "held together with chewing gum and bits of string." The whole thing was "straight out of the ark."[18] By that transient—that would have a lasting influence on radio. The very designation "disc jockey" did not always refer to a consistent role or position, unlike that of "announcer" on the BBC (or even "DJ" on Atlanta and Caroline). In the early days, especially, whoever was on the fort on a given day was quite likely to be pressed into service. This happened to Calvert's own daughter, Susan. It also befell a photographer, Martin Stevens, who twice found himself stranded by bad weather in early 1965. And several of the engineers, most notably Paul Elvey, found themselves in front of a microphone, often quite regularly. Moreover, of those who went out to Shivering Sands intending to go before the microphone, many were youngsters being given an audition. Partly as a cost-saving move and partly out of a genuine desire to foster talent, much as he had done at Clifton Hall, Calvert would hire them on a week's trial, paying £5 to cover expenses. It was more than an apprenticeship would usually pay. Many had a go. They did their week's stint and then usually disappeared back into the Kent economy. If they proved adept, however, then they might carry on. But Calvert still preferred to work without contracts, so even those who made the cut remained on an informal payroll.

How did one arrive on Shivering Sands? For Chris Cross, it was perfectly simple: strolling down Denmark Street one day in September 1964, he noticed the headquarters of Radio Sutch and walked in to volunteer. Calvert had him out on the fort the next day for the start of his week's audition, and he became a regular. No doubt many others started in much this way, perhaps after hearing the station on a transistor or car radio, or talking about it with friends in the dance hall. Several heard City's own commercials appealing for talent or technical help. Teenager Alan Clark was one: after his week's audition he refused to take Calvert's fiver for an answer and ended up staying right through to the end in 1967. Dick Dickson (or Dixon) likewise heard "a very faint signal" in Ramsgate, which led to his going out to the fort as an engineer/DJ. And the station's major engineer, Paul Elvey, happened to hear an appeal while at a loose end on returning from a project in Africa. As time went on and the station became better known, it attracted applicants with more experience, typically as club DJs. These often sent demo tapes to Denmark Street. But the initial informality did not disappear. In 1965 one Dave Gillbee, an air traffic controller at Gatwick, made the mistake of uttering criticisms of Radio City at his local pub. Eric Martin happened to overhear, and challenged Gillbee to do better. He was soon out at Shivering Sands.

The DJs we know of were a multifarious group. Most remarkably, perhaps, Shivering Sands had female presenters, in the shape of Calvert's two daughters, Candy and Susan, and a niece, Tamara Harrison. Susan Calvert only appeared on air once, but her sister, thirteen, became a regular. She had her own show, *Candy's Pop Shop*, which was recorded at Clifton Hall and broadcast from the fort. These aside, all the DJs were men, and almost all of them were young—the same age as their projected listeners. They were seventeen to twenty-two at the time when City was eventually shut down in 1967. The few exceptions tended to move on relatively quickly: Tony Brandon was in his thirties, for example, with a background in journalism and comedy; he departed for Luxembourg and then Radio London. Bob Spencer moved to Radio Scotland. Ed Moreno too was in his thirties, and had experience in radio from the United States as well as in club DJing in London. Moreno had worked on Caroline—and had been part of the abortive GBOK project before that—but his diabetes meant that he had to tape his shows on shore. He soon moved into management.

Many City DJs were local to London and the southeast. But others originated in a wide variety of backgrounds, from all over the United Kingdom and beyond. One came from the west of Ireland, another (Rick Dane) from Africa. A distinct group were Australian. Some had technical experience: Paul Kramer, for example, was a film engineer before joining City in July 1966. Others could cite prior work in entertainment. Some, like Alexander Dee and Karel Beer (one of the youngsters given a £5 trial), had attended drama school, or were still doing so. A few were even professional actors. Rick Dane had appeared at the Royal Court Theatre, and Peter Dolphin was a bit player in TV series. Tony Brandon had been a stage comedian, while Tom Edwards had hosted shows for an ITV company. And, of course, a number of DJs came from the music business itself. A handful, like Sutch, were musicians. Two (Woolf Byrne and John Edward) had played sax and guitar in a Maidstone band called the Manish Boys, the lead singer of which would go on to fame as David Bowie. Adrian Love and John Martin came from musical dynasties: Love's father had been a prominent band leader, Martin's a BBC manager. Love himself had played in jazz bands and orchestras. And several others graduated from club DJ to radio DJ, often after sending a demo tape. Peter York, for example, was DJing in Southampton before he briefly broadcast from City in 1966. Ben Healy had been a club DJ in London, working at major Soho and West End venues for three years before he sent his demo to Calvert in spring 1966. Calvert, impressed, told Healy he wanted him for a new station he was planning to launch. Events intervened, and he ended up with Radio Scotland.

Several of the older City DJs had already been before a radio microphone by the time they arrived on Shivering Sands, usually while doing national service in places like Aden. Phil Jay, for example, worked with British Forces Broadcasting on Cyprus while serving in the RAF. On his return he became an assistant to Larry Parnes, the original British pop manager, and organized dances in central England before sending his demo to Denmark Street. His distinctly Calvert-like experience stood him in good stead and he became a mainstay of the station. But the only DJs with real experience of civilian commercial broadcasting were the four from Australia. Ross Brown had worked at several stations before coming to Britain and being hired by Dorothy Calvert, by this time City's program manager. Ian MacRae had broadcast in his native Melbourne before joining City in February 1966. Both Brown and MacRae were successful and popular, and would remain until City was shuttered in February 1967. Dennis "the Menace" Straney and Norman St. John, who had also broadcast in Australia beforehand, had shorter runs. Arriving in early 1965 while on a round-the-world tour to convalesce from illness, St. John was persuaded by Reg Calvert to join the station. But he found its equipment, living quarters, and food unbearable, and left for Caroline South. Straney departed from City to join Wilf Proudfoot's Radio 270, anchored off Scarborough.

The least experienced City presenters, on the other hand—the teenagers who answered the station's regular calls for DJs—tended to live nearby, in northeast Kent. Some had been born there. A number were still at school when they went out to Shivering Sands. Bob Le Roi, a Canterbury teenager, graduated at fifteen from making "tender tapes" (recordings to be played on air while the entire crew helped haul up supplies from the tender) to presenting in his own right. In 1965 he may have been the youngest presenter broadcasting anywhere in Britain. Another teenager, Eric Johnson, was listening to the station in Gravesend when he heard repeated references to the Record Centre in Whitstable; he visited, spoke with Martin, and ended up going out twice to broadcast from the station. Cliff Cuttelle, a Whitstable native, was an apprentice at a printing works that had done jobbing work for Martin, and knew the manager's daughter from school. Martin had him go out to the fort on days when the station was short-staffed, and after a while he became a fixture. Cuttelle would be part of the group Martin recruited to go to Knock John in late 1965. Six months later, an eighteen-year-old named Eric Martin (no relation to the manager) auditioned on the fort, and after finishing his A-levels returned to stay as a DJ until it closed. Howard Michaels, a nineteen-year-old laboratory staffer at Wilkinson Sword and a precocious club DJ, sent a demo tape that resulted in the standard week's audition—but he ended up stranded at Shivering Sands for two weeks in atrocious weather. Eventually a thoroughly fed-up Michaels denounced the station and its management on air. As soon as the storm subsided he was hauled back to Whitstable and replaced.

What emerged from this unstable mixture of experienced hands and absolute beginners was unlike anything else on the airwaves. Radio City had an endlessly varying, sometimes quite original schedule, for all that it favored Calvert's own bands. *Candy's Pop Shop* was one example, unusual in having a young, female presenter and an irregular slot. Ian MacRae and Alan Clark presented a satire called *The Aunty Mabel Hour,* while Clark co-hosted a requests show entirely devoted to the Beatles and Rolling Stones. Toward the end of City's life it also broadcast programs recorded in New York by a soul DJ named Ralph Cooper, introducing a rapid-fire rhyming talk quite comprising in reality two largely autonomous operations, Caroline North and Caroline South (the old Radio Atlanta); Radio London, a new and well-organized competitor; Radio City, the scrappy but imaginative fort station; and another fort station named Radio Invicta. This last had started transmissions only a week after Radio Sutch. Based on Red Sands, another of the Army forts, it was the creation of veterans of the Voice of Slough project, who had joined forces with a Kent salvage tug master going by the alias Tom Pepper. Pepper ingeniously claimed salvage rights to the fort by an ancient marine law. It seemed a success, but at the start of 1965 Pepper and two staff members drowned when their tender sank. Invicta closed soon afterwards, but the other three stations persevered, and before long the prospect of profit was attracting more ventures into the fray. It is impossible to know how many pie-in-the-sky projects were mooted, but a few got on the air. Radio King was one; it began broadcasting in March 1965 from the fort vacated by Invicta. Its instigators included two of Pepper's old comrades and Oliver Smedley's cousin, Austin Churton Fairman, who had resigned from Atlanta at the time of the Caroline merger and now tended to use his microphone alias of Mike Raven off air as well as on. Unlike the other offshore stations, King adopted a smooth, middle-of-the-road idiom, the major exception being Raven's own show devoted to R&B. It struggled to find an audience, and in September it closed.

The next station on Red Sands was Radio 390. Like King, it avoided the pop format, employing "announcers" (not DJs) to target housewives with a stream of "sweet" music. The format was the brainchild of a public relations adviser turned radio entrepreneur, Theodore ("Ted") Edward le Bouthillier Allbeury (1917–2005). A tall, imposing, and occasionally distant man, during World War II Allbeury had been a senior intelligence officer in Britain's Special Operations Executive (SOE). He was said to have continued to serve in the Secret Service during the cold war. Mystery allowed a panoply of legends to grow up about his activities, but it was widely reported that he had been involved in interrogating high Nazi officials, particularly Himmler. Later he would parlay his experiences into a successful career as an espionage novelist. But he had also pursued an overt

AS THE PIRATE boom took hold, it challenged more than just the BBC. Despite what is often taken to have been its eclipse by the rise of television, thanks to the pirates once again radio occupied center stage in a series of debates about the very constitution of culture. What, if anything, was valuable in mass or popular culture, and was it under threat by modern media? How could it be studied, evaluated, and enhanced? Such questions had been posed with increasing urgency since the early fifties. Those convinced that there was indeed a critical, constructive sensibility among mass readers and listeners—one that needed and deserved to be nurtured—saw in pirate radio a profound threat to Britain's cultural future.

In a sense, this took up themes that had originated in the 1920s, with the advent of broadcasting itself. The enterprise had always provoked questions about its relation to cultural enrichment, and in particular education. As early as 1926, Reith received a plan for a "wireless university," but did not pursue it.[21] In the 1930s, such questions came into focus again when the BBC wrestled with the question of listening. Jennings and Gill's *Broadcasting in Everyday Life*—that extraordinary account of working-class listeners in Bristol that inaugurated its efforts—concluded with an appeal to integrate the cultivation of critical listening with more formal educational processes, contending that the fate of democracy itself might depend on this being done successfully. And in succeeding decades, the corporation worked fitfully with schools and other institutions to this end. In the late 1940s, the historian E. L. Woodward likened these efforts to the revolution in cultural literacy that paperback books had brought about.[22] Now, the question of the listener was once more alive. Once again it merged with that of forming citizens.

The early sixties were a time of radical uncertainty about the state and future of education in the UK, and in particular about higher education. Concern about the lingering elitism of the universities combined with awareness of a looming crisis of scarcity. At this time, full-time students numbered about 216,000 nationally (about 7 percent of nineteen-year-olds). Forecasts projected that by 1980 there would be 560,000. More alarming still, a surge in the birthrate immediately after the war meant that a quantum leap in demand for places—of the order of 30–50 percent—was imminent. And alongside this "battle of the bulge," as it was called, were fears that Britain was losing its best researchers to America in a "brain drain." The upshot was that the country might well face defeat in a technological race with the United States and the USSR—and each new canceled prestige project, from the TSR-2 bomber to the Blue Streak missile, seemed to confirm the prospect. It was alarmingly reminiscent of the anxiety that had gripped Britons in the twenties, the last time when radio and popular science had been central to such fears of national decline.

None other than Lionel Robbins, the LSE economist who as a young man a generation earlier had created the intellectual environment for Coase and Hayek, led a thorough investigation of the problem. His report took two years to complete. It swiftly became the most famous and influential document on higher education in modern British history. In a telling reversal of Robbins's earlier convictions, it responded to the "emergency" by arguing that what had hitherto been haphazard should be managed as a "system" and dramatically expanded. Not only was this necessary to preserve Britain's place in the world, Robbins warned, "it is an essential condition for the realization in the modern age of the ideals of a free and democratic society."

In practice, the expansion called for by the Robbins Report was already under way. But it was clear already that that would be too little and too late.[23] In this context, ideas for using the ether as a tool of cultural improvement consequently revived and multiplied, at exactly the same time as the commercial pirates were laboring to launch their ships. Schemes went by various names, but the commonest was a phrase that had been heard intermittently ever since the 1920s: the "university of the air." Political scientist Sir George Catlin proposed a "University of the Air" at the time of the Pilkington Committee, for example, but his view was relegated to a minority report. Meanwhile, the Institution of Electrical Engineers suggested its own plan for a "televarsity." And Michael Young, chairman of an education think tank, called for "an 'open university'" to deal with the looming crisis. Young himself actually launched an experimental "Dawn University" project, with Cambridge dons lecturing on television and a National Extension College coordinating the pursuit of London extramural degrees. As proposals multiplied, even the Conservative government drafted plans for a "college of the air," although its focus would be on a lower tier of education.[24]

It was the Labour Party—or, more precisely, its new leader, the forty-seven-year-old Harold Wilson—that took up the torch. In March 1963, the physician and longtime Labour politician Lord Taylor of Harlow submitted a report to the party articulating reasons for adopting a "university of the air" in response to the coming crisis. If "a good society is a highly educated society," Taylor argued, then "all who are capable of benefiting from higher education must have access to it."[25] And the only way to achieve this democratically transformative change—to make higher education a right, not a privilege—was both to increase the number of conventional universities (he wanted to double it) and to deploy broadcast media to extend their reach across the population. Wilson seized on this radical proposal, and soon learned that the use of broadcasting was already being proved possible in America. A U.S. senator, William Benton, publisher of *Encyclopaedia Britannica*, told the Labour leader of a University of the Air operated by a commercial television company in Pennsylvania in collaboration with local colleges and universities. It broadcast free lectures to some 250,000 "students," 84 percent of them women, who could now "attend college without leaving home."[26] The idea caught the imagination of Wilson, who was eager to portray himself as a forward-looking technophile. That September, he used his speech launching the general election campaign to announce his own idea of a university of the air. It would provide adult education across the land, under the management of a "trust" comprising universities, broadcasters, teachers, and publishers. And a few weeks later Wilson returned to the theme in what would prove the most successful speech of his entire career.

It has become famous as the "white heat" speech. At the party's annual conference in Scarborough, Wilson stood to proclaim a "scientific revolution" that must transform Britain. Technical advance was moving with unprecedented rapidity, and automation would soon allow factories to operate without human workers. Computers were already supplanting human powers of memory and intellect. Under a free enterprise system, Wilson warned, these technologies threatened only mass unemployment. "If there had never been a case for Socialism before," he announced, "automation would have created it." A Labour government would therefore have to act. It must ensure that Britain produced more scientists, and that those scientists remained in the UK. The country and its industry must also make better use of their innovations. The key to the national future, therefore, was what Wilson called "a revolution in our attitude to education." It was in this context that a "university of the air" must be created—and when it was, it would make "an immeasurable contribution to the cultural life of our country." A new Britain was on the cards, "forged in the white heat of this revolution," from which old practices and snobberies would have disappeared. The revolution in public knowledge would be its foundation.[27]

Wilson's clarion call received widespread enthusiasm and praise. And, faced with a choice between "white heat" and tepid conservatism, the electorate narrowly but decisively opted for Labour. It was a victory for the university of the air—and a defeat for any prospect of commercial radio.

The idea of a university of the air appealed to Wilson and others as a futuristic counterpart to traditional bricks-and-mortar institutions, and one able to reach much further into the general population. Needless to say, however, the more ambitious sketches drew skeptical attacks, not least from those committed to traditional ideals of education. The chief educational officer of Norfolk, Lincoln Ralphs, published a particularly stinging critique in *The Economist* as early as March 1962. Ralphs lamented the "seductive and superficial" appeal of a notion that would, at its extreme, rob a student of all face-to-face contact with teachers and fellow learners. But Ralphs suggested that the more extravagant claims were in truth tactical devices, not serious plans—they were "pre-Pilkington manoeuvres," calculated to attract attention from the committee investigating the BBC. Sure enough, the committee devoted much time to the topic. Although it did not overtly endorse it, it did cast the possibility as a virtuous alternative to vicious commercialism. And that, as much as the committee's practical recommendations, framed the debate for the next decade.

Meanwhile, the idea found powerful allies, both within the BBC itself and among advocates of more local media. John Scupham, the BBC's first Controller of Educational Broadcasting, issued a manifesto in 1964 for what he called "a social revolution," to be led by the corporation in alliance with the government and major educational institutions. Scupham revived the idea that Pilkington had rejected: that learning should get its own channel. He added that the BBC should help create a "national library" of recordings to serve as the backbone of such a "university." It was in the same context that another senior BBC manager, Oliver Whitley, claimed that no democratic society could be a real success without the general inculcation of a "philosophic outlook" among the population at large, and that the BBC and the university of the air should endeavor to achieve this. (It is disconcerting for a modern reader to find at the top of Whitley's list of praiseworthy BBC programs *The Black and White Minstrel Show*.)[28] At the same time, dreams of a university of the air converged with schemes for local broadcasting. When pirate stations claimed that they wanted to become land-based local broadcasters, as they often did, politicians and the BBC projected in response a network of "local broadcasting universities of the air," as Director General Hugh Greene called them. In 1966, a conference co-organized by the BBC and the University of Sussex drew fresh attention to these possibilities, at levels ranging from primary education up to research.[29]

The university of the air thus came to stand as the principled alternative to capitulation to commercial culture. Invocations of education confronted invocations of freedom of choice. For proponents of a university of the air—as, ironically, for pirate fans—what was at stake in the debate in the radio contest was "culture," in a more direct and incisive sense even than in Hayek's day. This was expressed most clearly by the supreme opponent of commercial broadcasting, the champion of working-class cultural practices and their study: Richard Hoggart.

Hoggart had come to attention with the runaway success of his book *The Uses of Literacy* in 1957, which warned of the erosion of critical judgment among working-class Britons by commercialized mass media. After that success he had become the champion of public service ideals on the Pilkington Committee. When Pilkington reported resoundingly in favor of the BBC, one press wag described it as "going the whole Hoggart." Now, he was instrumental in founding the academic field of "cultural studies." Not at all the highly theorized and morally relativist enterprise it was to become, in Hoggart's view it was a committed and indeed moralistic endeavor. The point was to apply to the cultural practices of lay people the same attention that the Leavisites—admirers of the critics F. R. and Q. D. Leavis—had devoted to fine literature. It deserved such attention, and, when properly appreciated, warranted defending. Hoggart joined forces with the brilliant immigrant scholar of popular culture, Stuart Hall, to defend the project both by fostering its academic study and by campaigning against commercial broadcasting.[30] The terms and tone of their assault were striking:

> It has taken centuries to forge even those democratic structures—in law, in politics, in the provision of education and elsewhere—that we now have. Mass communications within prosperous centralised democracies are a new phenomenon and we have not yet found the organisational forms, or the general temper, which will allow us to use them in the best ways. It takes a long time, here as elsewhere, to move away from dominative and paternalistic modes. But if we cut short the effort and settle for rule-by-cash-register we shall be committing an act against democratic growth roughly comparable to reinstituting the taxes on knowledge.
>
> "Freedom and Independence" here does not lie in giving a handful of individuals the chance to make large profits, but in finding forms of organisation which will keep this powerful means of human communication free from exploitation by any man, whether for cash or for ideology.[31]

Prospects for the university of the air closely tracked those for pirate radio. It became a realistic proposition in 1965, just as commercial radio seemed set to become a national reality. After more than a year of delay, Wilson gave the task of fulfilling his commitment to Jennie Lee, MP and widow of the Labour MP and architect of the National Health Service, Aneurin Bevan. Lee now became the principal booster of the university of the air, driving it forward against determined opposition on many sides. Above all, it was Lee, more than Wilson himself, who insisted that the new institution be a true university. It must be "rigorous and demanding," upholding standards rather than talking down to what one critic called the "educationally underprivileged." Only if it offered a qualification equivalent to the degrees offered by conventional universities, Lee insisted, would it be worth having. It was in this uncompromising form that the Cabinet referred the idea to an advisory committee under her leadership—a committee simultaneously charged with addressing the pirates.

As a result, the conflict that pirate radio sparked in 1964 did not quite reproduce the old division between BBC and anti-BBC camps. This time, the BBC occupied more of a middle position. The real opposite pole to the pirate stations was a putative institution called the university of the air. For its advocates, the BBC's status should obviously be preserved, but there was now room in the ether for another power. It should be a force for knowledge and enlightenment, not for Spam and skin cream. An old notion, originally created in the very earliest days of broadcasting, the university of the air was now revived to capture an ideal for the positive use of broadcasting for the next generation. Contentions about a university of the air intersected at all points with those about the fate of the BBC and the virtues—or rather vices—of commercial broadcasters. And the BBC found itself pinioned between passionate advocates on two sides. One camp was Oliver Smedley's: it wanted laissez-faire and commercial competition. It is relatively familiar to us. The other was formed by the BBC's own fiercest defenders. They saw it as a vital cultural bulwark, alongside the universities, of culture, criticism, and intellectual diversity. It was a matter of moral politics, they believed, that neither be subject to commercial depredations. This camp argued that the BBC was admirable, but that it was not enough. Britain needed an ethereal academy.

The debate over pirate radio had become a contest over what was sometimes called the public mind. By its climax, everything that this camp believed to be most dubious about the pirate enterprise would be identified with Radio City. And for piracy's ultimate ideologue, City would represent the last chance for his media revolution. So the conflict over pirate radio would come down to two towers: the ivory tower and the tower of power.

BY MID-1965, REGINALD Calvert was restless again. The popular appetite for commercial radio was burgeoning, and he was itching to expand Radio City to feed it. He had his eye on another of the old anti-aircraft forts: Knock John, a Navy fort further out to sea than Shivering Sands. It was less stable, and, with a smaller footprint, less suitable for a large antenna. But it was potentially promising nevertheless.

Calvert had Eric Martin send a small team of youngsters including Cliff Cuttelle out to Knock John with cleaning supplies. They were to spruce up the fort in advance of engineers bringing transmission equipment. The men managed to scramble up onto the platform, to find a scene of squalor and decay untouched for at least a decade—complete with rusting antiaircraft guns. They set to work and cleaned up enough of the fort to imagine putting it to use for a station. They did their job, and the engineers landed on the platform a few days later, intent on setting up Radio City II. But for the first time Calvert found himself confronted by a determined and potentially violent antagonist. His men ran into a rival band sent by Roy Bates, a fisherman and entrepreneur from Essex who had hit upon the same idea at the same time. There was a brief confrontation before Bates's gang won the day. The City crew were sent packing. When he found that Dick Dickson had left equipment behind, Calvert angrily dismissed him. Dickson promptly went back and joined Bates.

The short-term result was that Knock John became the home of Radio Essex, which started operations in November. Its equipment was rudimentary (antiquated military technology powered by old World War II generators) and its aerial homemade, but it worked. The longer-term consequences were more serious. In denying Calvert the opportunity to use Knock John, Bates left him casting about for other opportunities. That search would soon lead him to Radio Caroline. And to Oliver Smedley.

6

"THINGS ARE GETTING HOT"

It was ten days after Radio Caroline began transmitting, and the station was still on the air. Rumors of more pirates about to set sail were multiplying. Yet the government had done nothing, and showed no signs of intervening. Labour MP Roy Mason, a Yorkshire coal miner now serving as shadow to the Postmaster General, rose in the House of Commons to demand action before it was too late. He warned of "the inherent dangers of allowing such a station to continue," and asked the Cabinet to consider the extreme step of jamming Caroline's broadcasts. Mason's sense of urgency derived not from the existence of Caroline alone, but from the possibility that it would soon be joined by other commercial stations—not just Atlanta and City, both of which soon started up, but others too. The government must act now, Mason declared, to prevent the creation of "a radio network round our shores."[1]

This idea of a rival network to the BBC's, rampantly commercial and untrammeled by concerns about copyright infringement, interference, or public service, may sound exaggerated. After all, the pirates were in competition with each other as well as with the BBC. But it was not an isolated prophecy on Mason's part. And recent experience with commercial broadcasters in the realm of television suggested that they were all too willing to merge into monopoly conglomerates. Press speculation was already rife that something of the sort might come

into being. And Postmaster General Reginald Bevins announced publicly that an "armada" of ships was in the offing. Similarly, for Oliver
Smedley, on the other side, a single pirate was not enough; he wanted
a network to challenge and defeat the BBC and its public corporation model of society. So as Caroline was joined by Atlanta, and then
by a growing number of other pirate stations, it was all too easy to
identify the proliferation as heralding this threatened "network." It
came to seem that the fears of both political parties—and the hopes
of Smedley's Atlanta—were on the mark.

But any hopes Smedley had of expanding Atlanta into a network
soon ran into serious trouble. By far the most professional of the
new pirate stations, Radio London, saw to that. As we have seen, it
appeared in December 1964. The station's capital came from Texas,
its holding company was based in the Bahamas, and its ship was registered in Panama. Another company, Radlon, oversaw sales from
London, with accounting in dollars filtered through Swiss accounts.
With this structure the operation managed to avoid major tax liabili-
ties in Britain and America alike. Radlon's managing director, the
experienced advertising executive Philip Birch, was a pirate broadcaster with a skill that no rival matched. London soon proved itself a
strong competitor, especially for Crawford's Caroline South. A revamp
of Crawford's station did little to help, and by mid-1965 it was clear
that the Atlanta camp was in serious trouble.[2]

In the summer of 1965, Calvert and Crawford met and discussed a
merger between Caroline South (the old Radio Atlanta) and Radio
City. It is unclear which of the two sought out the other; Dorothy
Calvert later said that the initiative was Crawford's, while participants
on his side tended to think that it came from City. But there were
clear incentives for both. For Calvert, Caroline might provide a much-
needed injection of capital and professionalism. Radio City needed
both. If it could be put on a firmer footing, his own domestic situation
might stabilize. And he might even be able to pursue his own vision of
expansion. He continued to talk to journalists of launching a pirate
television station.[3]

For Crawford, and for Smedley behind him, the opportunity was even more important. Radio City could survive without Atlanta; it was by no means clear that Atlanta could survive without City. Caroline South was still leaching listeners, and Project Atlanta was fast approaching a crisis point. It had never made money, and now there was little prospect that it would do so in the future unless some radical change took place. An alliance with City would certainly be a step toward the "very powerful combine" needed to create a nation-wide network, but more immediately it could cut costs, remove competition, and provide a secure location. Shivering Sands fort itself was the critically important attraction. Ships were expensive to crew and maintain, and they were always liable to mishap, or even, given the sometimes ferocious weather conditions of the North Sea, disaster. Indeed, in January 1966 the *Mi Amigo* would be driven aground during a storm and narrowly miss being destroyed. A vessel's need for stability also limited the height of any antenna that could be mounted on board, and hence the range of any transmission. None of these constraints applied to a fort. The broad footprint of Shivering Sands in particular was its crucial asset. By running guy cables to its separate towers, engineers could hope to erect the tallest aerial of any offshore site anywhere around the UK. This stable, secure location might well present the solution to Atlanta's gathering problems.

It was now that Smedley first met Reg Calvert. In his guise as finance maestro for Atlanta, he visited the fort several times. He soon came to recognize its potential (and, apparently, to advise his new acquaintance to move his own personal investments offshore). No contract was signed, but with Smedley's approval the two stations created an informal alliance. Caroline would receive all of City's income, and in return undertook to meet its smaller partner's day-to-day costs. Calvert, his wife later testified, was to be paid £1,500 a month plus 50 percent of City profits, and would manage the programming and technical aspects (she remembered him being charged with managing the ship as well as the fort).[4] As the deal got underway, City began rebroadcasting Caroline's news programs and promoting Caroline's schedule on its own shows.

For this potential to be realized, however, Radio City would need new equipment. That meant a new transmitter (and perhaps the generator to power it) as well as a new antenna. In October 1965, Smedley phoned the Calverts from the United States, and announced excitedly that he had found the first of these. The transmitter would be expensive, but it would dramatically improve City's reach. The device was quickly flown across the Atlantic and transported to the Kent coast. There the Caroline tender, the *Offshore I*, was waiting to ferry it out to Shivering Sands.

As soon as the tender drew close to the fort, it was clear that something was going to go badly wrong. The transmitter turned out not to be the new, efficient, and powerful unit that Smedley had described and that City needed. It was a massive and antiquated hulk, which had seen long service at a station in Fort Worth and had over the years degenerated into what City man Philip Perkins called "a home brew lash up." It arrived in three forbiddingly large crates, each eight feet tall and six wide. Lifting such weights the 60–70 feet onto the fort would test the rebuilt crane to its limit. In the event, it could just about bring up one of the boxes, but it could not hold it steady long enough to be manhandled onto the fort. The crate lurched back onto the tender's deck, narrowly missing the crew. They tried again, moving the boat away for safety. But now the crate hit the side of the tower and fell back. Its harness caught for a moment on the structure of the fort. Then, as Alex Dee and Perkins moved to wrestle it onto the tower, it broke free. The massive crate fell through the yawning space from the chamber to the sea and disappeared beneath the waves.

That night, Calvert called on the fort's ship-to-shore radio and learned what had happened. "I do believe he had a seizure," recalled Dee. But he pulled himself together quickly, and arranged for divers to salvage the lost crate. They came out the next day and managed to raise it. Finally, the transmitter made it up to the transmitter tower. There, West, Perkins, and two engineers from Caroline laboriously took apart the entire cabinet, washed every component in fresh water, and reassembled it. The effort proved largely futile. The mammoth device never worked properly—and it demanded too much of the generator in any case. West and Perkins returned to their own transmitter and concentrated on keeping that going.[5]

All was not lost: a good aerial could overcome to some extent the problems of a weak transmitter. Elvey had asked for one repeatedly. Typically, Calvert initially insisted on making his own. He had scaffolding paraphernalia shipped to the fort to build it, and in a feat of bravery and resourcefulness the City crew erected a homemade antenna. It worked, more or less. But it was soon felled in a storm. At that point Elvey got his way, as Calvert accepted the need for a professional device. He realized that a large antenna would be too expensive to buy, but arranged to rent one from an aerial engineer named Alan Arnold, a thirty-nine-year-old with a heart condition who found Calvert's pluck worthy of the gamble. In early 1966, Arnold's men came out to Shivering Sands and erected a towering 200-foot aerial. Combined with the height of the towers themselves, this gave Radio City by far the tallest antenna of any pirate. It potentially transformed City's fortunes. The new antenna became the icon of the "Tower of Power."

The Caroline-City pact, although impelled by the needs of each side, took effect amid a number of attempts to remake offshore radio into a responsible, "respectable" endeavor. These attempts impinged upon the very idea of "pirate" stations.[6] They had always been called that primarily because they disregarded the international regime for allocating wavelengths. But another reason for the moniker was that they were intellectual property pirates. The copyright and performing rights agencies had long trumpeted the need for action against them on that basis, and did so once again in December 1965. In practice, the record companies made sure that the pirate stations got new releases in good time to air them; but this was largely unacknowledged. What was acknowledged was that Atlanta had agreed a *modus vivendi* with the Performing Right Society in its early days, and in February 1966 Philip Birch's Radio London finally announced a deal, too.[7] London would pay the society thousands of pounds in deferred royalties, and in future contribute a proportion of its advertising revenue. It was not an orthodox agreement, to be sure, and London persisted in regarding it as *ex gratia*. For that reason the PRS remained committed in principle to shutting down the offshore stations. But it did provide a measure of respectability. Sir Joseph Lockwood, the chairman of industry giant EMI, certainly saw what it implied: he denounced the PRS for accepting "derisory" sums from pirates who continued to abuse "other people's property." (They offered amounts like £3,000; the BBC paid roughly £15 million a year.)[8] The point was that one by one the offshore stations were being brought within reach of probity. At the same time, they won over the trade associations of the advertising industry, and Birch announced that "he hoped the word pirate would now be dropped from broadcasting terminology." By June 19, 1966, even the *Sunday Times* could report that "radio pirates are growing respectable."[9]

But for Calvert's alliance with Caroline it was too late. Toward the end of 1965 the payments from Caroline had dried up—it is not entirely clear that any were ever made. Crawford himself had gone to ground—he "disappeared," as Dorothy Calvert put it. When Calvert pressed for reimbursement, he was told that all City's checks had in fact been passed straight on to Project Atlanta. And there they stayed, unopened. Project Atlanta had collapsed.

Atlanta's future had come to depend on Shivering Sands. But by autumn 1965 government statements cast a new shadow over the fort stations. Postmaster General Anthony Wedgwood Benn told Parliament that action would be taken against them; the Copyright Council was once again pressing him to take decisive measures, which he acknowledged would be welcome to those "whose performances are being pirated."[10] This new uncertainty coincided disastrously with Atlanta's looming financial crisis. On December 17, the company's creditors lost patience and presented an ultimatum. Smedley gave in. He sold Project Atlanta's assets to Caroline, hoping to pay off most of its debts. The company remained in existence, but with no further role to play. Smedley said that commitments would be honored, and Calvert's secretary continued to send bills to Atlanta for payment. But in practice the alliance had foundered. Smedley's personal assistant, Aubrey Boutwood, certainly believed that the sale had brought the alliance with City to an end.

So, as Radio London and the other offshore stations negotiated for respectability and an end to pirate status, one station ended up outside all such agreements. That station was Radio City. Calvert had to take the reins again at a moment when Radio City found itself, in a sense, the one true pirate left.[11] And it was a more viable site than ever. The new antenna was part of the explanation, but perhaps as important was the return of Dorothy Calvert. The Calverts' daughter, Susan, had managed a reconciliation between Reg and his wife, and Mrs. Calvert now became the station manager for Radio City. Her inaugural trip to the fort on Good Friday was only the second she had ever taken. She swiftly took charge, instilling discipline and dynamism at once. The waywardness that had prevailed since its days as Radio Sutch came to an end. Her letters to the DJs on the fort show that she listened constantly to the station, and took pains to correct what she saw as its flaws and blemishes. DJs were to refrain from singing, stop rambling between records, focus relentlessly on Top 50 discs, and disregard anything that was on its way down the charts as simply "dead." And on some specific musical choices, too, she put her foot down: "NO Sinatra." Under her management the station became at last more predictable.[12]

But as it improved, so Radio City became more attractive—not just to listeners but to piratical challengers.

IN EARLY JUNE 1966, the phone rang in Racity's Denmark Street office. The caller did not give his name, but he had a warning to impart. He had heard of a threat to Shivering Sands. Some piratical rival was scheming to send a gang to the fort and take it over. That kind of aggressive action had always been a possibility—the press had reported plots more than a year earlier.[13] But this sounded serious. Calvert's guess was that the maverick Roy Bates of Radio Essex, with whom he had already tangled over Knock John, was responsible.

Calvert was right. The caller was in fact Ted Allbeury, boss of Radio 390. A onetime employee at Allbeury's company, Estuary, had gone on to work for Bates, and on a social visit had happened to let slip that his

new manager had designs on the fort. Bates was apparently considering extending his triumph at Knock John by seizing Shivering Sands
too. Indeed, he claimed to have paid a reconnaissance visit already,
and to have taken away equipment at the dead of night. Presumably
it was just long-abandoned stuff on the unused part of the structure.
But the claim was nevertheless worrying. And a frightening pattern
seemed to be emerging, for there had been rumors recently of threats
against the Calverts themselves.

Dorothy Calvert sent word to Shivering Sands: Lock down the
hatches. Be watchful.

OLIVER SMEDLEY FELT an increasingly acute sense of urgency and
frustration. It was humiliating enough that his own Project Atlanta
had all but given up the ghost. But now, so soon after its collapse, he
could see offshore broadcasting expanding rapidly. Shivering Sands
in particular seemed to be thriving. He faced the prospect of a new
media landscape being carved out in front of him. If he wanted to
establish the network he needed for his political vision to come about,
then he would have to move fast. He had to get back into the action.

In February or early March 1966, Smedley contacted Calvert again.
He knew of a company, he said, that wanted to buy Radio City for
£10,000. He even turned up in Denmark Street and spent the day
examining City's accounts. Calvert refused to sell, feeling that the
station was now worth far more. But he did vouchsafe that he would
be prepared to do a deal for what he regarded as the right price. He
was restless once more, and wanted to either expand or sell. He clearly
had in mind a major upgrade, whether or not the existing station
remained his own: he would soon contact the aerial engineer, Alan
Arnold, to ask about erecting an antenna on a rock in the middle of
the Bristol Channel, the aim being to launch a new station covering
the west of England and Wales. But any sale would have to be done
quickly, he warned Smedley. A general election was in the offing, and
were Labour to win, their Postmaster General, Benn, would surely
move against the pirates. Sure enough, at the beginning of June, Benn

urged prosecutions against the fort stations, if only to demonstrate his intent to destroy the pirates.[14]

It seems that Smedley took Calvert's willingness to sell seriously enough to continue searching for investors. At any rate, Aubrey Boutwood believed this to be so. Once or twice he seemed close to netting one; in early May, a potential investor came to Denmark Street to examine the books of Radio City. But none of Smedley's sanguine prophecies ever seemed to come good, and this was no exception: a few days after the visit, he wrote to say that he would not be investing. Still, never one to let an absence of actual capital get in the way of practicing capitalism, Smedley forged on. He now began to think in terms of commanding City himself. He would do so, he thought, through a revived Project Atlanta.

On May 24, Smedley wrote to Alexander Horsley, a fifty-nine-year-old pilot for Trinity House (the sixteenth-century institution that still oversees lighthouses and pilots in Britain). Sandy Horsley had been involved with Project Atlanta since as early as 1963, having heard tell of it when Richard Harris, the nascent company's general manager, came to his house for a cocktail party. Horsley had arranged for friends to buy shares in the ill-fated venture, and had himself advised on where to anchor the *Mi Amigo*. Now he opened Smedley's letter to find draft documents for a new company. It was to be called Seagull Publicity Ltd. Smedley's plan was that Seagull would effectively take over Radio City. Smedley himself would be a director, and the headquarters would be at his IGMS office, where the IEA had started out. The company would sell airtime to advertisers on behalf of Project Atlanta, which would run the Shivering Sands station. The other director would be Calvert, who would become manager of the station. There was to be the usual Smedleian arrangement of cross-ownership: Atlanta would get half the 5,000 shares in Seagull and give them to Calvert, and buy 500 more in its own right. He also provided that in the event of deadlock between Calvert and Atlanta, one side could buy the other out. Smedley proposed to raise capital for the scheme by selling the rest of the shares, with a requirement that all who bought them must lend the new company £10 for every £1 spent on its stock. As ever, he sounded confident: people were already rushing to subscribe, he told Horsley, and anyone interested should act quickly. "As the station is already on the air," he added, "the risks involved are considerably less than in some other cases we have known."[15]

But Smedley did not know that his time was fast running out. Calvert had lost patience with his repeated promises, and had contacted rivals on his own behalf. First he approached Ted Allbeury of Radio 390. Calvert proposed a collaboration. But Allbeury rejected the approach. He suspected, as he later put it, that the Radio City boss would be "a very difficult man to control," and a safely middle-of-the-road station like 390 would not accommodate him well. Calvert then went to Philip Birch of Radio London. Here he found himself in much more sympathetic company. The two met at Calvert's flat on May 12. Calvert told Birch that he wanted to leave the radio business; music publishing and management were his forte, and he had ideas he wanted to pursue in those realms. They entered into secret negotiations to sell Radio City.

Birch found the prospect appealing for all the reasons that Smedley and Crawford had done the previous autumn. With the new antenna in place on Shivering Sands, the fort was a very attractive proposition, and he had the experience and capital to make the most of it. He and Calvert swiftly concocted a plan: they would create a new station, under the aegis of a Bahamas company to be called the Sweet Music Association. Calvert's Tarpon and a firm acting for Birch would share ownership. Radio London would continue unchanged, but City would be replaced by this new station, which they agreed to call "Radio Sweet Music"—a name they soon changed to "UK Good Music," or UKGM. As that name suggests, they hoped to capture the middle-of-the-road audience that Allbeury was targeting with Radio 390. Calvert would get a monthly stipend. The two men verbally agreed on the terms, and drew up a draft document. Among other things, Calvert confirmed that he owned all the equipment on the fort free and clear (except the antenna and a 6kW transmitter, which were rented)—and that the 10kW transmitter brought aboard the previous autumn from Texas would be made fully operational. He put the draft in the glove compartment of his car so that it would be ready to hand. It was dated just one day after Smedley's charter for Seagull Publicity.

Calvert and Birch agreed to move forward quickly. They set a debut date for UKGM of July 1, giving them less than six weeks to complete all the details. It was a hard target to meet, but Calvert was delighted to be proceeding so fast. Come July 1, the long months of insecurity and tension would be over. Not only would he finally be free of pirate radio; he would garner a monthly income of £1,000 for his pains. Keeping quiet about his scheme, he made plans for a long-overdue family holiday. The Calverts would leave for Portugal as soon as everything was in place. But his family noticed he was edgy. He tried to persuade them to go ahead of him, but would not say why. He had never been a keen holidaymaker, but this was different. Worried, they refused to go. Only then did he announce to their surprise that he planned to sell the station to Radio London. Later still, they would learn about the rumors of threats. Whatever was going to happen, he had wanted them out of harm's way.

At about this time, a tender unexpectedly drew up alongside Shivering Sands during Alan Clark's afternoon show. Two Radio London DJs jumped from the boat and came up into the studio deck. Keith Skues and Duncan Johnson were on a secret visit, they explained. It was part of the UKGM scheme: they were there to vet the Radio City facilities. By all accounts they were dismayed by what they found. The character of Radio City was utterly alien to the highly capitalized professionalism to which they were accustomed. But it was evidently good enough. Soon after, all the City DJs were summoned one by one to Radlon in Curzon Street to be told that the change was on. The move spread anxiety through their ranks. None of them had any formal job security anyway, but none knew who, if any, would survive in the new order.

It was now that disaster struck. Smedley found his long-sought investor. It is not known whom he had in mind, or even if the prospect was really any more solid than the others he had touted earlier. But on about June 5 he telephoned Calvert in euphoric mood to tell him the good news. Jill Wileman took the call. She alerted Calvert, who immediately saw that he had no choice. He called Smedley back and told him about the deal with Radio London. Smedley's euphoria vanished instantly, to be replaced by resentment. He accused Calvert of playing "a dirty trick." Dorothy Calvert, who was present in the room, saw Reg's surprise as Smedley grew more abusive. Eventually Calvert told Smedley that he had given him ample time to make good on his promises to launch a new company, and "talk was not enough."[16] Smedley announced that he would instruct Atlanta to stop paying any of City's bills forthwith—rather an empty gesture, as it had not transferred any funds for months, if ever. But it was a signal of finality nonetheless.

It is easy to see why Smedley should be so dismayed. The longer the pirates survived, the harder it became to silence them, yet he could see the final end of Atlanta looming in this deal. It destroyed his last hope of getting in on what he still believed would be a politically epochal—and personally profitable—moment in media history.

Something had to be done. And Oliver Smedley was nothing if not a man of action.

SMEDLEY FEARED THAT in a matter of days Shivering Sands would fall into Birch's hands and his hopes would be gone. At this moment of crisis, he returned in his mind to the alliance that Atlanta and Calvert had had in late 1965. And he remembered the ill-fated Texan transmitter that had been intended as its centerpiece. Whose was it?

The answer to that question has never been clear. Dorothy Calvert later told the police that there had been a "gentleman's agreement" about the transmitter. In the event of the alliance breaking down, she said, it would become Reg Calvert's property. In the draft agreement with Birch to set up UKGM, Calvert effectively took the same stance. And Smedley may well have seen things in the same light in 1965. But in June 1966 he thought very differently. Atlanta now needed every single asset it could count, and a transmitter worth, by Smedley's accounting, thousands of pounds was not to be given away. More to the point, it could be used as a lever to gain greater ends.

The idea of some kind of raid on Shivering Sands now began to seize Smedley's imagination—and, no less, that of his ally, the dramatic impresario Kitty Black. It is entirely possible that the notion originated with Black, although she was cagey when quizzed on French TV about her role, explaining only that she participated because "I was asked" (*On m'a invitée*). "She is a very shrewd woman," concluded the police, who came to believe that she might well have been the instigator. At any rate, she was at least as determined as Smedley to rescue something from the Atlanta fiasco, and the two of them embraced the risky venture equally.

Black and Smedley knew that they would need professional help for any such expedition. Smedley called a meeting at Project Atlanta's Dean Street office, and Black phoned Sandy Horsley, the Trinity House pilot, to ask him to come. She refused to say why, but he attended anyway. When he arrived, Smedley got straight to the point. Would Horsley do something for them?

Yes, Horsley replied, but then hesitated, perhaps guessing what might be about to come. "As long as it's legal."

"Are you aware," Smedley asked, "that Radio London has bought Radio City?"

No, Horsley replied, he had not known. He had thought that Smedley himself owned part of City, given that he had sent him the Seagull prospectus only a little while earlier. At least, he believed that Smedley had expensive equipment on the fort.

Smedley pressed him. "I wish to contest the deal with Radio London and repossess my property." Could he board the towers?

"Are you sure this is legal?" asked Horsley again.

Smedley deflected the question: he promised to take legal advice before acting. He would also take advice about negotiating with Calvert under duress if the seizure happened. But, he added, "the Tower has no known law." Its very autonomy, so appealing for a pirate site, made the question of law moot. Conventional measures such as injunctions were unlikely to work. The answer had to lie in direct action.

Horsley shrugged and decided to play along, thinking it would be a "lark." They would have to go in under cover of darkness, he began. The doors would be shut on them if they tried anything by day. The best time would be the dead of night, when he knew from experience that security on the forts would be lax.

Smedley pressed again: it would have to be done soon, as before long Radio London personnel would swarm over the tower and make any attempt impossible. Could Horsley get to work and "find some assistance as secretly as possible"?

The pilot agreed to do so. But then he observed that the operation would inevitably cost money. It ought to amount to £700–£1,000, he supposed. Where would this come from? "Why don't you ask the Atlanta board?"

Smedley refused. "They don't know about it," he revealed. "I'm going to present them with a *fait accompli*." It was the most fateful moment of the conversation.

Smedley and Black now volunteered to put up £250 each, and after some prodding Horsley said he would lend another £250. They split up. Horsley was set to recruit a gang for the raid.

Two days later, the conspirators met again at Dean Street. Horsley brought along another pilot, Donald ("Dodge") Jones, who was also an Atlanta shareholder. Crawford, who had been uncomfortable and largely silent at the first meeting, now withdrew altogether. He wanted nothing to do with such a risky adventure. From now on, Project Atlanta was not to be responsible for events. He left. Whatever happened next would be a purely private exploit, planned and paid for by Oliver Smedley and Kitty Black.

Smedley, Black, and the pilots got down to planning. They agreed that the "operation" would take place in a week's time, on the night of Sunday, June 19. Horsley had that long to organize tugs, personnel, and stores. He would have the help of Jones, but they would need to work fast. As they departed, the cabal ended on a strange note combining self-justification and ambition. He was doing this, Smedley said, "solely to get the shareholders' money back." One of his own aunts had invested in Project Atlanta, and he had a duty to people like her who had entrusted their savings to his venture. Horsley said that this was exactly his own view too. But then Smedley added that Horsley might well gain a one-third share in any deal that Calvert signed as a result of the seizure. The remarks attested to what were, at best, split motives: either Smedley was acting to protect Atlanta's interests, or he was plotting to force Calvert into a new venture. Horsley saw the distinction immediately. And he rejected the second idea. He would give his take, whatever it might be, to those he had lured into buying Atlanta shares.

HORSLEY GOT TO work. On Monday morning, June 13, he contacted Max Hamilton, the managing director of a tug firm in London, to ask about chartering a boat. Three days later he confirmed the charter, booking the *Vanquisher* with its captain, Percy Smith. Hamilton was curious, because Horsley requested a smaller boat too, which implied that the tug was not going to meet a conventional ship—it would usually simply come alongside. Horsley declined to say what was going on. He remarked cryptically that this ship had an overhanging superstructure, but would say no more.

On Wednesday the 15th Horsley phoned Henry Maxwell, a Trinity House pilot based, like him, at Gravesend in Kent. He gave no details but asked if Maxwell wanted to do a job. Jones too then met with Maxwell on the pier at Gravesend. He explained what he knew—that they were to seize Shivering Sands on behalf of Atlanta shareholders. They arranged to meet at Jones's house in Strood on the Sunday morning.

The next day, Horsley called his friend Peter Buckland, a taxi proprietor and another Trinity House pilot. Buckland went that evening to speak in person. Horsley told him that a Major Smedley had property on Shivering Sands that had to be "protected" in the face of a rumored takeover by another company. If interested, he should come the next day and meet Smedley himself. Buckland duly showed up, and the four of them discussed the plan. By the time they had finished, Buckland had agreed to recruit a "gang"—a term of art in the riggers' trade, meaning a set number of men and a foreman. The four pilots would meet only one more time together, at Jones's house on the Sunday morning. Their task, he told them, was to keep the station off the air until Smedley was paid. Horsley asserted that Smedley had £35,000 of equipment on the fort—roughly five times the highest plausible value, and ten times what the transmitter had cost Project Atlanta in the first place.[17]

Buckland, meanwhile, set about building his gang. He found a liaison in Fred Bradish, a sixty-seven-year-old master rigger. It was Bradish's business to corral together teams of riggers to handle the loading and unloading of ships. He got 25 percent commission for each job. Buckland phoned him out of the blue midmorning on Thursday and asked for seven men to go downriver to protect some "stuff" for Horsley. Bradish, who had never heard of Horsley, asked what ship it was. It was not a ship at all, Buckland replied. But beyond saying cryptically that the stuff really belonged to "the major," he would say no more. A couple of days later he phoned again, presumably after hearing more about his mission. They were going out to the forts, he revealed. And he would need not seven men, but ten.

Bradish knew what to do. Alf Bullen had phoned on Saturday to ask after work, and he would be an ideal leader of the gang. Bullen was a big, heavy fifty-nine-year-old from Northfleet, a Kent town on the Thames estuary that had fallen on hard times. With long years of experience on the docks (he may even have helped erect the forts during World War II),[18] he was used to working with Bradish and knew how to pull together a gang quickly for a one-off job with no questions asked. Bradish put him in charge. The rendezvous would be at the Royal Terrace Pier, Gravesend, he said: be there at eleven thirty on Sunday night.

Then Bradish and Bullen hit the phones and did the rounds of the Gravesend pubs, calling in favors. Henry Collier, fifty-nine, another rigger habitually employed by Bradish, was one of the first to be collared. Bradish met him at a pub on the Saturday night. He told Collier to contact him on Sunday evening; he thought he had a job for him.

Collier called at seven o'clock. "Is it engine work, or deck repair?" he asked.

"No, it's nothing like that."

"Right, Fred."

Collier was in.

Alf Law, a boiler fitter at the new Tilbury B power station, was next. Law was a younger man, only thirty-six, and was unusual in having a steady job away from the docks. But he was a friend of Bullen, and that weighed in the balance. He was eating lunch at a Gravesend pub when Bullen caught up with him and drew him aside. He needed Law for a secret job, he said, that would mean going to sea, perhaps for as long as two weeks. Law did not hesitate. He called the power station and took a holiday. He was ready to go.

Most of Bradish and Bullen's conversations went like this. As Albert Jarvis, picked up at the Pier Hotel bar in Gravesend, put it, the men "didn't ask." Theirs was a world of casual jobs, arranged by a trusted overseer. As they came into focus at the last minute, it was not uncommon for some mystery to attend them. This was no exception. Most of Bradish's regulars were used to telephoning him on a Sunday evening to ask after work, so it took until nightfall before he could reckon on ten helpers. But by eight o'clock he had his gang. Not all were regular riggers; apart from Law, there was also the manager of the Chase pub at Gravesend. But all were members of the same loose community of casual labor, and they could be assured of getting the usual rate of £54 16s for a week's work. Bradish and Bullen knew and trusted them. None failed to be at the pier that night for the rendezvous.[19]

At nine twenty the same evening, Smedley left his cottage at Wendens Ambo, drove the short distance to Audley End, and took the train for London. Pamela Thorburn saw him off. Now twenty-three, Thorburn had known Smedley since she was eight. She was technically an employee of IGMS, and had long been Smedley's secretary in the Coleman Street office—a job she had recently resumed. But two years earlier, at the time of his divorce, she had moved to Wendens Ambo and become his housekeeper and occasional child-minder. She had also become rather more. As she would later put it, the two of them did not share a bedroom, but they did occasionally share a bed. When she saw Smedley off at the station and returned to their cottage, she knew that he was headed for a rendezvous, and then for the fort.

At Liverpool Street Station Smedley rendezvoused with Kitty Black, who had come in from Norfolk. They took a car to the Royal Terrace Pier in Gravesend, where the tug *Vanquisher* was moored along with a smaller motor launch. Black had dressed for the part—all in black, her blond hair starkly silver in the moonlight under a dark head scarf. They arrived at the pier just after Bradish. Smedley came forward and shook hands, and at his nod the men started loading supplies from a van onto the tug. Then Bradish watched as the *Vanquisher* quietly slipped her mooring and moved away from the quay. She carried "Big Alf" Bullen, the gang of ten, the four pilots, and Smedley and Black. Only the last two knew what was afoot, and Smith and his crew wondered. Why had Horsley insisted on bringing a ladder and heaving lines? What about the ominous presence of the riggers? Nobody had warned Smith to expect such an incongruous mix of passengers. One waterman suggested that Black—who had sat down and begun knitting—was a film star and that the venture was connected with a movie. But that hardly squared with the appearance of the riggers, who had been drinking and were now playing cards.

Only once the tug was safely away from the shore did Smedley and Black call Big Alf into the cabin and reveal what was going on. "This job I want you to do," Smedley began, "you needn't worry about any trouble, as it's all perfectly legal." But when he explained, the situation sounded less reassuring. "I own a lot of property on the towers on the Shivering Sands and I want you to help me get it ashore." They were going to board the fort, see that Radio City stayed off the air, guard what Smedley called his property, and in all likelihood carry it off the fort at the end of the affair. Bullen later thought he remembered this upright military man claiming that he actually owned the towers themselves, or at least was a majority shareholder in them. But there must be "no strong arm business," Smedley cautioned. When they got there, they would try all the towers in turn to find an open trapdoor; if all were closed, they would rouse the Radio City men and try to argue their way aboard. Alf nodded, and went to tell the rest of the riggers what was expected of them. Finding Collier on deck, he shouted the news to him over the gathering wind; then he went below to let the others know.

It took three hours for the tug and tender to make the voyage out to the fort. When they arrived, at about 3 am, everything was quiet. The pilots went across first in the small motorboat, along with Bullen and another rigger. They found a ladder leading up to the southeast tower, and climbed. At the top they found the trapdoor leading into the studio chamber open. They pushed it up and clambered into the empty chamber. There they waited, listening and catching their breath while the motorboat returned to the *Vanquisher* and brought Smedley and Black, along with Collier and another rigger. Then a third trip brought the rest of the riggers. The riggers now stayed put. Black and Buckland crossed by the gangway to the central tower, where the living accommodation was, and Black remained there while Smedley caught up. Then they entered the tower. After this moment, they could not turn back.

There were seven Radio City men on the fort: DJs Alan Clark, Ian MacRae, and Peter Dolphin, engineers Paul Elvey, Ian West, and Philip Perkins, and a cook, Leslie Dunne. All were asleep. Elvey was the first to awaken. "What the hell's this?" he demanded, jumping out of bed. Smedley started to reassure him. "I've been sent by Mr. Calvert," he said. He had come to protect the people and equipment on the fort and to prevent a "takeover." But Black was having none of it. She interrupted Smedley. Their real interest, she declared, was in equipment that belonged to them and that Calvert had failed to pay for. Elvey got the message. He warned his colleagues not to resist, fearing strong-arm tactics and believing that he had seen a revolver on one of the riggers. (Whether they were in fact armed is unclear. They insisted that they were not, and that in the event of violence their instructions were to "pick up and leave"; but they may have carried blades as tools of their trade, and in any case they doubtless appeared intimidating enough.)

Elvey went across to the generator and switched it on, the lights momentarily blinding everyone. Ian West—who recognized Smedley from his earlier visit to Shivering Sands—got up too. His first move was to make tea for everyone. Then he went across the causeway to the transmitter tower with Smedley and Black, and at their insistence removed from the transmitter the all-important crystal that maintained its output frequency. Without the crystal it was useless. West gave it to Black, who put it in her bag. The microphones also disappeared. Everybody seems to have assumed that she took the crystal and microphones with her when she and Smedley departed shortly after, leaving Jones and the riggers aboard the fort. At any rate, from that moment Radio City was silenced.

At first the Radio City crew seemed to accept the invasion with what Black would later call "philosophical calm." Elvey perhaps excepted, nobody realized yet that this *was* the takeover that Smedley spoke of. But one City DJ did respond rather strangely. Peter Dolphin was a newcomer. An actor by trade, with a minor television career, he had met Reg Calvert only on Thursday, and had agreed to come to Shivering Sands the very next day on the usual trial basis. Secreted away in his baggage was a high-quality camera. As the incursion got underway, Dolphin quietly fetched it and began photographing the raiding party and the tug. Elvey guided him to the southeast tower as the best vantage point; but some of the boarders headed across the catwalk toward them. Dolphin hastily thrust the camera into Elvey's hand and asked him to hide it. Climbing up to the old gun platform on top of the tower, Elvey knelt and pushed the camera as deep as he could under the armored platform.

With Big Alf controlling the hoist, Black and Smedley descended back to the *Vanquisher*. Then the tug moved off. The vessel had to return briefly to pick up Peter Buckland, who had been left behind drinking his tea, but then set out for the voyage back to Gravesend. Dodge Jones and Big Alf remained on the fort in charge of the riggers. Their orders were simple: to prevent Radio City from getting back on the air. Without a crystal or microphones, there was little chance of that happening anyway. An uneasy calm descended on Shivering Sands. It would remain that way for the next week.

AT 7:45 AM on Monday, Philip Birch stepped out of his house in the rural Kent village of Meopham, five miles south of Gravesend, ready to take his children to school. He got as far as the front gate before Oliver Smedley accosted him. Smedley had diverted from the drive from Gravesend into London to intercept Radio London's boss. In the car, Birch noticed, was a woman he had never seen before. Smedley told Birch to come to Atlanta's Dean Street office at eleven thirty. Calvert was due at noon. Smedley did not know how far negotiations between Birch and Calvert had got, so he was not sure with whom to negotiate.

Birch got to Dean Street just before 11:30 am. He was early. The woman from Smedley's car met him and introduced herself as Kitty Black. Horsley was there too, and had brought with him as a witness a seventy-year-old retired businessman, Horace Leggett. All were strangers to Birch. They chatted awkwardly for a few minutes, before Smedley arrived and the real business got underway. Smedley announced that his gang had taken over the Radio City fort. "Possession is 10 points of the law," he remarked. "We have been messed about by so many people in the past that this is the only way I can protect their interest." But now Atlanta and CBC were in the driver's seat. If Birch really wanted the fort, he would have to deal with them. It would cost him: £5,000 up front, plus 50 percent of advertising profit, or 30 percent of advertising revenue. Smedley was ready to do a deal.

Birch was at first nonplussed by this unorthodox mode of bargaining. But he decided at once that he was not interested. Atlanta and CBC had no "moral, legal or other right" to the fort, he declared, and any disagreement with Calvert should be worked out legally. He would never do business with anyone who acted in this manner. He "got a little bit irate," Leggett recalled, and denounced Smedley's ultimatum as "blackmail." Horsley tried to defend Smedley by saying that Calvert had effectively appropriated Atlanta's property, but Birch was having none of it. He departed, leaving the room in silence. The conspirators had been confronted with the stark possibility that their high-risk "lark" could go very wrong indeed.

Reg Calvert arrived shortly after Birch left. He had traveled down by train from Manchester and come straight from Euston. He knew nothing of the boarding, assuming rather that the Atlanta group wanted to discuss meeting their unpaid bills. He entered the room, therefore, in a good mood. What confronted him within the next few moments came as a profound shock.

Calvert's response to that shock was to become the focus of contention for months to come. It is therefore all the more important to realize that after the event nobody had unmediated access to his reactions: how he acted, what he said, and how he said it. At this crucial meeting in Dean Street, in particular, the only others present to record their impressions were partisans for Atlanta. Their accounts were recorded quite promptly after the event, and it is unlikely that they were concocted. Yet they were also, naturally and necessarily, interested. The impressions they conveyed—and in all probability the impressions they themselves got—were those of participants, complicit with Smedley in a battle of wits and wills. It is significant that of those present that day, only Smedley himself had even a passing acquaintance with the Radio City boss. The others had no prior experience of how he thought and spoke. They had no basis on which to calibrate his expressions and words. What they portrayed was a dramatic, intense performance, and at moments even a menacing one. To those who knew him best, however, key elements of the story told by Horsley, Smedley, and especially Black rang false. The events of the next year and beyond would hang on how far the Atlanta group's version of events in this half hour was believed.

According to the Atlanta group, when Calvert entered the room, Smedley bluntly told him the true purpose of the meeting. His station was off the air, Smedley announced, and would remain so. Calvert should be under no illusions: if he tried to retake the fort, then the riggers would destroy all the equipment on board. But on the other hand, he continued, City could resume transmissions readily—if Calvert agreed to a deal. He then laid out the same terms as he had earlier offered to Birch.

Calvert was first shocked, then angry. But the collaborators recalled that he began calmly enough. He told Smedley that he himself would not be affected by City's silence, because thanks to the deal with Birch he had secured a regular income regardless. And in any case he was pursuing other schemes—schemes like that for a station in the Bristol Channel. Perhaps they might even join forces to develop it. But then he added that he would take it as a personal challenge to see the boarders off the fort. By the time he was finished, he added, they would be "screaming to come off." At this point Calvert changed tone, and launched into what Black, at least, represented as an increasingly strange string of threats.

Eyes averted, Calvert began his monologue by telling the conspirators of his past. He had been brought up in Huddersfield, he said, amid the slums. He had "come up the hard way." Life had taught him that if he wanted something he had to be ruthless, even to the extent of somebody getting killed. He had run dance halls, at one point controlling thirty-two of them. And dance halls were a "pretty rough, tough business." Through that business he had come to know "the best fighters in the country." One of his friends was a crack shot. And he himself was not to be trifled with. "He explained that he was a better than average amateur chemist," Kitty Black recalled. He was an expert in explosives and gases, and had recently discovered a "nerve gas." Calvert even mentioned some formulas, based, apparently, on ammonia. But he had so far only been able to test the gas on animals, and was keen to try it on humans. Perhaps he could do so by firing mortar shells onto the tower. The others stared at him, not knowing whether to be appalled or incredulous. Then he reached inside his jacket pocket and pulled out a device resembling a fountain pen. "It's in there," he said. It was the gas-pen. It proved that he could "look after himself," and he was prepared to use it if necessary.

Was he bluffing? Horace Leggett was at a loss, but found the references to chemistry convincing and wondered if he might not be serious. "You must be mental, man," stammered Horsley. "I know," Calvert replied; "I am most unusual; perhaps I am a little mental. My wife can do nothing with me when I've made up my mind." Black was more skeptical. She found the idea of mortars and nerve gas outlandish, and her surmise was that Calvert was "dramatizing." Yet even she told the police later that she had found Calvert hard to appraise.

Black brought the meeting back to order. Dowsing Shivering Sands with nerve gas, she pointed out drily, would be "extremely bad publicity." In fact, it would be disastrous for all concerned: it would immediately destroy public sympathy for the enterprise of commercial broadcasting itself, and would surely lead to the shutting down of both forts and ships. So she urged Calvert again to accept a deal. If he did, she said, then City could be back on the air almost immediately. "I can't do that, love," Calvert replied. "I want to play this my way." And with that he marched out of the room.

There was silence for a moment. It was Horsley who broke it. "He's a paranoiac," he declared. Before he could go on, Smedley cut him short. "A good deal of talk has gone on," he cautioned. "I think we should all forget what has been said in this room." Nobody dissented.

At the foot of the stairs, Kitty Black ran into Calvert again. She walked with him out to the street. There followed a brief but revealing exchange as they stood together on the pavement for a moment. Calvert had evidently come to the conclusion over the previous half-hour that Black was the real power behind the gang. "I like you," he said ingratiatingly. "I'd like to work with you. But those three up there"—he gestured back at the Atlanta office—"are a lot of old women." He moved off, adding as he left, "Go back and ask if this is just some of Reg Calvert's bluff or not."

Black did in fact go back and report this to Smedley and Horsley over lunch. At the end of the meal Horsley suggested to Smedley that the scheme had failed, and that they should acknowledge as much by withdrawing the riggers from Shivering Sands. Smedley was having none of it. "No," he replied, "we are in possession of the tower, looking after our own equipment." The men would stay. The stakes would go on rising.

WHETHER OR NOT he had been consciously performing a role, as Kitty Black suspected, Reg Calvert's monologue had been bravado.

The act had worn off by the time he arrived back at Racity's office. Wileman could tell immediately that something was seriously wrong. The fact was that the deal with Radio London was not quite complete. His own fate may still have been tied to that of the fort. Moreover, he felt suddenly responsible for the physical safety of a group of young men whose presence on the fort was at his behest. And if Radio City could not broadcast, then the curtailment of revenues would soon destroy its viability. Calvert's other operations—the bands, the dance halls—were still making money, but Radio City would cease to be a going concern, and at a time when the Loughborough hall was still leaching money. It was only recently that Dorothy had rejoined him, after a six-month separation motivated largely by worries about financial prudence. The urgency that Smedley had felt so keenly now fell just as heavily on Calvert. His station was facing closure at just the moment when his venture ought to have paid off handsomely, and, worse, the men on the fort might be in imminent danger. Something had to be done.

The next day and a half saw increasingly frantic maneuvering by both camps. Reg Calvert went first to Birch, and the two agreed not to acquiesce to Smedley. Then he and Dorothy decided to send the engineer Tony Pine out to the fort to investigate. In fact, Pine had already noticed that the station was off the air and decided to go. Fred Downes took him on *Harvesters*. Pine climbed aboard the fort, where he found the riggers in occupation. They were there to guard Smedley's transmitter, Don Jones told him, and had orders to prevent the station from broadcasting. Pine left again, and when they got back to Whitstable, Downes contacted Calvert to tell him that the crystal and microphones were indeed gone.

Meanwhile, the silence of Radio City was starting to get noticed. Ted Allbeury got in touch. He had warned earlier of a threat to Shivering Sands, and now he had heard that the fort had been boarded. Was it true? Calvert's reflex reaction was to deny it. Allbeury immediately got confirmation from Birch's office. But Calvert was still reticent later that day when he himself came to Radio London. As it happened, Radio City DJ Tom Edwards was there discussing the prospective formation of UKGM. The two met up again in the evening at Calvert's flat in Welbeck Street, just north of Oxford Street. Calvert did not mention the crisis. But Edwards could tell something was wrong: his manager was nothing like his usual "chirpy" self, and he disappeared into another room at one point to make a long phone call. While he was gone, Edwards pressed Dorothy Calvert about what might be up. Only now did he hear of the boarding. Edwards was shocked. But over cake in the kitchen Calvert insisted to family and guest alike that he would find some way to get the riggers off. Plans were half-forming in his mind. At one point he said he would remove all the City staff from Shivering Sands, but almost immediately he thought better of it. Better, he decided, to go to Scotland Yard. By the time Edwards left to catch the train for Whitstable, this seemed to be the plan. The next day the DJ would be out at the fort—just in time to see the standoff worsen.

The last thing Calvert did that evening was to call Allan Crawford, Smedley's partner in Project Atlanta. As Crawford recalled it a few days later, Calvert was talkative and nervous, in rather the same way he had reportedly been at the meeting with Smedley earlier in the day. He demanded home addresses for Black and Smedley, apparently proposing to beat them up. He implied that he could have them kidnapped and smuggled out of the country, and, Crawford said, "rambled about a gang in Leicester who could break arms and legs." Crawford listened with mounting incredulity. Calvert could not mean all this to be taken seriously. He guessed (and this seems plausible) that the City manager must be hoping that he would pass word of these threats on to Smedley, and that Smedley would then be intimidated into ordering the riggers to leave. Calvert did not get those addresses. But neither did his dramatic gambit pay off. Unknown to him, Crawford had never really liked Smedley, whom he had long found doctrinaire and undiplomatic. The raid on the fort was the last straw. He sat tight. Smedley never heard the threats he was supposed to hear.

But Calvert now knew for sure that Black and Smedley had taken not only the transmitter crystal but also the microphones from the fort studio. With those there was no tricky issue of ownership. He had a case he could take to the police.

SOME TIME EARLY on Tuesday the 21st, the phone rang at the home of Churton Fairman. Fairman was no longer with Project Atlanta. He had resigned over the merger with Caroline, and after a stint at an iconic sixties music venue on the Thames, Eel Pie Island, outside Richmond, he had gone to work for Ted Allbeury. He now combined duties as an assistant to Allbeury with those as a DJ on Radio 390. When he picked up the phone that morning, he found himself talking to Smedley. His cousin was cock-a-hoop. He had something Allbeury might well want—the Shivering Sands fort. Could Fairman set up a secret meeting?

Fairman arranged for Smedley and Allbeury to talk over lunch that day at the Special Forces Club in Knightsbridge. Smedley recounted the story of the raid. He proposed that Allbeury's Estuary Radio buy Radio City on the same terms as Birch had rejected the previous day: £5,000 down and half the profits. Needless to say, like his earlier offer to Birch, this went far beyond Smedley's stated purpose of protecting the Texan transmitter. Allbeury stalled, saying that he would have to talk it over with the Estuary board of directors. Shortly after they parted, Birch telephoned. Allbeury had let him know in the morning that Smedley wanted to meet, and now Birch was curious about what he had said. The whole justification in terms of the transmitter, he insisted, was simply false. But had Smedley offered to sell the station to Allbeury? Allbeury would not say. He revealed only that Smedley had made an offer of some kind. It would need to be discussed with the Estuary board, and once that had happened he would let Birch know.

Scarcely had Allbeury hung up when the phone rang again. It was Calvert.

REG CALVERT HAD left his flat at 10 am. On a normal Tuesday he would have gone out on the *Harvesters* to Shivering Sands. Today he stayed put. Most of the day he would be at Denmark Street, phoning IGMS unceasingly in a bid to contact Smedley.

When Smedley could not be tracked down, he called Tony Pine and asked him to go out again to the fort to see that no violence or damage had taken place. This time Pine would take a message with him. "The blackmail threat Mr Smedley and Company arranged has failed," Calvert dictated. Scotland Yard had been asked to deal with the situation. "We send this letter as a caution to all people who have taken part in this subterfuge that they might know the severity of what they are doing." Pine was to offer to take back to shore anyone who wanted to leave; otherwise they should know that most of them had been photographed, and it was only a matter of time before their addresses were discovered. "I beg you," he ended: "take heed of this note as this is your last and only chance to leave peacably [*sic*]." With that he left and went down to Bow Street police station to make good his statement. With him he took a onetime music journalist named Brian Harvey, who had been working on publicity for the Fortunes. Calvert had Harvey in mind to run the new promotion and publishing company that he planned to form once Radio City was off his hands.

At Bow Street, Calvert and Harvey sat down with Colin Rutter, a detective sergeant in C Division. Calvert began by recounting the story of the previous day's meeting at Project Atlanta. He accused Smedley and Black of stealing the crystal and microphones and urged that they be prosecuted. Rutter was uncertain how to respond. The long-standing problem of jurisdiction over the forts—which had enabled the pirate stations to operate in the first place—made him hesitate about offering to enforce property laws there. But Calvert was insistent. He was losing money by the minute, he retorted. If the police would not get rid of the boarders, what about his doing so himself? He rather guilelessly asked Rutter for his own advice about getting them off with hired "assistance." Rutter's advice being to do no such thing, Calvert agreed to wait. Yet Rutter also suggested that if he could get in touch with Smedley he should ask him to phone the detective. Calvert left declaring his intent to get a message to the riggers telling them that the police were involved and asking them to "capitulate."

That message actually arrived at Shivering Sands while Rutter and Calvert were talking. The *Harvesters*, with Pine and Edwards on board, chugged up to the fort at about three o'clock. Pine was carrying Calvert's ominous note. Both stayed on the tower, while Clark, who was due for shore time, departed with Downes. A big firefighter tug approached as they left. She carried the first of what would become a daily dose of supplies for Smedley's men. They were digging in.

Through that night none of the City men were allowed to reach the studio, and all Pine's entreaties to let Radio City resume fell on deaf ears. When Downes got back to Whitstable, Calvert heard that the boarders were in no mood to leave. In fact, they were getting more threatening. The danger of violence seemed all too real. Downes continued to watch, and continued to worry. "This really is piracy!" he would tell the press. "'Pirate radios' was a silly term, but this is piracy in the old-fashioned sense."[20]

Back in Denmark Street, Calvert and Wileman continued to try to find Smedley by phone. They also searched for Kitty Black, and it seems that Wileman did manage to speak with her before she left for the country. She asked Black if she had Radio City's crystal. Black denied that she did, and said that only Smedley could resolve things. Wileman inferred that he truly was the ringleader, and redoubled her efforts to track him down. She never did. But she did succeed in discovering his address in the Essex village of Wendens Ambo. In the end, as she got ready to leave work, Wileman rang Coleman Street one last time. She put her hand over the receiver and asked Calvert whether he wanted to convey a specific message. At the forefront of Calvert's mind was the failure of his note to the riggers to budge them, and the report that they were becoming more threatening. "Yes," he said. "You can tell her things are getting dangerous."

Fielding those calls all day at Coleman Street was Pamela Thorburn, Smedley's housekeeper/companion. Wileman and Calvert had been ringing "continually," she later told police. According to her, their messages had become more unsettling every time. Calvert had told her at one point that Smedley was about to be arrested by Scotland Yard, but that if he phoned back immediately then the affair could be "hushed up." He added that he had sent a message to the riggers that their photographs were in police hands and they too would be arrested when they disembarked. Later, he declared that "he was going out to the Tower personally with poison gas and that he intended to kill them all." As Wileman recited Calvert's words at the end of the day, therefore, Thorburn heard them as the latest in an escalating sequence. She dutifully wrote them down on a blue notepad. And then she showed the line to Smedley—who, far from being away, was standing next to her. He had been at Coleman Street much of the day, considering options for disposing of the fort. Detached from Calvert's preoccupation with the situation on Shivering Sands, the words could be construed as distinctly ominous. Smedley laughed—as far as he was concerned, no theft had occurred—but decided to stay aloof. He did not want to get involved in "unpleasantness," and would ignore Calvert until he adopted a "civilized" manner. As for Thorburn, she assumed that Calvert was "bluffing." It had been a long day, and she and Smedley thought little more of it as they left to catch the 6:36 out of Liverpool Street.

IT WAS IN the midst of his increasingly frustrating attempts to find Smedley that Calvert telephoned Allbeury. His exasperation came out in a flood. He began by asserting that he had had the Radio 390 boss followed. He knew he had had lunch with Smedley. Allbeury recalled that Calvert said he had had Smedley "framed" for theft, and that he had by now probably fled the country. "I want to warn you," he added, "that tomorrow I shall personally kill everyone on the fort and to do with the operation." He spoke again of his nerve gas, and of his pen-gun. He also hinted that he had killed someone before who had tried to blackmail him, and remarked that it was easy to make such a death look like an accident if one knew how.[21] "You have a nice little business," he concluded; "I have lost my business and if you have anything to do with this I'll see you lose yours. I haven't got these scars on my face for nothing."

Allbeury was taken aback. "This is absolutely ridiculous, Mr

Calvert," he said, and hung up. Immediately he picked up the receiver again and called Birch. He was responsible now for Calvert's behavior, Allbeury told him. Attempts at intimidation were not appreciated. Birch tried to protest that all the violence had been on Smedley's part, but Allbeury was unreceptive. Calvert was sounding like "a dangerous man," he said—even a "psychotic." But he concluded with the distinctly deflating suggestion that Birch should have Calvert take an aspirin and get a good night's sleep.[22] Allbeury, like Birch, was still inclined to assume that it was all bluster. And when he called Smedley a moment later to recount the exchange, the Atlanta man's only response was to ask drily, "Whatever in the world will he get up to next?"

Boutwood, who ran into Smedley at around this time, agreed that he was not ruffled by Allbeury's call. His boss, he said, "did not seem at all concerned." But Allbeury and Smedley were old military and SOE hands, inured to this kind of talk and perhaps even inclined to relish it. For a civilian it could be very different. When Churton Fairman got home that night, he drew the curtains and paced the room agitatedly, returning to the window every few minutes to cast a furtive peek out at the street. His wife asked what was up. Probably nothing, he told her. But Allbeury had told him he might want to hire bodyguards.

REG CALVERT HAD seemed happier that afternoon, returning to Denmark Street with Brian Harvey. Rutter had at least sounded sympathetic. Perhaps the police would now act. He laughed as he recalled his anger at the Dean Street meeting with Smedley the previous day. "I could have picked up a chair and hit him on the head with it." A little later, he even joked with Harvey about outlandish plans to get the boarders off the fort. They might rent a helicopter, he proposed, or hire police uniforms from a props company and fool the riggers into leaving with them. Yet the jocularity had a slightly ill-omened— or perhaps fatalistic—edge to it. That edge came to the fore at six o'clock, when Harvey was ready to depart.

Calvert had made a decision. He announced that he was going to drive out to Smedley's home to discuss removing the boarders. He was dogged by the memory of Smedley telling him that any attempt to force them off would result in the transmitter equipment being "smashed." He wanted things settled peacefully before there was a chance of their getting out of hand.

"Would you like me to come with you?" Harvey asked. As long as nothing violent was on the cards—he was "chicken," he said—he would be happy to help.

Calvert grinned. "No," he replied; that would not be necessary. But he would be grateful if Harvey remained accessible, as he was exhausted and might need someone to drive him home afterwards. As they parted, Harvey felt that his boss seemed "slightly depressed." But he did as he was told, and went home to wait for a call. Later that night, when Dorothy Calvert phoned to let him know that Calvert had indeed gone to see Smedley, Harvey's sense of foreboding had still not left him. "I hope he won't do anything silly," he said. Then he asked whether her husband had taken a gun.

"Of course not," she replied shortly.

But had Harvey heard Calvert's exchange with Rutter he would have been even more concerned. The detective had made an appointment for Calvert to speak with a Detective Inspector J. A. Barker at New Scotland Yard the next morning, and phoned at seven o'clock that evening to let him know. Calvert's answer was disquieting: he might miss the appointment, as he had decided to go out to the fort and try to expel the boarders. As a policeman, Rutter naturally found the idea of lay enforcement distasteful at best. He tried to dissuade Calvert by pointing out that he would be heavily outnumbered and that any attempt on the fort might well result in injuries.

"But not if I was suitably armed and peppered some of them with lead."

Startled, Rutter tried again. He now argued that if Calvert did indeed take weapons out to Shivering Sands, and if the police turned out to have jurisdiction there, then he would be committing a serious offense—more serious, implicitly, than anything Smedley might be responsible for. Calvert took the point, but still protested. All the time that action was delayed, Smedley was edging closer to selling the fort. He had to be stopped before that happened. But Kitty Black seemed to have disappeared, and Smedley was proving impossible to contact. The only people he could negotiate with were the men on the fort.

Sergeant Rutter stood firm. A precipitate move against the gang on Shivering Sands would do no good. It would only cause "complications." Much better, he said, to talk first to Barker. Calvert reluctantly acquiesced. But he also intimated that he meant to try talking to the riggers. They could not be intimidated, and apparently he could not try to force them off, but perhaps they would listen to another kind of argument. Money might talk.

SMEDLEY AND THORBURN arrived home at Wendens Ambo at seven forty-five. The phone rang almost as they came in through the door. They were expecting it—the press were sure to be clamoring for quotes, and Black had sold the story of the boarding to the *Daily Mail*. Smedley picked up the receiver. But it was a wrong number: someone looking for a Mrs. Hurst. No matter; the journalists would call soon enough.

In Welbeck Street, Dorothy Calvert placed the receiver back in the cradle. "He's in."[23]

Reg Calvert left the flat a few minutes later. He felt fatigued and unwell; his arm was stiff and sore. As he closed the door, his wife put a wad of notes into his hand. It came to £440. It was their last resort: if Smedley proved stubborn, Calvert would go on to Whitstable, sail out to Shivering Sands, and try to buy the riggers' loyalty.

Calvert drove the big Ford Zodiac to Hertford. Just after nine he pulled up at the home of Alan Arnold, the aerial engineer who had installed the Tower of Power two months before. The two men did not know each other well, but Arnold had developed a real admiration for Calvert's resilience and creativity. And he was almost certainly the person Calvert had had in mind in warning Smedley and Black of his ability to call on the services of a crack shot. Arnold was a skilled target shooter, and had even taken a pistol out on their first trip to the fort together to practice in an open area.

Arnold had telephoned Calvert that morning, having noticed that Radio City was off the air. He was concerned that his antenna might have a fault. Calvert had reassured him, but then added cryptically that "there was a bit of bother." Would Arnold lend him a shotgun? "This is a stupid thing to want," Arnold replied. Not least, they were too valuable to be "dropped in the drink." No, he should go to the police. Failing that, his best bet was to "wander round to the nearest gym and try and recruit some people."

"I've been to the police," Calvert said. "I don't think they can do anything about it." He might hire a helicopter to land on the fort to try to evict the boarders.

Like Allbeury, Birch, and Smedley, Arnold was not too concerned. "From my association with him I formed the impression he was rather inclined to exaggeration [*sic*] and at times seemed to be very impulsive." So when Calvert telephoned once more in the early evening to ask him to drive to Wendens Ambo and provide "moral support," Arnold agreed.

Calvert paused at Arnold's house to telephone home. It was a quick call. He reassured his wife that he was going peacefully, and—this perhaps as a result of Harvey's suspicion—that he and Arnold were unarmed. He had had "a long think about it," he said, and would do it her way. He hung up promising to ring her later. Then he turned to Arnold.

"Come on, let's go."

THEY TOOK CALVERT'S Zodiac rather than Arnold's E-Type. Arnold drove. As they moved north out of suburban Hertford, only now did Calvert say where they were going. They drove north through the countryside while he told Arnold the story of the takeover, apparently relaxed and at ease. They went through Bishops Stortford, and as they approached Saffron Walden stopped at a pub for directions. Calvert got out, and returned five minutes later with an unopened bottle of cider. He had had the good luck to meet a courting couple, one of whom lived in Wendens Ambo and knew the very house they were seeking. They drove on, Calvert navigating from the directions the drinker had given him.

Calvert's car had a radio-telephone fitted in it—one of the few at that early date. The system operated more like a telegram than a conventional telephone: messages had to be routed via an operator, who kept a record. During the drive north to Wendens Ambo, two messages were conveyed. The first was from Calvert to his wife in Welbeck Street. It read: "Warn, other people arrive 6 no trouble." He was anticipating having to make that voyage out to Shivering Sands at dawn the next day.

The second message was from Welbeck Street to Calvert. Sent at 10:25 pm, it was a warning, but of what is unclear. It read, simply and starkly: "Things are getting hot."

Calvert never received it. At the moment it was composed, his car was drawing close to Wendens Ambo and the home of Oliver Smedley.

Duck Street was a small lane heading off to the southwest from the main road through the village. Late at night it was easy to miss. They passed the black mirror of a pond to the left, and then the tall shadows of hedgerows and overhanging trees closed in on them. In a moment they passed the lights of the last cottage, and the empty dark of the open countryside surrounded them. Calvert had Arnold stop the car while he went to the door and asked for Smedley. He had the wrong house, the woman who answered told him; Smedley was three doors down. Turning the Zodiac around, Arnold let the car nose back down the road at a walking pace while his passenger peered out into the darkness and counted down the houses.

And then, all of a sudden, they were there. "Stop here," Calvert instructed. The Zodiac pulled to a halt on the gravel drive.

Calvert drew a deep breath and got out.

7

THE WAR AGAINST THE PIRATES

The doorbell rang at 4 am. It was the police, bringing the news from Essex. Dorothy Calvert was helped into a car and driven through the deserted streets of predawn London, then out on the A-road to Saffron Walden. By eleven she had met with PC Christopher Kearney and confirmed the unthinkable. At the hospital in Bishops Stortford she identified her husband's body. Then it was back to Saffron Walden police station. There a woman police constable named Snipe helped her relive the events of the last few days and construct an account of how Reg had come to arrive at Wendens Ambo. As they spoke, something made her look up and across the room. The moment was heart-stopping. Standing there was Oliver Smedley, staring expressionlessly at her. Later that day she came home with the beginnings of a suspicion: somehow, Smedley would not be held responsible for what he had just done.

PC Kearney had brought Smedley to the station in the early hours, and spent the rest of the night with him. Smedley had lain down but not slept. As he rested, Kearney took the opportunity to write notes on what he had said earlier. By six, Smedley was up again and talking as if he had not stopped. At about 10:40 am, Detective George Brown arrived, and shortly after eleven o'clock there was an impromptu court hearing. It lasted only a few minutes, and Smedley sat mute in a leather armchair before the justice of the peace, Lord Braybrooke—a man he may well have known personally, as the occupant of Audley End, on the grounds of which he had resided a few years earlier. By ten past eleven Smedley stood formally charged as a murderer.

THE RIGGERS REMAINED on Shivering Sands, immovable. News of Calvert's death reached them by a journalist's launch early on Wednesday morning. Big Alf was nervous now. He had not been prepared for this. Nobody knew what the gang would do, least of all themselves, and the risks were clear to all. The City men shouted from the fort that the boarders had threatened to destroy the towering aerial if Dorothy Calvert approached. That would put Radio City out of action forever.[1]

Some seemed set on escalation regardless. Sir Alan Herbert of the British Copyright Council publicly demanded that the government send in the Navy to end the occupation by force. Any idea that Shivering Sands might be outside jurisdiction he declared "a dangerous delusion."[2] Meanwhile two lawyers claiming to act for Dorothy Calvert tried to railroad her into bringing a case against the riggers as *actual* pirates. They compiled a long and tendentious brief for this farfetched strategy, and at first would not accept her refusal to adopt it; at one point they forced their way into Scotland Yard demanding that she comply. In the end she had to repudiate them altogether, for fear that their misconduct would lead to more violence. Nobody wanted Shivering Sands liberated more than her—and she was determined to see it happen. But not at such a cost.

Then, on the morning of June 26, that problem solved itself. The boarders suddenly embarked on a tug and disappeared back into Kent.

The gang had been kept supplied since the initial boarding by tugs from the mainland (and by creature comforts given them by the Radio City crew). But Horsley, who had reluctantly continued to finance their occupation in the forced absence of Smedley and the voluntary one of Black, had become increasingly hesitant to keep footing the bill, which now stood at some £1,600. He telephoned Project

Atlanta and presented an ultimatum: after Friday, June 24, they were on their own. At that Kitty Black finally came to see him. She volunteered almost no money, but did agree to take on responsibility for the occupation from then on. It was presumably her decision, therefore, that they leave. Horsley saw to it. The motor barge *Kethole* picked them up. On Sunday evening they docked at Sheerness, piled into a maroon Mercedes 220 and a Jaguar, and dispersed. The next day all of the men were back to their casual labor rounds. A journalist who tracked down Big Alf asked him if he was pleased it was over. "Well," he said, "now I'll have to go back to my missus."[3]

Seeing the boarders leave, the Radio City men on the fort were at first nervous that they might have booby-trapped the studio tower. But after waiting a few minutes to make sure that they were truly alone, they cautiously crossed the causeway and ventured into the studio. Finding it largely intact, they almost ransacked it in search of the crystal for the transmitter. Eventually it was found—it seems that Kitty Black had hidden it there rather than taking it away with her. They lost no time in reinstalling it into the transmitter.

Radio City came back on the air just after 9:30 pm. Ian MacRae chose the first record, intended for the riggers' ears as they sailed home. For once, it seemed permissible to play something by Sinatra: MacRae fired up the turntable and put on "Strangers in the Night."

DOROTHY CALVERT MOVED quickly to reassert control of Shivering Sands. There was no question of the deal with Birch to create UKGM going through now, so the station would just have to continue independently. She fielded a flood of letters from security companies (or ambitious individuals) in the days after broadcasting resumed, offering to patrol the forts and prevent a new boarding. In the meantime, there was a mess to clear up and damage to be repaired. She tried to claim more than £800 from Horsley to cover this, to no avail. She also tried to claim rent from Atlanta on the Texan transmitter. A remarkably defiant move, it inevitably met with no greater success: even the initial shipping costs, still unpaid, had eventually to be met from her husband's estate. Although the purpose of the raid had allegedly been to protect this device and bring it back, it was abandoned on the tower after Reg Calvert's death. Its remains are still there today.

Radio City's fate was precarious at first, but it survived. By late summer it was broadcasting from 6 am to midnight every day. But several of the staff who had endured the occupation were not there for much longer than the riggers. Rumors of betrayals had long swirled, and several of the DJs themselves had wondered why the hatch through which Smedley's men had come that morning had not been locked. First to go was Paul Elvey, the engineer. When he returned from his stint on the fort, Mrs. Calvert declined to re-employ him. Like everyone else on Shivering Sands, Elvey had no contract, but worked from stint to stint. As she recalled it much later, she believed him to be in contact with the Caroline operation, and suspected that he was responsible for leaving the trapdoor open that allowed Smedley's party to enter the fort. *Somebody*, at any rate, had disobeyed her warning of a week earlier to make sure it was locked. The tale of Peter Dolphin's camera, last seen in Elvey's hands, only added to the mystery, and now she had heard a report that as soon as Elvey made landfall he went to a pub and telephoned Kitty Black.[4] Whatever the truth might be, rumors and suspicions were rife in those anxious days, and she took no chances. Elvey was not invited back to Radio City.

The other absentee was the newcomer, Peter Dolphin, whose camera Elvey had hidden under the gun platform in the first minutes of the raid. Within an hour, the camera had disappeared, never to show up again. Meanwhile, Dolphin had given the impression during the first day of the occupation that he was acting as a journalist. Elvey dismissed this as pretense, but in fact Dolphin did communicate with Fleet Street during the occupation, and it seems plausible that the camera—a sophisticated device, which Inspector Barker thought far above Dolphin's level of proficiency—had been given to him in the expectation that he would have something to shoot. In any case, Dolphin jumped into a launch at the first opportunity and returned to London, saying that he had had enough. Once back in the capital he indulged in an extraordinary piece of self-promotion, claiming to have been kidnapped by fake police officers and interrogated about Radio City over a weekend in an East End hideway. The tabloid press leaped on the tale avidly. But as soon as the real police asked him about it, Dolphin's confidence evaporated. The whole story, he confessed, was imaginary.

This would not to be the last time that pirate radio was mixed up with fantasies of East End criminality.

SAFFRON WALDEN MAGISTRATES began their preliminary hearing on July 18. It may not have seemed so at first, but the odds were stacked in favor of Smedley. The principal witnesses were sympathetic to him. Kitty Black in particular, who was a powerful presence, was determined to defend his actions, as she demonstrated in an interview she gave at this time for a French television station. She used the occasion to present Calvert as a violent intruder and Smedley as a justified defender of his household.[5] Alan Arnold, by contrast, who might have been more helpful, seemed nervous and ill at ease— perhaps even fearful. Moreover, the distinctions of class and culture between Smedley and Calvert appeared stark—starker, perhaps, than they really were. And, not least, there had been a month of relentless public exposure by the time the hearing commenced.

During that month, the affair had fallen prey to a newspaper industry under threat. On the surface, Fleet Street was still the thriving and self-assured beast that it had been a decade earlier. Newspapers were large, journalists plentiful, and they enjoyed circulations that were among the highest in the world. But in reality a crisis was at hand. Readerships were static at best, and television and commercial radio were eating into advertising revenues. At least half of the national press was now unprofitable, with no prospect of improvement. Some papers had closed, and others were facing amalgamation. The industry had commissioned an investigation from *The Economist*'s well-respected Intelligence Unit, and in 1966 it received a massive and sobering report. The viability of all newspapers was likely to erode even further, it projected, producing heavy losses across the board.

And the situation was worst for the tabloids: not all would survive, and in all likelihood only one could hope to make a profit.[6]

So in mid-1966 there was a sense of desperation abroad in Fleet Street. It was made only worse by the fear, imminently to be realized, that the government would respond to the crisis of the seamen's strike which had left Big Alf and his men at a loose end by a drastic tightening of economic policy, which would inevitably hit sales and advertising revenues hard. In this context, any sensational story was bound to be seized upon even more avidly than usual. And the Radio City confrontation came at just the right time. The result was a frenzy of stories about the supposed demimonde of pirate radio, each trumping the last. The police dutifully collected and filed many of them, noting bemusedly that almost none should be regarded as trustworthy. By mid-July, this lurid spectacle had continued for almost a month. It had focused relentlessly on tales—frequently exaggerated, sometimes invented—of Calvert's own background and his maneuvers in the last few days of his life. The cumulative image was of a man violent and uncontrollable. It was not surprising that that image now dominated the hearing. Naturally, Smedley's defense would want to play it up.

What was less predictable was that the prosecution would stress this image too. The prosecution barrister, Peter Palmes, began by displaying Calvert's gas-pen. This device, having reportedly been flaunted by Calvert himself in his confrontation with Black and Smedley at Dean Street, had become a totem of the tabloids. Palmes went along. He then recited a brief version of the story of Radio City's elusive alliance with Project Atlanta. Smedley, he said, had put a transmitter worth £10,000 onto the fort, which Calvert had never paid for and which therefore remained Atlanta's property. When Smedley had heard of the prospective deal with Radio London, he and Kitty Black decided to send a gang onto Shivering Sands "to protect their equipment." Black herself, the first witness called to the stand, recounted her version of the raid and the meeting the next morning. On Palmes's account, having achieved this, Smedley had then urged Birch to include Project Atlanta in the UKGM deal. But Birch rebuffed him. Palmes then recounted the "extravagant threats" that Calvert had made, which, he contended, "no one took very seriously." But that night Calvert burst into Smedley's home and brandished a "heavy" metal statuette over Pamela Thorburn's head.

On the second day, Arnold and Thorburn both described the struggle at Smedley's cottage from their different perspectives. Each gave the impression that Calvert had been out of control. Arnold had been "absolutely flabbergasted" by the eruption, he said, concurring with Smedley's lawyer that Calvert had used violence. When Smedley shot him, Thorburn added, her first feeling had been one of relief that he had stopped attacking her. Palmes even quoted Smedley himself: " 'What could I do under the circumstances? I probably saved the girl's life.' "

Calvert's family listened in disbelief. In their eyes the pen was a red herring, and the story of the confrontation at Wendens Ambo implausible in the extreme (the statuette that Calvert had reportedly brandished was produced in court, only to fall apart before their eyes). The transmitter was worth nothing like £10,000 and had never worked, and, far from being owed money, Atlanta had left City in the lurch. Most of all, Smedley's claim that the raid had been to protect property was a smokescreen for a bid to expropriate Shivering Sands itself—what other interpretation could his dealings with Birch and Allbeury bear? And as for Calvert's threats, while he could be dramatic, he had never committed violence.[7] They had been characteristically impulsive gestures, theatrical, perhaps daft, and certainly unwise, but not serious—as all at the time had registered. The idea that he would intend to kill someone was to them absurd. The very words that Kitty Black attributed to Calvert did not sound like his. On the other hand, even if the fracas that night had been as intense as Thorburn recalled, Smedley could not have been aware of its intensity: as Detective Brown's internal report pointed out, Smedley had gone directly to his bedroom and then out to accost Neil Warden. He had returned, armed, and fired at almost point-blank range without a word passing between the two of them.[8]

The sense of foreboding grew into alarm on the night before the

final day of the hearing. At half past midnight, the burglar alarm
went off in Welbeck Street. The Calverts dialed 999, fearing for their
lives. The police sent a patrol, and for an hour or two the flat was
full of constables. But nobody was caught, and nothing was missing.
By the next morning the police seemed to have lost interest in the
incident altogether. But as they entered the courtroom, the Calverts
heard Smedley's barrister declare that his cottage in Wendens Ambo
had been broken into that night, too. A pillowcase full of silver had
apparently disappeared. If the story was true, then the coincidence
seemed outlandish: two households, separated by about fifty miles,
but entwined in the same fatal incident, attacked at almost exactly
the same moment. And in both cases the intruders got away unseen.
What could it mean? Not for the first time, an oppressive sense of
trepidation descended. The experience had left the Calvert family
badly shaken, and for months and years to come they would continue
to feel themselves to be living under watch.

Their sense of foreboding proved accurate in a more immediate
sense. That afternoon, after three days of hearings, the magistrates
concluded that no jury would convict Smedley of murder. They committed him to trial at Chelmsford Assizes in October on a manslaughter charge, and released him on £500 bail.

ON JUNE 28—EXACTLY a week after the shooting—Smedley's only
public defense of pirate radio appeared. It was published in a Liberal
magazine called *New Outlook*.[9] Entitled "Issues Raised by Pop Pirates,"
Smedley's piece offered a short but sharp defense of the pirates on all
the grounds familiar from the polemics of Coase, the liberal economists, and the IEA. He hailed them for eroding not only the BBC
monopoly but also that of the record companies. And he made explicit
the affinities between his pirate program and his broader economic
ambitions. The piece had clearly been scribbled off hastily, and it
appeared as a desperate self-justification. But it was no less emphatic
for that. "In our highly protected and therefore rigid economy,"
Smedley proclaimed,

the really provocative thinkers rarely get a look in—such statements [as] that the people of Britain would be twice as well
off with a Government dedicated to policies of maximum
unemployment, to removing the protective tariffs that keep
a grossly inefficient motor car industry in being even at the
expense of the possible disappearance of the industry altogether, to the reduction of agricultural subsidies so that more
food might be imported and thus give more work to our shipping and shipbuilding industries or that we should soon learn
to get along very well without a B.B.C. at all would be taken as
signs of incipient demention. Nevertheless it was views such
as these that influenced me to help Alan Crawford and Kittie
Black [*sic*] to get their original scheme for off-shore commercial radio off the ground, or rather on to the sea.

Pirate radio was not against the law, Smedley insisted. It was against
the intentions and interests behind the law. Those interests were the
preserve of monopolists in media, particularly the BBC, the recording
industry (dominated by Decca and EMI), and the musicians' unions.
These three acted in concert, with the union imposing needle time
and the record corporations buying exclusive airtime on Luxembourg
and, de facto, the BBC. Nor was piracy necessarily antagonistic to
copyright or performance right, as Sir Alan Herbert always claimed
with his hyperbolic calls to send in the troops. Most of the pirate
entrepreneurs were closely aligned with musicians, and they had made
deals with the PRS. As for the unions, in Smedley's view they were
merely agitating to protect their parochial interests. Pirate radio's
essential virtue was that it "prised open the market to new entrants."
In contrast to monopolies, it gave exposure to unknown and unpredictable artists. "The thieving is not done by the pirates," Smedley
concluded, eerily catching the defiantly moral tone later adopted by
early computer hackers confronting critics of their intrusions into
proprietary data, and by the bit-torrenters of the 2000s facing the
RIAA: "they have merely lessened the degree to which it was already
being done by others."

The key pirates, Smedley maintained, were the "more controversial" fort stations. Sir Alan was on "stronger ground" in attacking
these. Nobody seemed to know under whose jurisdiction they fell.
But as time went on, confidence was growing that the government
could not simply shut them down without either allowing the BBC to
broadcast advertising or, much more probably, licensing land-based
commercial radio. The longer the state delayed, the more likely investors in the pirates would reap dividends. Smedley neglected to mention that his own pirate venture had essentially collapsed, but in his
coda quietly conceded the point. "Whether they make money or not,"
he concluded, the pirates "served a purpose." They "put a curb on
the expenditure of the public's money," and inflicted change on the
hidebound BBC. "The liberty and safety of the people have been
enhanced," Smedley concluded, by "our modern-day pirates of the
air."

But Smedley himself had now brought that charmed life to an end.
Not only was Calvert's death an outcome of pirate radio's peculiar
culture; it was about to become the catalyst for its destruction.

THE BRITISH GOVERNMENT had long complained about the pirate stations, and had listened sympathetically while the BBC and the rights
agencies wailed about interference and copyright theft. But it had
been content so far to stand back, reasoning that the popularity of
the pirates was such that acting precipitately to shut them down was
not worth the candle. The Cabinet liked to claim that it was await-
ing European consensus, but the Scandinavians had acted quickly
enough. As time went on, and the stations signed deals with rights
societies and reached agreements with advertising bodies, so intervention became even harder. It was on the very day that Smedley and his
men set out for Shivering Sands that the *Sunday Times* reported that
pirate radio had finally achieved respectability.

Calvert's death transformed everything. Shooting people was unac-
ceptable. After the March 1966 general election, Labour had a majority large enough to ride out any backlash from silencing the pirates,

but not large enough to permit it to be insouciant about gun violence. Immediately MPs posed questions in Parliament. Surely this episode proved that tolerating piratical illegality would inevitably lead to worse. "Piracy is an aspect of anarchy," stormed Hugh Jenkins, chairman of Labour's backbench Communications Committee. "When the Government condones anarchy, as it has done over the last few years, the anarchists soon take over."[10] The Conservative William Deedes demanded that the forts be brought under government jurisdiction by *fiat*. There were now ten pirate stations, MPs noted: how many more need there be to merit prosecutions?[11] Before the week was out, Jenkins himself had moved to answer that question by proposing a bill to outlaw the pirate stations, establishing in their place on-shore local radio and a national pop station. It would all be overseen (along with a fourth television channel) by a unified national Television and Radio Authority. Such was the grand scale of response that Calvert's death seemed to demand.

The pirates themselves realized that a potentially fatal crisis was at hand. Several took to the press in a bid to limit the damage. They often did so by highlighting their civility and good conduct. Dorothy Calvert herself paid tribute to Birch for refusing to submit to anarchic practices, and for persuading the other offshore stations to shun them too. Birch, speaking anonymously, told *The Guardian* that all the stations had agreed to hold fast against Smedley. Atlanta was a failed venture, he continued, that had shied clear of City when the government had seemed likely to close the forts, only to change its mind when UKGM appeared on the horizon; its precious transmitter "does not appear to be worth a darn." And Allbeury took to the *Daily Telegraph* to conjure a future in which commercial stations would broadcast business news, and would all enjoy the kind of polite arrangement that his Radio 390 had reached with the Performing Right Society.[12] Along with arguments for laissez-faire and the obsolescence of Copenhagen wavelength allocations, this insistence on the civic-minded character of the enterprise seems to have been intended to head off the storm now imminent. Only Smedley's *New Outlook* piece struck a sour note in the midst of all this sanctimony—frightening babies, indeed.

The Postmaster General, Anthony Wedgwood Benn, saw that he would need to act. He lost no time. On July 1, Benn told Parliament that the government had decided to make it a priority to pass legislation. Parliamentary schedules proved suddenly malleable in the face of such violence. Benn, however, had always had interestingly mixed feelings about confronting the pirates: as a devotee of Britain's long history of popular radicalism, he felt distinct unease at the prospect of having to silence voices so clearly popular and independent of state control. He had privately told Harold Wilson in 1965 that "there is nothing I look forward to with less enthusiasm." Within days, his problem of conscience was solved. Wilson held a reshuffle and moved Benn to the Ministry of Technology. He was replaced by Eric Short, a much less sensitive soul who lost no time in proclaiming his intention to act. Legislation would be introduced immediately to close these "squalid" enterprises, Short declared. In his eyes they were clearly illegal. "It is no use talking about lawlessness in our cities if we are prepared to allow this to take place on the high seas."[13]

Short presented his bill on July 27, just over a month after Calvert's death. Called the Marine etc. Broadcasting (Offences) Bill, it proposed to outlaw all involvement with offshore stations. The bill had been drawn up extremely rapidly, and met with some disdain in the press. The Economist, always a reliable critic of the broadcasting monopoly, denounced it as "a ripe cartload of needless rubbish." But it was modeled closely on the laws passed earlier in Scandinavia, and it ought to be robust. Short pronounced the pirates "doomed." Presented with rumors that yet another fort station (called, with unconscious irony, Radio Albatross) was gearing up, his response was swift and unequivocal: it need not bother, as the forts were going to be demolished. The state planned to make it illegal for British companies to advertise on the offshore stations, cutting off the pirates' lifeblood. And if any pirate thought of relying solely on overseas companies—a possibility that Birch had mooted, guessing that Japanese transistor radio manufacturers might be interested—then the government would consider banning the sale of their goods. "It must be realised what a chaotic situation is developing," Short contended. "Do not forget that the freedom we have in this country—the freedom the pirates claim the Government are trying to interfere with—only exists because we have grown up to respect the law." From now on, he added, any "wealthy American" planning to create a pirate station "had better get that straight."[14]

ALL OF THE pirate stations, including the revived Radio City, geared up to campaign against the new bill. They were quick to raise the political stakes, and the press was keen to help them do so. They once again argued that they had proved their popularity, implying that MPs who acted against them would pay a political price. (That had less impact now, but it is worth noting that one of the listeners to pirate radio, Cabinet papers imply, was Prime Minister Harold Wilson.) Birch claimed that Radio London alone could boast 12 million regular listeners in the UK—and his rumored income of £20,000 a month carried its own message. Any MPs who rushed to vote in favor of suppressing such a phenomenon would be, as Ronan O'Rahilly put it, "idiots." They would make themselves look like devotees of that "old-fashioned Puritanism" that sensible Britons had abandoned at the time of the *Lady Chatterley* trial in 1960.[15] Moreover, to clamp down now, Allbeury maintained, would raise fundamental questions about "how democracy works." It would become a question of freedoms— freedom of choice, freedom of the press, and intellectual freedom. Radio, Birch agreed, was like newsprint: as a means of communication, it should be "free from pressure." Radio 390, in common with the others, regularly broadcast paeans to this principle of "freedom of the air." And the pirates repeatedly proclaimed that government action against them would be arbitrary and spiteful. Across Europe some three hundred broadcasters, including Voice of America and the Vatican's official mouthpiece, were currently operating outside the Copenhagen allocations. Why single out these ten?

The pirates' best hope was to ride out the storm that Calvert's death had unleashed. Their likeliest political allies were the Conservatives, 65 percent of whom told a survey in spring 1967 that they favored the pirates. There was a chance that the Tories might return to office before they were silenced, and the pirates might then hope to resurrect themselves on land as licensed local stations. So they assiduously courted Conservative politicians, using the language of choice versus centralized control. Allbeury twice addressed the Conservative Broadcasting Committee, while Tory MPs visited the ships, making sure that their presence was noted on air. One or two Labour members went out too. It must be said that neither displayed deep affinity for the enterprises, whose staff tended to be less than half the age of the MPs. One exception might have been the young Labourite Chris Rowland, but as an ex-BBC man he was no friend to the pirates. He found the Caroline staff avid to convince him that "they had nothing to do with those terrible people who ran the towers," and declared himself bemused by "bizarre snobberies" that he assumed were somehow elemental to pirate life.

On its face, the public movement for pop radio was formidable and mounting. MPs like Rowland (who died shortly after his visit to Caroline) received letters from some 100,000 constituents about the fate of the pirates. The first pressure group was formed by the Young Liberals: their Save Pop Radio Campaign appeared less than a week after Smedley's trial in autumn 1966. Others followed. The most vociferous, the Free Radio Association, came into formal existence in February 1967, claiming massive public support. The FRA circulated "more than a petition" that supposedly garnered 15,000 signatures. But it seems more significant for its Hayekian language than for any practical hopes its endorsers may have entertained for it:

> The Free Radio Association is fighting for free speech, free enterprise and free choice. The Government is trying to crush all competition over the air by silencing the commercial stations—thereby preserving the monopoly of the BBC and depriving us of the freedom to listen to the stations of our choice. This is a step toward dictatorship. If the Marine etc. Broadcasting (Offences) Bill becomes law in its present form, free speech will be suppressed. . . . We, the British people, will

fight for freedom of the air as we have fought before when our freedom has been threatened.

Yet the risk of a massive popular backlash remained just that: a risk, not a certainty. And if anything, it receded in the face of parliamentary facts. The FRA's actual membership was small, and few marched to Trafalgar Square for its cause. Short dismissed its 15,000 signatures outright as "fraudulent."[16]

The effect of the campaign was therefore paradoxical: it convinced MPs that their constituents' anger existed, but that it could be faced down if a fundamental overhaul of radio broadcasting took place at the same time. As Jenkins put it, "you can't take away the sugar without providing a little saccharine." The bill was only halfway to a strategy. It was "a simple pirate-basher." His powerful committee had been pushing for more since the "squalid" incident of Calvert's death. To replace the pirates there would have to be a national pop broadcaster, or a network of local stations, or, preferably, both, to preempt the perennial demand for "free enterprise local stations." Perhaps they could even be funded by advertising. To turn a BBC channel into "a quasi-official Caroline" would be "loathsome" to many in the corporation itself who cleaved to its mission of cultural improvement, but that problem would have to be faced.[17] Even Short conceded the political point. He promised that the government would create a public alternative to the pirates, and that it would be "better than anything the pirates are doing." "I like pop music," he told the tabloids, allowing himself to be photographed holding a transistor radio somewhere close to his ear.

A "legalistic blitzkrieg" against radio piracy was imminent. It started well before the new law was passed. The authorities already had powers at their disposal, and in the wake of the Calvert shooting they finally deployed them. The first summons was issued on September 21, 1966, against Allbeury's Radio 390, for unlawful use of "apparatus for wireless telegraphy." Roy Bates's Radio Essex received a similar summons a week later. Their hearings were set for late November.

As Smedley's trial approached, national attention focused on the antithesis of everything he had once envisaged Project Atlanta achieving. Instead of "the new voice of freedom" catalyzing the end of the public corporation and a revolution in economic culture, the pirate sector was set to be subsumed into the very social model that he had wanted to overturn. After years of "hot words and no action," a channel was about to be created for "some kind of State pop." The *Sunday Times* put the question explicitly: "Will pop be nationalised?"[18]

THE THINK TANK that Smedley had set up a decade earlier, the Institute of Economic Affairs, found itself in the front lines of this prospective war—a war whose implications extended to the shaping of an emergent information economy. In Yorkshire, Wilf Proudfoot's Radio 270 allied with the IEA to republish its *Competition in Radio,* adding a new preface underlining its timeliness.[19] The station circulated the tract free to its supportive (but perhaps rather bewildered) Scarborough listeners. And the Institute itself chose this moment to publish the latest in its sequence of polemics on information, under the title *Copyright and the Creative Artist.* It appeared just as the government was moving to close down the pirates, and broadened the case against that policy dramatically. It extended the case for piracy into an indictment of the central principle of the information economy itself.

Copyright moved on from the cases of television and radio to clarify in general what it called "the possible conflict between the producer and the 'consumer' of intellectual property." Its argument was essentially that of Arnold Plant, revived for a new generation. It frankly denied that copyright had anything to do with creativity, declaring that "it can never have been remotely responsible for a masterpiece." Term extensions merely restricted the circulation of works to no public benefit whatsoever. Meanwhile, it noted, "piracy flourishes," especially in the developing world, where it was widely approved for making educational works available. British and American publishers risked the appearance that they were campaigning against education in Third World countries in order to preserve ludicrous profit margins. In the realm of music, the problems were even more apparent.

The Performing Right Society and Public Performance Ltd. exercised collectivized monopolies. They restricted the broadcasting of records through the needle-time agreement. According to the IEA's tract, it was this that constituted the recording industry's major objection to pirate radio. Its real concern was that the broadcasting of records would cut into sales. The belief derived from an older world of sheet music, the IEA noted—a world in which copyright actually did lead to works being unavailable for purchase (publishers would only hire them out), and to their being continually amended in order to extend protections indefinitely. By 1967, two thirds of Verdi's music was unobtainable; none of Liszt's could be found "undoctored." Much of Mozart and Schubert was in the same state. Puccini's *Turandot* was restricted. The radical implication was that information monopolies of all kinds—not just the BBC's, but copyrights and patents too—should be cropped back drastically. This marked a convergence of arguments that had begun half a century earlier and been refined in the tracts on radio and television. And the IEA came closer to expressing its official support for the position than for any other argument it had ever published.

IN THE WAKE of the magistrates' hearing, Dorothy Calvert's lawyers complained to the Director of Public Prosecutions. The case was being mishandled, they charged. Attention had focused not on Smedley but on Reg Calvert, and in particular on his conduct in those last two days. The impression had been created that he was the real "criminal" in the case. The fact that the hearing had begun by reconstructing the meeting at Dean Street meant that his words there took on overwhelming significance, yet the only witnesses called to attest to what he had said were on Smedley's side. It was especially notable that Kitty Black, who had never met Calvert before that moment, had been encouraged to describe his character, whereas his widow and Birch were never permitted to testify at all. The magistrates had not been alerted to the fact that Calvert had been carrying £440 to offer to the riggers, which was surely "most relevant" as it confirmed his pacific intent.

Nor had the hearing broached either Smedley's prior "transactions" or the real nature of the boarding. Claims that it had been peaceful had been allowed to go uncontested, as too had those that its motivation was to protect property. In fact it had been carried out with deceit, with the "ulterior motive" of forcing Calvert into a deal—as evidenced by Black's seizing the crystal of the working transmitter as well as the one purportedly owned by Atlanta. And if the transmitter were so important, why had it been allowed to languish on the fort ever since? Finally, the representation of events at the cottage had been one-sided, too. The gas-pen had been invoked as though it were some kind of lethal weapon: a "pistol." It was no such thing, and in any case Calvert had never brandished it—in contrast to Smedley, who had resorted without hesitation or warning to a real and deadly firearm. Moreover, the magistrates had never realized something about Calvert himself that might have altered their perception of events: he had very little sight in his right eye. He suffered from cataracts, and had taken to relying on John Wileman, Jill's guitarist husband, to drive him around. If Thorburn's scratches had affected his left eye, his family felt, then it was quite possible that during the fight he had been virtually blind.[20]

The complaint did no good. Prosecutors briefly considered reinstating a murder indictment, but decided against it. Fearing as much, Calvert's daughters, Candy and Susan, approached their MP. He happened to be the eminent QC Quintin Hogg (later, as Lord Hailsham, to serve twice as Lord Chancellor). Hogg was one of the most experienced and respected legal experts in the country. As they recall it now, Hogg declared a belief that Smedley would get at least several years in prison. But he also hinted at deeper issues at stake.[21] As it was never very clear what those issues might be, the hint only contributed to the sense of uncertainty that had arisen around Radio City even before the boarding of Shivering Sands.

THE TRIAL OF Oliver Smedley for manslaughter began at Chelmsford Assizes in Essex on October 17. If the Calverts already had their suspicions about the outcome, they cannot have been reassured by the identity of the presiding judge. Sir Aubrey Melford Stevenson was sixty-four, and had a well-deserved reputation for idiosyncratically conservative views, which he was not slow to voice from the bench. He also had a record of siding with defendants who, in his view, had been warranted in taking actions that would normally be beyond the pale.[22]

Predictably enough, the trial mirrored the hearing back in July. Much time was spent on Calvert's outlandish statements before the confrontation, and the prosecuting QC remarked that the jury would need to "assess the effect of this sort of talk." In addition, Smedley's version of events had changed slightly. He now spoke of Calvert "kicking his way in," and asserted that he had assumed at the time that the Radio City man would have brought men he "commanded" with him. He had also been "practically certain," he said, that they would be armed. When he came into the room, he claimed, he had seen Calvert brandish something, and had intuitively reacted on the assumption that it was a gun and that he was about to fire. Calvert had not said anything. ("He was too frightened to say anything," someone in the audience interrupted. "He thought Smedley was going to shoot him.") So he had himself fired first, "instinctively." He had not aimed. In fact, Smedley claimed, Calvert's lunge forward at him had forced the issue. "He ran onto the gun, really." At this, Susan Calvert cried out. Melford Stevenson had her ejected.

Melford Stevenson's summing up was emphatic. Calvert had acted like a "lunatic," he told the jury. "Would anyone who saw, who learned, who had an opportunity of observing the consequences of that conduct, have had much doubt that the person committing himself to conduct like that might well be intending to do serious physical injury to that young woman?" If the jury believed Smedley's story, he said, it was "entitled" to acquit him. Even the prosecutor had told the jurors that if they thought Smedley had really believed himself or Thorburn to be in imminent danger, then it was their "duty" to acquit. Smedley's defense had claimed that there was no case to answer, because Calvert was in effect a burglar. Melford Stevenson demurred, but only so as to make the same point more emphatically. There was a case to answer,

he remarked, but "I do not think it will take very long to answer it."
The jury should not even bother to withdraw.

Taking the hint, the panel took no time at all. It acquitted Smedley.
For good measure, he was awarded 250 guineas in costs.

Leaving the court, Smedley tried to be conciliatory. "The whole
thing has been a tragedy," he lamented—"an appalling wastage of
a very brilliant human life." Calvert, he added, had been "the sort
of man I regard highly." But the Radio City boss had found himself in a situation beyond his control. He was out of his depth. And
here Smedley hesitated, in what sounded like a rare moment of self-
reflection. "Presumably we all were."

Smedley then announced that he would abandon all involvement
with radio until commercial broadcasting became legal. "No more
piracy."[23]

A MONTH AFTER Smedley's acquittal, his closing phrase had started
to come true for the United Kingdom at large. The political furor
created by the Calvert shooting had not died away, and the government remained determined to act against the enterprise that had, it
felt, led to the outrage.

Radio 390 was the first to be silenced. On November 24, Allbeury
and his assistant David Lye pleaded not guilty to charges of violat-
ing the Wireless Telegraphy Act. They claimed that Radio 390 stood
outside territorial waters. By an ingenious piece of hydrographic sur-
veying, the government was able to claim that it was within them—
barely. Allbeury and Lye were convicted. Although the penalties were
slight, and Allbeury immediately announced an appeal, he decided to
close down the station. It ended transmissions the following night. In
the event, the appeal was dismissed in mid-December, and Allbeury
declined to pursue it to the House of Lords.

Radio Essex (or BBMS, as it now was) followed 390 into oblivion
at the end of the year. Roy Bates's hearing had taken place a few days
after Allbeury's, and had had the same outcome. Unlike Allbeury,
Bates tried to keep his station on the air in defiance. But with no

THE WAR AGAINST THE PIRATES

advertisers it could not continue to operate for long, and some time around the end of December it fell silent. By this time the first summons had been issued against a ship station, Radio Scotland, and it was clear that the government was resolute. Yet Bates was still not prepared to admit defeat. He dismantled the station's equipment and moved it to another fort, Roughs Tower, which was unambiguously outside territorial waters. Whether he intended to restart broadcasting from this distant location is not entirely clear. But no transmissions were ever heard. Bates and his band remained secure but silent on their lonely redoubt.

That left only one fort station in operation: Radio City. The government had delayed acting against it while Smedley's case pended. It then delayed again because the initial verdict against Allbeury seemed to imply a definition of territorial limits that would have left Shivering Sands outside.[24] But it was only a matter of time. At the end of January 1967, the summons finally came. The hearing was set for February 8.

BUT DOROTHY CALVERT had another, more immediate threat to confront. It looked like Oliver Smedley might be back—this time in alliance with Radio City's old rival, Roy Bates.

In January 1967, rumors began to swirl around Whitstable and London that another attempt might be imminent to seize Shivering Sands. Police heard from an informer about a new plot to storm the fort and evict Radio City. Big Alf Bullen confirmed to a reporter that he had been approached again to participate. In the last week of January, the rumors became louder still. Finally, Dorothy Calvert felt she had to warn Inspector Barker at Scotland Yard.

Barker had already heard and disregarded some of the talk. But he had learned to trust Mrs. Calvert's word, and he acted on it now. He immediately got in touch with officers in Kent and Essex, with the Home Office, and with the Admiralty. He had, he told them, "reliable information" about an imminent attack on Shivering Sands. The new information came from three different sources on the same day, and deserved credence. It seemed that two Whitstable men, Anthony Pine and Philip Perkins, were planning to take over the fort, in alliance with a Southend figure calling himself "Uncle." Barker did not mention—although he almost certainly knew—that Pine and Perkins were ex-City men: Perkins had once been the transmitter engineer, and Pine had been dismissed in November for unreliability.[25] He asked for Navy help, requesting that a military tug be put on standby to ferry police officers out to the fort at short notice. After all, if Shivering Sands lay within British waters for the purposes of prosecuting Dorothy Calvert, then Britain must surely accept a "moral responsibility" to try to stop acts there that might produce another death.

It was not hard to conjure a motive for a new assault. "Uncle," Barker believed, was Roy Bates. Radio Essex/BBMS having recently lost its base, and, Roughs Tower being remote and ramshackle, he would be in dire need of a new studio. But Barker also suspected that Bates might not be acting alone. "It is also suggested that Smedley is associated with this plan," he reported. Nor was this so implausible. Smedley had never relinquished his claim to equipment on the fort. And Mrs. Calvert had just heard from Allbeury that Smedley had once more been in contact offering to sell City to him. Allbeury claimed to have rebuffed him even more emphatically than the first time, but the information was ominous. Dorothy Calvert now telephoned Bates herself, and he too admitted receiving new overtures from Smedley, which he insisted he had rejected with contempt. (He spoke of physically throwing the Atlanta man out.) She warned him off for good measure, at which point Bates made sure to call Barker to deny all involvement. Smedley, he said, was still "the one to watch."

Barker was skeptical. "I am not prepared to accept an assurance from Mr. Bates," he noted, even though Bates was certainly well aware that the police were keeping an eye on him. "He is firmly convinced of his right to take over just what he fancies in the estuary. . . . Bates is the type of man who would take over the fort and then defy anyone to do anything about it." But the idea of an alliance between Bates and Smedley was one to be taken very seriously indeed.

Whitehall accepted Barker's logic and put a Navy vessel on standby, with cars ready to whisk police to Wapping if need be. As the court date for Radio City approached, however, it seemed that they would not be needed. Finally, Dorothy Calvert appeared in the courtroom in Southend on February 8, to be prosecuted on the same grounds as Allbeury and Bates before her. She too was found guilty and fined. Like Allbeury, she had no desire—or resources—to fight on against the state, and from the steps of the court she announced the closing of Radio City. It went off the air for the last time at midnight.

But as the last hours of Radio City ticked away, all those rumors of an attack on Shivering Sands suddenly turned into warnings of an imminent raid. At 8:30 pm, a Post Office agent who had been instrumental in the prosecutions of all three fort stations reported getting information from someone he knew as a reliable informant. The caller claimed that an attempt was about to be made on the fort. A boat would collect eight men from a beach at Whitstable, ferrying them out to make a landing at dead of night. The story seemed to relate to a man named Smythe, who had telephoned another known only as Barry earlier in the day and discussed the adventure. The agent knew who Smythe was: he lived in the same house on Whitstable's seawall as Pine. That was enough to make the story ring true. He immediately picked up the receiver again and called Scotland Yard.

Inspector Barker's plan went into effect. The Navy readied its ship for departure, while Barker and his men rushed to a car and drove at full speed to Wapping to meet it.

Kent police initially reacted just as energetically. But before Barker could leave the dock, they thought better of it and called to cancel the naval expedition. The story was a hoax, they now believed. Smythe and Barry were jokers, acting on instructions from Phil Perkins and Tony Pine—perhaps they were really Perkins and Pine themselves. Like the Calvert family, Perkins and Pine had felt sure ever since June 1966 that their telephones were being tapped. They had cooked up the idea of a plot in order to test that suspicion, by seeing what reaction a telephone conversation about a boarding party would provoke. There was never a real plan to rendezvous on Whitstable beach, then. But Perkins, standing in a nearby telephone box, had stayed to enjoy the result. He laughed delightedly as the seafront filled with a crowd of fretful constables straining their eyes to spot a gang of toughs who never came.

Back at Wapping, Barker and his men relaxed and disembarked, heading at a more restrained pace back toward central London. Yet they did not entirely believe the Kent force's reasoning. Both Barker and the Post Office agent remained convinced that there *had* been a real scheme afoot, even if Pine and Perkins had exploited it for their own ends. It had evidently been called off in the face of their prompt action. Or so they told themselves reassuringly.

Whether Barker was right would remain unresolved. But in one sense it did not matter. If Smedley or Bates—or whoever else was behind the supposed plan—had indeed thought better of it at the last moment, they had missed their last chance. With Calvert removing the studio equipment after Radio City's closure, the fort lost much of its appeal to such men. That same night, Barker told the Navy to stand down. They would not be needed again.[26]

THE MARINE OFFENCES bill had its second reading in Parliament in February, and sailed through with a large majority. The Conservative opposition proposed amendments, but they were designed principally to delay passage until some public counterpart to the pirates had been established, not to protect the stations themselves. Only in the Lords in May did a real obstacle appear to the bill's progress. The Lords voted to delay implementation until an alternative existed to fill what Lord Denham called the "void" that would be left in listeners' lives by the end of the pirates. The government overturned this quickly, and the bill became law on July 14, 1967.

It took effect a month later. All the remaining pirate stations except Caroline swiftly capitulated, realizing that they could not hope to retain enough advertising income to survive. Even Radio London, which until the last moment had kept up a brave front of defiance, bowed to the inevitable and shut down on August 14. Radio 355, Allbeury's newer venture, closed on the 5th with an eloquent speech by Allbeury himself contrasting the restrictions of British society to the freedoms of America. Wilf Proudfoot closed Radio 270 and put its ship up for sale. Radio Scotland likewise went off the air, finishing with a ball in Glasgow and a ceremonial pitching of the station's entire record library into the sea. A week later the Royal Navy blew up Sunk Head tower, one of the old forts, to ensure that no future pirate would be tempted to commandeer it.

Only Caroline made a serious effort to survive. As an Irish citizen, Ronan O'Rahilly was not personally affected by the new law. He remained in London, operating, as it happened, from Project Atlanta's old Dean Street office. But even Caroline found the going extremely hard. It resorted to program cuts, crude forms of plugging, and spurious commercials. By March 1968, the organization was in irremediable debt. Tugs chartered by creditors turned up one day and seized both Caroline ships, towing them to Amsterdam. There they remained, impounded and silent. The war on the pirates that Smedley had unwittingly and unwillingly launched when he pulled the trigger on Reg Calvert was over.

BUT NATIONALIZING POP music still remained to be done. At the same time as announcing the anti-pirate bill, the government had also announced a review of broadcasting policy in general. For the first time since at least the early 1950s—indeed, given its radical scope, for the first time since the formation of the BBC in the mid-twenties—a reappraisal of the structure of radio broadcasting was at hand.[27]

It proved a tricky business. Ironically, given the prominence of intellectual property concerns in the anti-pirate war, a major stumbling block was copyright. The BBC had begun floating plans for an all-day music station as soon as Atlanta and Caroline first launched. But the needle-time agreement was a huge obstacle to any such venture. Frustrated, the corporation had been reduced to issuing statements that the pirates were "stealing the legal property of British musicians, gramophone companies, and other copyright holders." Even Short had discovered that "unless Parliament sees fit to amend the copyright laws (and amending laws to meet special circumstances is not a particularly happy practice) it must remain a very open question whether the BBC can negotiate enough extra needle time on affordable terms for the projected pop service to be economically viable." But the death of Calvert had made it imperative that something happen. Copyright could no longer be regarded as impervious to reinterpretation. A way around "needle time" had to be hastily found. Suddenly under intense pressure, the Musicians' Union conceded a deal at a meeting in November 1966 that extended long past midnight.[28] Needle time would not disappear altogether, but the BBC's allocation was almost tripled. Plans were immediately laid for a "Programme 247" to replace the soon-to-be-defunct ships, and the government quietly hired a public relations firm to plan for eroding the pirates' popularity and building that of the BBC's substitute. Through the spring and summer of 1967, intense talks took place within Whitehall over how to shut down the pirates, how to create an acceptable substitute, and how to sell the change to the public.

Just before the anti-pirate law came into effect, the new regime of BBC radio was proclaimed. In place of the old Home Service, Light Programme, and Third Programme—the national channels created at the end of World War II—there would be a radically reshaped schedule. Pop music—the preserve of the pirates, and of the mooted Programme 247—would be catered for by Radio One. The old Light Programme would be shorn of its more pop-ish elements and become Radio Two. The Third Programme, with an uncompromising schedule of classical music and high culture, turned into Radio Three. And the old Home Service, focused on speech and news, became Radio Four. This new system would come into effect at the end of September 1967. BBC radio had been completely restructured, to a degree without parallel since the creation of the corporation itself.[29]

In galvanizing action against the pirates, the death of Reg Calvert also galvanized action for the university of the air. On September 18, 1967—less than two weeks before Radio One was due to come on air—the Cabinet launched a planning committee devoted to this long-delayed venture. The new group, chaired by Jennie Lee, was destined to shepherd what was now called the "Open University" into existence.

Six months later, its outlines were in place. When it eventually opened in 1971—with the support, somewhat mysterious to contemporaries, of the new Tory education minister, Margaret Thatcher—the Open University would have almost 20,000 students in its first intake. In a decade it would grow to become Britain's largest higher education institution.[30]

In the meantime, the BBC had no experience of presenting the kind of radio that the pirates had offered. The controller of the new Radio One, Robin Scott—a veteran of BBC television—would need to find skilled DJs somewhere, and quickly. He naturally turned to the pirates. The initial list of Radio One DJs was thirty-three names long, and over half—seventeen—were pirate radio graduates. The majority of those, eleven, came from Radio London, the most respectable of the pirates. BBC men had quietly visited London's vessel even before it shut down, in a bid to recruit its best presenters. (Radio One would also closely mimic London's slogans and jingles.) Another four had links to Caroline, but only two came directly from O'Rahilly's operation, and both were quickly fired. One more presenter, Stuart Henry, came from Radio Scotland. And the other ex-pirate to join Radio One was Mike Raven (Churton Fairman), Smedley's cousin, once of Atlanta, later of King, and most recently to be heard on Radio Luxembourg. Not a single person from Radio City made the transition to the new public pop station.

The new station came on air at 7 am on Saturday, September 30. The first DJ to be heard was Tony Blackburn, ex–Radio London, from which he imported his old program format, and even its signature tune. Blackburn had the breakfast show six days a week. Yet his was one of only two scheduled programs devoted entirely to records—needle time remained a constraint, despite the Musicians' Union's compromise. And for much of the rest of the day Radio One shared programs with the tamer Radio Two, resorting to the corporation's familiar live bands and cover versions. In the period that followed Radio One's inauguration, moreover, Scott treated all his ex-pirate presenters as on trial. They were on short-term contracts, the idea being that only a few would be kept on after an initial audition. Some flourished. Raven was one, despite being the oldest of the ex-pirates to join up. Another, to become much better known, was John Peel. The corporation also gave a grudging and sporadic home to the one unquestioned original genius of the medium that the pirate stations had bred. Originally named Maurice Cole, Kenny Everett had thrived on Radio London, where he had developed his distinctive style of comedic virtuosity, experimenting with multi-track tape to record his diverse voices. Like Peel—and, in his way, Blackburn—Everett would do much to define the style and ensure the quality of British popular radio for the next generation.

But these were exceptions. Most of the other pirate veterans were cast aside rapidly. In-house presenters proved more amenable to the ways of the BBC, even in its institutionally revolutionized form. In that light, the new station's upbeat tone came across to many listeners as artificially bright and contrived. George Melly's jaundiced summary in the *Observer* was much cited. "The solemnity with which the conventions evoked by the pirates have been plagiarized is almost Germanic in its thoroughness," Melly remarked. "The effect is of a waxwork." *New Society* denounced it all as a "phoney revolution."[31] And Calvert's old partner Screaming Lord Sutch concurred. The managers at Broadcasting House might have hired the best pirates and adopted their best tunes, but they had looted rather than learned. "They've turned out to be the biggest pirates of them all."

8

A MAN CALLED UNCLE

One morning in February 1967, around the time of the closing of Radio City, a man walked into the King Music office on Denmark Street and asked to make an appointment to meet with Dorothy Calvert. A commercial acquaintance of Reg's, he told Jill Wileman, wanted to discuss business with her. Wileman noted the request, and after work that evening Mrs. Calvert walked with the man to a night-club off Clifford Street. There a group was waiting for them. They all climbed into a taxi and drove to the Astor Club in Berkeley Square, where a cabaret was underway. Only now did she encounter the man who seemed to be in charge: a dark-haired, intense, heavyset fig-ure, who finally revealed the point of the rigmarole. He wanted Radio City to continue, he said. She should not concern herself about the government; he had the government in his hands. He could ensure that the station would be left unmolested. Would she keep City on the air?

The question made Dorothy Calvert distinctly uneasy. These men were East Londoners, with Cockney accents and a hard edge. She found it hard to imagine that Reg could really have worked with them. No, she decided. She would not keep the station on the air if it meant breaking the law, whatever power this man might possess. He made an effort to argue, but soon recognized that she was resolute. At length he gave up, remarking that he could see that she was a lady who would not change her mind once it was set. His Rolls-Royce delivered her back to Welbeck Street.[1]

She was lucky. Reggie Kray was in an unusually personable mood that day. Even though he was the more stable of the Kray twins, whose criminal rule over the East End was then at its bloody peak, he was a fearsome figure whom not many dared to cross.

It was probably inevitable that speculation would link the Radio City affair—and for that matter pirate radio in general—to the Krays. The brothers were the acme of what has been called the louche side of sixties media culture, and in 1967 they were at the height of their power.[2] Crude and brazenly violent, Ronnie and Reggie had managed to survive in the open for years, partly because the local community in the East End was too frightened of them and their band of heavies ("the Firm") to testify against them. But it was not only a matter of terror. They also exploited a conservative, masculine social order in the East End, with distant roots in the dissenting traditions of previous centuries. In Bethnal Green and Mile End, the police seemed a relatively distant presence, whereas the Krays embedded themselves in the local round of boys' clubs, pubs, and boxing gyms. And from that base they were extending their reach into the West End. A *frisson* of risk attracted sports personalities, media stars, and politicians to their orbit.[3] The most fashionable society photographer of the day, David Bailey, took glamorous shots of them. They enjoyed the attention and the prestige. It was no wonder, then, and no surprise, that Reg Calvert was occasionally said to have boasted of links to the brothers. Nor was it surprising that on the other side Smedley's imaginative financial ventures seemed to make him a natural associate. As far as can now be ascertained, there was never any evidence linking either man to the Kray Firm. Certainly the police at the time gave no credence to the tales about Calvert, and it seems that on that day in 1967 Dorothy Calvert was not even sure who Reggie Kray was. Most likely, the proposal she rejected was an opportunistic one. Reggie had seen a chance to expand his protection rackets into another corner of the glamorous world that he so relished, and was inclined to pursue it. Had she said yes, no doubt the demands would have followed. At any rate, if Radio City was not attuned to the Krays, the Krays were attuned to Radio City.

This was not the last time that the Firm would cross paths with a veteran of the Calvert affair. Early 1967 was a tense time for the Krays, and it would soon get worse. Frank "the Mad Axe Man" Mitchell had disappeared on Christmas Eve, and the authorities suspected, rightly, that the brothers had had him killed. Reggie's wife had already attempted suicide once, and in June she would succeed. Dorothy Calvert had seen Reggie himself in a rare sober moment, for he was under severe strain and drinking heavily. Ronnie was in hiding, isolated in a flat near the King's Road in Chelsea. There he was spending his lonely hours elaborating fantasies of an international murder syndicate.

In the summer Ronnie emerged from hiding with a resolve to put his grandiose plans into action. To impress the American Mafia, he set out to organize an assassination. The chosen victim was a nightclub owner named George Caruana. A contract had been put out on Caruana as a result of some now obscure underworld quarrel. An American named Cooper, who had wormed his way into becoming Ronnie's trusted adviser, urged the brothers to take this opportunity to make an impact. One possibility, he suggested, would be to kill Caruana by radio. And he had the ideal man to do that. At a pub in Bethnal Green, Cooper introduced Ronnie to an expert radio engineer who could be the hit man. He was tall, pale, and balding, with a manner that in the 2000s might be called geeky. It was Paul Elvey—the same Elvey who had been chief engineer on Shivering Sands.

Elvey had already been involved in one failed hit that Cooper had undertaken for the Krays: a bizarre attempt to kill an underworld figure in the very heart of the legal world, the Old Bailey. Elvey had been set to use a James Bond–like secret weapon involving a spring-loaded hypodermic full of cyanide hidden in an attaché case. He lost his nerve in that attempt, or so the Krays heard, but now he had another chance. After rejecting other options (including a diver's speargun and a hunting crossbow), the idea was that he would detonate a car bomb under Caruana's Mini. Cooper said he could get gelignite from a contact in Scotland. Ronnie liked the idea: its technological quality would impress the Americans.

A couple of days later, Elvey flew up to Glasgow and picked up three dozen sticks of dynamite in a sky blue suitcase. He took a taxi back to the airport, heading for the return flight to London. The police arrested him as he got on the plane. He had intended to put the case in the overhead luggage bin.

For the police unit charged with bringing the Krays down, Elvey's arrest promised the crucial break they had long been looking for. The detective in charge, Leonard ("Nipper") Read, flew straight to Glasgow to interview him. After a little stonewalling, Elvey told his tale. He led Read to Cooper—who turned out to be a U.S. Treasury agent, acting as some kind of loose cannon *agent provocateur.* The American's actual role remained murky. But he claimed that he had recruited Elvey because the engineer needed the £1,000 fee while being clearly incapable of killing anyone. That, at least, made sense: Elvey himself testified that he was "hopelessly mis-cast in the role of a professional liquidator." Conceivably, he too had always known this. In any case, it could truly be said that he ended up playing a crucial part in bringing down the Kray empire. For it seemed clear that the Krays had been eager enough participants. Detective Read therefore decided to take a gamble. With the evidence he had from Elvey and Cooper, he ordered the Krays and their entire Firm arrested in a coordinated series of raids. With the Firm behind bars, he hoped, the terror that had kept East Enders silent would dissolve.

The twins had just left the Astor Club when the police swooped, picking them up without a fight. Within hours, every member of the Firm was behind bars. And almost immediately it became clear that Read's gamble would pay off. As the aura of impunity that had surrounded the Firm dissipated, people began to talk. By the time the Krays appeared in court in mid-1968, there was a crowd of eye-witnesses arrayed against them. One of them was Paul Elvey, now a prosecution witness. Thanks largely to his testimony, the twins were committed for trial at the Old Bailey. In March the following year they were convicted of an earlier murder, after the longest trial ever held in the UK. They were sentenced to decades in prison. And it was only now, seeing their photographs in the morning paper, that Dorothy Calvert realized who had taken her to the Astor that day a year earlier. She was stunned to see Elvey in the same story.

The fall of the Krays represented a turning point. By the end, their blunt and brutal methods looked not so much frightening as merely tawdry and dated. Monty Python's "Piranha Brothers" pastiche caught the tone of public disdain very well. Britain was set on moving forward, with new, modern sensibilities, and new, modern media to sustain them. As chance would have it, the judge who told the Krays that society had "earned a rest from your activities" had played an inadvertent part already in creating the latter. He was the same Melford Stevenson who had presided over Smedley's acquittal.[4]

AT THAT INSTANT late on Midsummer Night 1966 when Smedley took his fatal decision, two kinds of piracy came into collision. Reg Calvert represented one kind—a kind whose history can be traced back centuries. He was an ingenious and imaginative entrepreneur, opportunistic, ambitious, and relatively young. He spoke in grandiose terms, but his operations were undercapitalized, seat-of-the-pants adventures that might bloom or collapse—as so many radical ventures initially are. Ted Allbeury portrayed him as cultivating an image as the outsider, resistant to all rules. If, as Lord Morrison said, pirate radio was "one of the most anarchistic developments and experiments in our history," then Calvert represented its more experimental side. He was unconventional—as mercurial, in a way, as the experimenters of the 1920s, against whom the big media conglomerates had first defined themselves.[5] But an experimental life could be highly taxing, and by mid-1966 Calvert wanted to escape into a reliable and respectable livelihood. Smedley's boarding party threatened to make that impossible.

Calvert represented the kind of pirate or privateer that the Institute of Economic Affairs hailed as holding the key to social and cultural progress. In the aftermath of the shooting, even Smedley called him a genius of sorts. But as the Institute had discovered, established business culture was often hostile to such folk. And Oliver Smedley's own vision of a return to laissez-faire required—as he often reiterated—that the offshore stations uphold every norm of propriety. Smedley therefore stood for a different kind of pirate altogether. He was the rational capitalist, well versed in both the maxims of accountancy and the more abstract principles of liberal ideology. While Calvert came into piracy from below, as it were, Smedley entered it from above. Privately educated, metropolitan, and professional, he saw himself as what he had really almost been: an agent in the political and cultural affairs of the nation. He now wanted to be a player in remaking the industry of creativity. By ending the monopoly of the BBC, Smedley hoped to pave the way for a revived society of individualism, conceived in his uncompromisingly radical terms. Atlanta was to be a cultural and political vanguard. It was this—the point of all his labors for decades—that seemed on the verge of destruction in spring 1966. What made Calvert so appealing was therefore precisely what also made him so dangerous. And as in military and political life, so in financial and entrepreneurial: Smedley's instinct was to stand fast. Hold his ground.

This might seem to run athwart a constant refrain in the pirates' representations of their own activities, and one that played a real role in the tragedy of 1966. When pressed about why they had launched their expedition to seize Shivering Sands, Smedley's party told different stories, but those stories shared one common feature so obvious that it was never commented upon. All involved said that they had seen it as, in Horsley's term, a "lark." Sitting with the constable next to Calvert's body, Smedley himself ascribed the whole episode to "a joke gone sour." Kitty Black too was inclined to invoke its playful, if in her eyes theatrical, quality. It was a jape, an act, *not serious*. The notion probably never attracted attention because of the constant association, then as now, between piracy in general and happy-go-lucky escapades. It is an association that has all too often been restated almost unconsciously, as if it were natural. Yet in the case of pirate radio it was not natural at all. The offshore stations cultivated the impression designedly, carefully, and relentlessly. Being unserious was a serious matter.

Presenters gave the impression that life on the ships was a constant breeze because profits might depend on sustaining that attractive impression. The notion of freedom played a similar role. Constraint had to mean the BBC, and the BBC had to mean constraint. In reality, offshore DJs were often very strictly limited in what they could broadcast, and how. Very few indeed had the leeway to create a program like John Peel's renowned *Perfumed Garden*, transmitted at dead of night from Radio London. Radio City was at first a rare, perhaps unique, exception. But under Dorothy Calvert's control even City grew increasingly disciplined—as it had to if it were to survive. "Freedom" of this kind carried its own obligations, some of them quite constricting. Nobody knew that better than Oliver Smedley.

Smedley's acknowledgment of the tragic quality of the confrontation over Shivering Sands was not, therefore, merely a gesture made for public effect. It reflected real ambivalence toward someone who was challenging the same resented monopoly, in the name of an alternative that was more vital than Smedley's own. Calvert's venture captured an aspect of the appeal of pirate radio that Smedley and Crawford's more orderly Atlanta could not rival. Smedley could not deny or suppress a station like City, but this warrior of laissez-faire could not live alongside it either. For his planned "network" to have a chance at challenging for Britain's future, he had somehow to appropriate it. Until he did, Radio City would remain Mr. Hyde to Atlanta's Dr. Jekyll.

REGINALD CALVERT'S BOMBAST in those last days before June 21, 1966, should similarly be seen in context. He was an experimenter and a showman. Brian Harvey's summing up seems accurate: "a straight dealing type of person, albeit a trifle hair brained [*sic*] at times . . . a creator, or ideas man."[6] Every venture of his that met with success had done so because he had projected those "ideas." He had drawn audiences in countless dance halls into some extravagant domain of the imagination. Radio City started the same way. Originally the extension of a dance hall evening and a by-election campaign, it became

something more partly as a result of another piece of showmanship.
When the government withdrew its launch, Calvert trumpeted it to the
press as a great victory, only to realize that he then had to make good
on the claim. But by the first half of 1966 this was wearing thin. The
ambiguous fate of the alliance with Project Atlanta meant that bills
were being left in limbo between Denmark Street and Dean Street.
Calvert was receiving threats to take Radio City to court over unpaid
debts. And rumors were starting to swirl of physical dangers to his
family and his men. He himself seems to have become disillusioned.
He wanted out. He was elated when Birch agreed to take Radio City
off his hands. So when Smedley's men seized the fort, it seemed that
his hopes were about to be dashed.

In those last two days between the takeover of Shivering Sands and
the drive to Wendens Ambo, Calvert oscillated between two very different strategies to deal with the crisis. He could be the impresario
or the entrepreneur. As entrepreneur, he spoke of peaceful resolu-
tions and of protecting his men. As impresario, he spoke in terms of
grand, theatrical gestures—of nerve gas and mortars, helicopters
and fake police. In the often raucous press coverage that followed the
shooting, the more sensational of these remarks were presented in
isolation. They were construed as consistent and seriously threatening. Sometimes, no doubt, they *were* threatening. But they were not
consistent, and a close reading of the principals' testimony indicates
that nobody took them as such before 10:30 pm on June 21. Not
for the only time, it may have been Kitty Black who saw through to
the essence of the matter. Calvert, she supposed, was "dramatizing."
And everyone—Allbeury, Birch, Boutwood, Thorburn, even Smedley
himself—assumed as much. Until that last moment.[7]

Smedley said in his defense that "I knew he came here to kill me."
He may well have assumed it at the last. Wendens Ambo was a quiet
village where residents often did not bother to lock their doors, and
for London men to turn up late at night and present themselves in
aggressive tones would naturally cause trepidation or worse. But it
seems certain that Calvert did not go to Wendens Ambo to kill anyone, and probable that he did not even mean to seize Smedley for

the police. The £440 in his pocket proves that he meant to go on to Whitstable the next morning if he could not reach agreement that night. Still stronger evidence, not noted at the time, was the identity of his companion. Calvert had had a choice, but in Alan Arnold he brought along someone who had already had two heart attacks, and who was extremely nervous of getting into any situation more stressful than a staring contest. It would be hard to conceive of anyone less useful in the event of a real confrontation.

It is not possible to know definitively what would have happened if Smedley had shouted a warning at that critical moment instead of pulling the trigger, or if he had shot into the ceiling instead of straight ahead. He did neither. And what had been a tumult of arguments, representations, and meanings froze at that moment. They were then battened into place by the welter of press coverage that followed. When judges and jurors looked back, what they saw were those fixed meanings. They missed the tumult of possibilities out of which they originally came.

WITH RADIO CITY gone, Roy Bates represented the enduringly piratical wing of pirate radio. He had demonstrated as much in the struggle for Knock John fort, from which he had expelled Calvert's men in September 1965. From that November until the end of 1966, Bates had run Radio Essex from the fort, using an obsolete World War II transmitter producing a signal that rarely even reached London. But then his station was silenced by the courts. Bates was not the kind of figure who would accept such a decision passively, and the suspicions that he now schemed to seize Shivering Sands—with or without Smedley's assistance—sounded plausible, at least to the police. But even if he had pondered such a plan, he soon rejected the idea. Bates's attention turned instead to a different fort, further out in the North Sea.

Roughs Tower, like Knock John, was one of the Navy forts. It was a gun emplacement platform atop two broad, hollow legs. It was not ideal for broadcasting, as the relatively small surface area meant that a tall antenna like Radio City's could not be erected. But it had the great virtue of remoteness. By no stretch of the legal imagination could Roughs Tower be said to lie within territorial waters (in 1967, at least; later the British government would claim precisely this). It was clearly in the open sea, and yet no radio concern had yet commandeered it. When Knock John was ruled out of bounds for pirate radio, Bates therefore packed up his equipment and moved it lock, stock, and barrel to this isolated and barren fortress.

Bates was not the only radio entrepreneur to spot the potential of Roughs Tower. By late 1966 it was clear that the furor over Calvert's death was going to lead to the end of pirate radio as it was then practiced, and a scramble took place to find viable ways of carrying on in the face of the coming crackdown. In January 1967, the gaze of Radio Caroline fell on Roughs Tower. Ronan O'Rahilly hoped to use it not as a station in its own right, but as a supply base for the *Mi Amigo*. He sent men out to the fort, and even built a helicopter landing pad to provide for victualling. But Bates's party challenged Caroline's, and after weeks of uneasy cohabitation his men expelled the Caroline crew. They then repelled an attempted counterattack, using firearms and homemade petrol bombs. Bates's band were even said to have concocted flamethrowers. This "gang warfare," as it was called in Parliament, reminded MPs of Calvert's death. It concentrated minds and spurred passage of the new law.[8]

Yet the legislation could not touch Bates in his new castle. Nor was the Navy keen to try force, in the face of an arsenal that was reputedly formidable, albeit improvised. The government instead thought to buy him out. But he demanded twenty times what Whitehall thought a reasonable sum. Then the authorities considered subterfuge. They received an offer by a disaffected Bates employee on Roughs Tower to betray his boss and hand over the fort to the military. But suspicions about the man's character (he was a habitual criminal) and worries about violence (he wanted the Navy to blow the fort up, to provide a spectacular denouement to a planned book about pirate radio) dissuaded them from pursuing the offer. Finally Whitehall was reduced to what one administrator termed the Al Capone approach. Bates might be prosecuted on the apparently unrelated basis that his son

was not attending school. But this too showed no likelihood of getting him off.[9] In the end, realizing that he was probably secure, Bates
declared Roughs Tower an independent state. He called it "Sealand."

The Principality of Sealand was declared in September 1967. Still
in existence today, it is almost exactly the same age as the modern
BBC radio system. It is a strange, self-constructed fiefdom, with a
class structure unlike that of any other nation in history, comprising
as it does only aristocrats. There have been times when it looked like
it would go bankrupt or fall to invasion, but no such calamities have
transpired. The state remains semi-licit, but it is tolerated. It is apparently stable. What has never been so clear is what it is for.

Over the years, the Bates regime has proposed various schemes to
make this *soi-disant* nation a going concern. After the pirate radio era,
they projected a tourist hotel and the establishment of a free port.
At one point they touted a massive extension to form an artificial
landmass. None of these visions took hold. But in the late 1990s the
advent of digital networking seemed to offer a new future for Sealand.
It could become, as the *New York Times* put it, "the first independent
colony in cyberspace."[10]

The immediate opportunity came from Whitehall. In 2000, amid
public consternation about the Internet's scope for various kinds of
licentiousness and illegality, Westminster moved to legislate for all
Internet Service Providers (ISPs) to be brought under the purview
of official investigators. Sealand saw an opportunity. It announced
that it would offer a venue for anyone wanting to issue material to
the Internet beyond the reach of any such state oversight. Its London-
based commercial arm, named HavenCo, invited applications. The
plan was to take this relic of the pirate radio era and turn it into a
pirate data haven—and to do so by re-creating some of the same institutions that the old pirate stations had used. But as a state, albeit one
without a police force or surveillance, Sealand could offer facilities
that were stable and predictable while remaining invisible to conventional authorities. The only explicit restrictions that Sealand proposed
to impose were that it would eschew spam, hacker attacks, and child
pornography. Anything else would in principle be fair game. Bates's

nation let it be known that in practice its biggest takers were likely to be online gambling corporations.

The moment for such a venture seemed ripe. The Internet was already a proven and resilient technology—it had originated in the late 1960s—but as a focus of commercial and cultural attention it was growing fast from a tiny origin. Forecasts of its future political economy were all the rage. Many of them portrayed the Net in terms of either a "new frontier" or a pirate realm akin to the Port Royal of the late seventeenth century. Bruce Sterling's novel *Islands in the Net* was a key point of reference. Published in the late 1980s, it combined both motifs. It portrayed a world in which traditional states were fighting a rearguard action against the rise of piratical "data havens" that acted as the eponymous islands within a sea of information. One of them was Grenada, the Caribbean island that had recently hit the headlines when it was invaded by the American military. In effect, Sealand hoped to create a viable future for itself by making this fiction of piratical data havens into fact.

The individual charged with making Sealand a data haven was an MIT hacker dropout and radical libertarian named Ryan Lackey. Lackey had a reputation as the real thing: he was a committed cyberlibertarian, the new counterpart in some ways to Oliver Smedley in an earlier generation. In particular, like Smedley, Lackey was a devotee of tactics that might make financial transactions invisible to tax authorities, which now meant citizens' cryptography and online currency systems. He had just left a posting on a projected information haven in the West Indies island of Anguilla. He was named chief technology officer of the new venture, which started operations in summer 2000. He brought with him as CEO Sean Hastings, a thirty-two-year-old American libertarian who had been in on the same Anguilla project. Breathless press coverage abounded. It was said that the fort was full of high-end servers, and that it had a fast line-of-sight link to the mainland and thence up to satellites.[11] Some versions had it communicating with the satellites directly. Sealand became a poster child of data futurologists. It even emblazoned the cover of *Wired*, the house magazine of wannabe digerati. Whether or not the business itself succeeded, it was already clear that it had scored a major public-ity coup among futurologists of information.

But the data haven was less fortress in the sea than castle in the air. Lackey resigned in frustration in 2003, and took to the stage at a DefCon convention in Las Vegas to explain why. He had been frustrated by interference on the part of the Bates family, who in his portrayal sounded like a particularly quarrelsome branch of the Habsburgs. In particular, he had grated at their insistence on uphold-ing the principles of multinational copyright owners, which was to him unaccountable. But more than that, it seemed that the whole scheme had been poorly realized from the start. Far from being crammed with ultra-modern equipment, Sealand was lumbered with antiquated computers and a network link that remained slow and unreliable. A year later Lackey could be found in Iraq, selling ersatz Internet linkup services to forward operating base personnel of the U.S. Army as the country descended into the worst phase of the insurrection.

It seems plausible that the failure of the Sealand data haven reflected a distinction that has long plagued upstart media. The persistent suc-cess of pirate radio, in large part, depends on the fact that a transmit-ter is cheap to set up and readily portable. A data haven inevitably requires huge up-front investment. The only reason that information "wants to be free" is that it can ride atop very expensive data infra-structure, which can, for multinationals, be paid for incrementally. Moreover, not only is a data haven expensive to start; it also demands regular infusions of investment to keep it in sync with the state of the art. Sealand never had any way of achieving even the first of these. It never recovered from its failure, and in 2006 a fire destroyed what little equipment there was. The very survival of the principality seemed in doubt, for the first time in decades.

In early 2007, however, it seemed that a saviour might be at hand. The Swedish bit-torrent site The Pirate Bay launched a public appeal for funds to buy Sealand. The site's organizers were bent on combat-ing intellectual property restrictions in general, and, alongside form-ing their own political party in Sweden, they had decided to seize the opportunity to establish their own nation. In the event, their bid to purchase Sealand came to nothing. The appeal for funds—contributors were to get citizenship—raised far too little for a realistic bid. In any case, "Prince" Michael Bates told Canada's CBC that copyright pirates would make inappropriate suitors. The bid fell through, and The Pirate Bay returned to concentrating on its legal battles and its political campaigns within Sweden.

Yet the prospective alliance between Sealand and The Pirate Bay was an interesting moment in the continuing history of pirate media. Not least, it highlighted the fact that pirate media *had* a continuing history. They did not spring forth from nothing with the advent of digital networks. As Bates himself has noted, there are distinct parallels between the business of pirate radio in that earlier age and the business of this data haven, at least, in our own. They hint at a history that may account for some of the reputedly unique properties of digital creativity today. Unfortunately for Sealand, those properties have helped to make its own digital ambitions obsolete. Digital pirates do not need nations.

THE REPERCUSSIONS OF violent death are inescapable and lasting. Neither side could evade them after June 1966. But for Calvert's family they proved especially bitter. Continuing to run Radio City, struggling to head off threats to Shivering Sands, and seeking what she saw as a just outcome to the prosecution, Dorothy Calvert came to feel that she was living under surveillance. The family telephones, she grew convinced, were being tapped, and the mysterious break-ins at Welbeck Street and Wendens Ambo on the last night of Smedley's hearing seemed calculated to convey some terrible message. She heard rumors of more threats, and a journalist let her know that the government was keen to suppress news coverage of her, apparently by imposing a D-notice (an official request to the press not to publish about a given topic for national security reasons). It is all too easy to dismiss such anxieties. A D-notice in particular seems unlikely, as these were imposed only rarely and were, as far as is known, recorded. Yet the burglaries did happen. And the state did have an interest, more or less avowed, in learning how pirate stations like Radio City operated. The Post Office certainly made great efforts, some of them clandestine and only recently brought to light, to discredit and upend pirate enterprises. It is not implausible that in that era of political anxiety, Whitehall or the security services should try to lean on magazines to limit potentially unhelpful coverage—this certainly happened with regard to the seamen's strike at exactly this time. Many authorities had the power to listen in on private telephone lines, too, without the decisions to do so necessarily ending up in the historical record. (Recently they have begun to be publicly logged, and it turns out that in 2008 more than 500,000 formal requests were issued by various agencies to authorize phone surveillance.) And Pine and Perkins's experiment did seem to furnish solid evidence that their phones, at least, were indeed being monitored. Why not Dorothy Calvert's too?[12]

The purpose of this book is not to venture into these questions any more than it is to re-try Oliver Smedley. They are worth asking—just as one can legitimately wonder who Smedley's new investor was in spring 1966, and whether there were real plans to retake the fort later that year or in early 1967. But to pursue these mysteries too far would be to divert attention away from broader, deeper, and longer-range issues. In any case, the skills needed to answer them properly would seem to be those of the investigatory journalist or the private detective, not those of the historian—and certainly not those of this historian. What can be said here, however, is simply that if somebody did indeed authorize surveillance or other clandestine work, it was presumably because more was thought to be at stake than a simple case of manslaughter. And that perception—whoever held it—was correct. By 1966, varieties of piracy and varieties of propriety had confronted each other repeatedly ever since the introduction of broadcasting. The BBC system itself was created amid the first of them. That system stood to be redefined by the second—which Reg Calvert's death had made suddenly inevitable.

Pirate radio never vanished with the silencing of the stations around the British Isles in 1967. It persisted in various guises in continental Europe, and also in the United States (where, in the absence of a

public broadcasting system, it had very different political meanings).
Before long it had revived even in Britain, too. In the 1980s–90s it
became once again a prominent and lively cultural force. But just as
the BBC changed, so pirate stations too took on new and different
forms. By this point, such stations were typically land-based. They were
small-scale, short-range FM enterprises that moved around within
cities, dodging government inspectors. The lumbering ships of the
AM era were largely a memory—and occasionally rather more, as in
1984–85 when a Caroline veteran ran a short-lived new shipboard
station, Laser 558. In their place were London Greek Radio, LWR,
DBC, and JFM. Many were not commercial at all, at least in any conventional sense, and some promoted particular political messages.
One study recorded the existence of almost 150 in 1985 in Britain
alone, and no doubt it missed many more. By the mid-1990s, these
new generations of pirate radio stations had shaped whole genres of
popular music and culture, and Radio One occasionally tried to snare
their better DJs, as in the sixties. Pulp's invocation in the 1995 song
"Sorted for E's & Wizz," in which Londoners learn of an upcoming
rave from pirate radio, captures a moment from that culture. In the
early 2000s, the British authorities were carrying out almost 1,500
raids annually on pirate stations of various kinds. By then, most of
the popular music that people listened to was a product, directly or
indirectly, of pirate radio.[13]

Now, in 2011, the events central to *Death of a Pirate* fall almost exactly
halfway between the invention of radio broadcasting and the present.
The history of radio piracy is what links the previous two moments
of transformation, in the 1920s and the 1960s, with our own time. A
third crisis of piracy is due.

PIRATE RADIO HAS become one aspect of a general cultural phenomenon of enormous significance worldwide: the advent of distributed creativity. In a world of digital networks, wired and wireless,
authorship and publishing are starting to dissolve, and the distinction
between reception and reproduction begins to lose any self-evidence

it once had. Common to the areas of contention in today's entertainment, media, and research enterprises, from music to science, are heavily moralized accounts of the nature of creative work itself. An "ethos" of openness or access is upheld as virtuous because true to the intrinsic character of genuine creative authorship. If there is hope, today's digerati hold, it lies with the proles—or the technologically literate ones, at least.[14]

Today it is increasingly evident that what is distinctive about our information age is not just a mode of storage and communication, or a technology of interconnection, but moral commitments and practices that have become commonplace and now seem inextricable from the technologies. They are definitive constituents of the digital revolution. Popular access and popular authorship are major cases in point. In the formative years of popular computing in the 1970s and 1980s, major debates took place among technorati about these principles, often in the form of exchanges about a putative "hacker ethic." Its elements included a rebellious stance toward intellectual property monopolies, a defiance of purportedly obsolete bureaucracies, and a pseudo-libertarian insistence on the primacy of creative artists over communal rules. By the nineties some of these convictions had been domesticated. Shorn of some of their earlier tabloid associations, they were now widely—if still controversially—recognized as characteristic of the generation that the Internet would bring into being. Sealand's bid for the limelight exemplified this. Such elements of the information age as these did not originate only with the seventies hackers and their antagonists. They had an older, more popular and yet less familiar history.

What is important is not just that this familiar moral tone is a product of history. It is the particular bit of history from which it has emerged that matters. The moral philosophy of digital libertarianism is usually thought to have derived from late sixties American counterculture.[15] That is true only in part. Digital libertarianism derives at least as directly from a very different history and politics—those of radio, and in particular British radio. That is the history of Ronald Coase and Arnold Plant, of Leonard Plugge and Peter Eckersley. It is also, at a pivotal point, the history of Oliver Smedley and Reginald Calvert.

Arguments about pirate media have never been solely economic or utilitarian, on either side. They have also been epistemological. That is, proponents challenge the kind and quality of knowledge that it is possible for humans to have. Hayek and his side famously argued that central planning constrained freedoms on the basis of an unsupportable claim to scientific knowledge. Followers of Coase would add that public intervention constrained communication and creativity—including science itself—on the same fragile basis. The *local*, discrete character of social reality was for them "the central theoretical problem of all social science."[16] What solves that problem must be a practice, not a theory, and one that could only be pursued by many people acting out in the field, not by one person in an office. For Hayek, the practical solution to the multifarious nature of society was the price system. But it would be "more than a metaphor," he himself said, to describe that system as "a system of telecommunications." What he left unsaid—and this is an inexplicable silence—is that the telecommunications system must not itself be an interested party. A monopoly in this realm, as no other monopoly, would corrupt social knowledge and make a Hayekian economy impossible. The assault on creative monopolies thus reflected imperatives buried deep in the heart of neoclassical economics. In the eyes of figures like Arnold Plant, the assault on the BBC was the same battle as that against the relentless expansion of copyrights and patents, and both were ultimately about the nature of the coming information society.

That assault reached a climax in 1966. During the early sixties, after the Pilkington Report, it looked as though a long campaign had just been lost. Plant, Coase, and their allies notwithstanding, the government was set against deregulating media. *De jure*, the BBC reigned. But at just this moment millions of citizens began using miniaturized, portable radios to tune out the monopoly broadcaster and search for unpredictable, semi-licit, and frankly commercial stations. Smedley's cohort saw in this the possibility for a thoroughgoing challenge to an entire political and economic system. Their Project Atlanta would begin by undermining information monopolies. Piracy for them was to be first a business force, then a cultural force, and finally a political force. It promised to transform media in Britain and Europe, and thereby become the thin end of a counterrevolutionary wedge in economic and political culture. The immediate objective was the untrammelled commercialization of the broadcast media; the more distant aim, a free market transformation of Britain itself. The Institute of Economic Affairs made this point explicit in its publications of the era. We know now that in the middle term, at least, the Coasians won on all fronts—and that pirate radio helped make Thatcherism what it was. But another objective took shape in the process, and perhaps an even broader one: the realization of an ideal of distributed creativity.

The ideal of distributed creativity is the principle that in our own day lies behind enterprises like "free and open source" software and the "open access" movement in science. It holds that creative achievement is no more likely to be best achieved by centralized systems of management than political or social achievement would be. Rather, creative endeavor is better visualized and organized as a process dispersed through communities, such that the irreducibly distinct perspectives and skills of disparate citizens can be brought to bear. Authorship on this model is an achievement by individuals acting collectively, and the rewards and responsibilities it incurs should reflect that. The technical abilities of the Internet help make distributed creativity of this kind practicable. But network cultures were mooted long before in the context of rivalries over radio, by radical experts like Peter Eckersley. Moreover, the economics of digital networked creativity, it has been argued, are best examined in terms pioneered by Coase in the mid-twentieth century. And the tradition of radio experiment represented here by Reg Calvert made the concept credible, by providing it with a history of enterprising practice as well as ideology. To understand why we now make the digital revolution into the realization of the ideal of distributed creativity, we need to appreciate why the ideal *already* commanded support. We need to tackle histories as long and intricate as this.

On the other side, the maintenance of cultural quality as well as

diversity—that old concern of critics like Richard Hoggart, and before
them of the BBC's founders—has never gone extinct. It too takes on
new force in a networked world. Questions of value, trust, probity, and
objectivity have never been as pressing as they are today. This does not
mean that the old principle of a single privileged information channel is tenable. It never was: as we have seen, the BBC was in practice
always one voice among many, several of which were always "piratical."
But after the radical changes that Reg Calvert's death brought about,
the tone of that voice changed permanently. The corporation began
to cultivate an ethos of skepticism toward authority that was largely
unknown before, and that extended to investing heavily not only in
creative works but in research to hold powers to account. The shift
came about partly as a result of having to face—and incorporate—
rivals. It also involved a fundamental transformation in approaches to
the practice of listening. What deserves respect in our day is the kind
of public broadcaster that emerged then. The BBC after 1967 became
a participant in a diverse media environment, seeking—on the whole
successfully—to blend a mandate for cultural quality with a place in a
new realm of alternatives and competitors. As it did, it found a skeptical, critical voice that it had hitherto lacked. It is perhaps ironic that
the virtues of an authoritative public broadcaster with a rich ethos
of service should become clearer precisely when its monopoly lapses,
but this is indeed what occurred. Given the real anxieties we face in
the networked society, its virtues are clear. But it is fragile. It needs
defending.

In short, the culture of information is not defined solely by technology and law. It is a matter too of norms, conventions, and values,
in three principal domains. One cluster centers on the notions of
the public good and the quality of the common culture. A second
concerns the optimization of creative endeavor, especially through
popular practices of research and experiment. And the third relates
to the balance of property rights and public access, both to ideas
and to a medium itself. All three derive from concerns central to
the history of radio. The first issue took shape around the notion
that a public monopoly was essential to the use of broadcasting

for cultural improvement, and thereby to the future of civilization itself. The second originated in the popular experimenters who were the first radio pirates; it is now conceived of in terms of the distributed creativity made possible by the digital networks. The third was initially theorized in the work of Arnold Plant and Ronald Coase—work inspired by the problems of British radio that resulted in arguments about intellectual property and spectrum allocation which would define the new information economy in the United State as well as in Britain. In each of these three domains, the contests traced in *Death of a Pirate* played a critically important part in defining our sensiblities in the age of networked information.

In the early twenty-first century, it looked for a while as though big media organizations like the BBC would reign. The digitization of everything seemed set to coincide with the corporatization of everything. To produce worthwhile online environments or multimedia entertainments required such massive resources that only multinationals could participate. But we are finding now that small media and small authors have a great future too. Diverse and tiny creative inputs can result in a more dynamic whole than uniform but monolithic offices. At the time of writing, the biggest deal in digital communications is also the smallest: Twitter is a format that allows only 140 characters to be posted at a time. It may well not last. But the experience of a small and simple medium capturing a major cultural moment is scarcely new, and doubtless it will happen again. We are entering a situation, plausibly, in which "stations" for distribution—not just of music but of texts, images, films, and programs—can be maintained by anybody. When every laptop or iPhone becomes a pirate station, that old question faced in their different ways by Reith, Coase, Plant, and Hoggart—the question of how to create and sustain the good society—returns in a new form.

Radio has an important place in the answer. The transition to networked digital media should create a golden age for this, the original "new medium." All the old arguments about ether scarcity are obviously otiose, and it becomes possible to listen from anywhere to "local" stations based in towns and villages across the world. But the risk

SOURCES AND ACKNOWLEDGMENTS

That the story of Reg Calvert's death can now be told is partly the result of a strange characteristic of British state record keeping. The papers generated in major criminal cases are preserved, but they are generally embargoed from public sight for a generation or so. I happened to be at the National Archives at Kew (then the Public Record Office) just after the files relating to Oliver Smedley's trial emerged from that embargo at the beginning of 2001, and I came across them at that time. The dossier, which extends to almost 1,000 pages, centers on the events leading up to the crime—if, indeed, it was a crime. It permits a finely detailed reconstruction of events, down to the very words spoken by the protagonists in the days, hours, and minutes leading up to the catastrophe—if you trust their testimony. But, more than that, it also contains a huge tranche of evidence about the world that both shooter and victim inhabited: the world of pirate radio. It is this that makes the file so valuable. Embracing testimony from every rank of participant, from managing directors in Mayfair to stevedores in Chatham and Whitstable, it throws light on all aspects of pirate radio at a moment when that phenomenon seemed to outsiders to be at a euphoric peak, but was in fact approaching a crisis. The investigation was carried out quickly and under sometimes risky circumstances, but it garnered recognition within the police hierarchy as an exemplary piece of work. Not much of it was adduced in the legal proceedings that ensued, however. Now, a generation later, it proves immensely revealing of the culture of pirate media from which the tragedy sprang. It provides raw materials from which something approaching an anthropology of that culture can be created.

In another respect, too, the police investigation that followed Reg Calvert's death proves valuable, and unexpectedly so. In the courtroom, jurists and jurors alike found Oliver Smedley—a decorated military officer, senior politician, and financial expert—an immediately comprehensible figure, deserving of a certain presumptive respect. So did the press. Kitty Black, too—well-spoken, urbane, multilingual—was a commanding presence. By contrast, Calvert, a self-made entrepreneur with a northern upbringing, enjoyed no such implicit deference. And, of course, he could not speak for himself. Much more time was therefore spent picking apart Calvert's activities, motivations, and character than was devoted to Smedley's, and always in a critical light. The police investigation was not altogether innocent of this predisposition. But the detectives do seem to have been more judicious, as it were, than the judiciary. Perhaps because they were accustomed to moving between social classes and demimondes, and had seen many sharp practices that spanned such distinctions, they were less prepared to accept an apparently authoritative figure at face value. By contrast, they registered explicitly their regard for Calvert's widow, whom they found resilient, shrewd, and trustworthy—to the extent of being prepared to call out the Royal Navy on her word. The files they kept thus act as a useful counterweight to the sometimes partial trial records.

Yet the police perspective is, for all that, a perspective. It rests on the kinds of questions detectives ask, and on the training and attitudes that they bring to their task. In this case, the portrait compiled by Detective Inspector J. A. Barker and his colleagues is itself partial in one important respect. It was naturally focused on immediate events and their causes. A longer historical perspective—one extending across decades—is essential if we are to understand not only what happened in June 1966 but also why it mattered. We must look at it in a broader and deeper context, as well as in its fine detail. This I have tried to do.

All the details recounted in *Death of a Pirate* are, I believe, true—at least, by historians' standards. That is, they are all attested in the historical record. This applies particularly to the words spoken by participants. I have never concocted them. Where dialogue is reconstructed, the words come from testimony recorded either at the time (by telephone operators, for example) or in statements recorded very shortly afterwards. Sometimes I have converted indirect speech in the statements into direct speech, but only where the conversion seemed straightforward and uncontroversial. Very occasionally, I have elided repetitive passages or reordered a sequence of sentences slightly to make the meaning clearer. Sometimes I have had to deal with differences between several witnesses' accounts of the same conversations, and in such cases I have tried hard to reconcile the various accounts to come up with a plausible reconstruction. But even here the differences involved have proven to be, in fact, rather inconsequential.

There is a problem with this evidence, however. Some of the speech attested in writing by participants like Kitty Black is dismissed by Reg Calvert's family as intrinsically implausible. They insist that Calvert never called women "love," for example, as Black said he called her; nor was he given to boasting about his prowess in chemical experiments. And he was unlikely to have talked about rising from the slums because in fact he had done no such thing. I do not feel qualified to adjudicate this question. In the end, I suspect it may be beyond adjudication, at least by historians like me. But to mitigate its effects I have tried to favor speech recorded by more than one witness, and that written down as soon as possible after the event, such that collusion was less likely to have occurred. I have also noted what seem to me to be the most significant issues at the points where they occur.

In the course of researching this book I have been privileged to meet with surviving participants in the pirate enterprises and their family members. For someone fortunate enough not to have encountered violence at close quarters, the experience has been a sobering one. It has brought home to me the extent to which violent death has repercussions that may not register in formal records but nevertheless remain acute, and do not attenuate over time. I am all the more grateful, then, that Dorothy Calvert and Susan Moore were willing to revive those memories for my benefit. They read through my original draft with a fine critical judgment. When Mrs. Calvert died in 2010, as this book was in proofs, Britain lost one of the most important, if largely unsung, figures in the sixties transformation of its broadcast media. So it is all the more necesary to note that she remained convinced that a major miscarriage of justice occurred in 1966—one made possible by unknown forces behind the scenes. Although extremely generous with their time and knowledge, neither she nor Susan Moore could in the end accept the account of the clash between Reg Calvert and Oliver Smedley given here, and they should in no way be thought to have endorsed it.

Oliver Smedley's son and daughter, Charles Smedley and Emma Currie, were most helpful in filling out his sometimes tangled history, and contributed their own comments about the text as it developed. Michael Bates of Sealand offered his own help. Colin Nichol provided important last-minute information on Kitty Black. And in a remote Cornwall farmhouse Mandy Fairman Dick, the widow of Austin Churton Fairman (Mike Raven), rustled up financial documents about Project Atlanta without which the story would have missed a crucial element. Finally, Ronald Coase, still going strong in his late nineties, was kind enough to meet with me and talk about his midcentury critique of the BBC. Others, too many to mention, have also selflessly provided advice, guidance, evidence, and corrections. I am grateful to them all.

Archival materials have been used from, among other places, the Mont Pelerin Society and the Institute for Economic Affairs holdings at the Hoover Institution, Stanford University; the British Library; the Royal Mail Archives; the BBC Written Archives Centre; Cambridge University Library; and the University of Chicago Library. John Blundell provided important help with the history of the IEA. My thanks to all of these.

I have presented earlier versions of this story at Northwestern University, Yale University, the University of Michigan, and the Google campus in Mountain View, California. I am indebted to the audiences at these events for their questions and suggestions.

My thanks also go to Steve Forman at W. W. Norton for much useful advice in shepherding the book into print; and to David Miller of the Garamond Agency for help at many points along the way.

In order to preserve the flow of the narrative in telling the central part of this story, I have tried not to interrupt it with extensive notes detailing exact source locations. I hope to provide a full citation record online for readers interested in following up specific details. But unless otherwise stated, information about the shooting itself and its circumstances comes from the files at the National Archives, MEPO 2/10939 and DPP 2/4207. Evidence about the broader pirate radio world can be found in a number of publications by amateur and ex-pirate authors, who have collected and made accessible huge tranches of material that would otherwise have been lost. The two most important books from this community are Mike Leonard's *From International Waters: 60 Years of Offshore Broadcasting* (Heswall, Liverpool: Forest Press, 1996) and Keith Skues's *Pop Went the Pirates II* (Horning, Norfolk: Lambs' Meadow, 2009). Skues was a DJ on Radio Caroline South, who gives a vivid account of life aboard Atlanta's old ship, the *Mi Amigo*. Robert Chapman's *Selling the Sixties: The Pirates and Pop Music Radio* (London: Routledge, 1992) is the only real academic study, but it is an essential work. In addition, enthusiasts have made substantial archives of photographs, documents, memories, and other material accessible online. The most notable entry points to this trove are *Offshore Echos* (www.offshoreechos.com); Jon Myers's *Pirate Radio Hall of Fame* (www.offshoreradio.co.uk); and the site maintained by ex-City man Bob Le-Roi (www.bobleroi.co.uk). I am grateful to the proprietors of these sites for their assistance.

I have provided more substantial references for my broader contextual argument about the history of broadcasting from the origins of the BBC to the transition to digital culture. It seems appropriate to be more explicit about sources here for three reasons: the argument is fairly provocative; it employs sometimes obscure or hard-to-find evidence; and it rests on my own readings of material that others have interpreted differently. Yet I have still attempted not to overwhelm the reader. These notes too are selective. They are intended to document the argument, not to provide a survey of the relevant literature.

Finally, a note is necessary on the term "liberal." I call the ideology of Friedrich Hayek and his followers (free trade, laissez-faire, anti-monopolist) "liberal," in accordance with their own usage. When I mean to refer to the Liberal Party—Britain's third party, which in the postwar era has embraced more collective, social democratic principles—I have capitalized the word. The modern American usage, in which "liberal" refers (often in a denigrating sense) to those very social democratic principles, was foreign to the Britain of the 1950s– 60s and is never intended in this book. Similarly, I avoid the term "neo-liberal," which is a later coinage.

NOTES

PROLOGUE   JUNE 21, 1966

1. For my use of the sources describing this confrontation, see the Sources and Acknowledgments section above. Here I have amalgamated accounts by Pamela Thorburn and Alan Arnold, with additional material from the others named, as recorded in statements made soon after the event; I have favored statements made earlier rather than later. The sources are all in the National Archives, Kew, MEPO 2/10939 and DPP 2/4207 (cited below as DPP).

1   A PIRATE PEOPLE

1. I. McIntyre, *The Expense of Glory: A Life of John Reith* (London: HarperCollins, 1994), 114–18.
2. Ibid., 56–57, 61–72, 114–16.
3. A. Johns, *Piracy: The Intellectual Property Wars from Gutenberg to Gates* (Chicago: University of Chicago Press, 2010). Readers wanting a more detailed account of the events in this chapter will find it in chapter 13 of *Piracy*.
4. Asa Briggs, *The History of Broadcasting in the United Kingdom*, 5 vols. (Oxford: Oxford University Press, 1961–95), I, 219–21.
5. Sir Oliver Lodge, *Talks About Wireless* (London: Cassell & Co., 1925), ix–xii, 3–11, 239–43.
6. Briggs, *History*, I, 229–30.
7. Ibid., I, 68–85.
8. P. P. Eckersley, *The Power Behind the Microphone* (London: Jonathan Cape, 1941), 54, 62.

9. J. H. Morecroft, "Will the British receiver license system fail?" *Radio Broadcast*, 7:1 (May 1925), 39–40.
10. "Marconi's next quest," *Daily Mail*, March 27, 1923.
11. C. A. Lewis, *Broadcasting from Within* (London: G. Newnes, 1924), 48; P. Scannell and D. Cardiff, *A Social History of British Broadcasting.* Vol. 1, *1922–1939: Serving the Nation* (Oxford: Blackwell, 1991), 278–79.
12. J. Rose, *The Intellectual Life of the British Working Classes* (New Haven, CT: Yale University Press, 2001), 202–06.
13. Briggs, *History*, I, 250.
14. *BBC Handbook 1928* (London: BBC, 1928), 350.
15. R. McKibbin, *Classes and Cultures: England 1918–1951* (Oxford: Oxford University Press, 1998), 457–62; C. Hilliard, *To Exercise Our Talents: The Democratization of Writing in Britain* (Cambridge, MA: Harvard University Press, 2006), 235–36.
16. D. C. Thomson, *Radio Is Changing Us: A Survey of Radio Development and Its Problems in Our Changing World* (London: Watts, 1937), 63–64.
17. Briggs, *History*, I, 352–60.
18. McIntyre, *The Expense of Glory*, 200.
19. R. H. Coase, *British Broadcasting: A Study in Monopoly* (London: Longmans for the London School of Economics, 1950 [distributed in the United States by Harvard University Press]), 46.
20. R. Skidelsky, *John Maynard Keynes*, 3 vols. (London: Macmillan, 1983–2000), II, 225–29.
21. S. Shapin, *A Social History of Truth: Civility and Science in Seventeenth-Century England* (Chicago: University of Chicago Press, 1994); Shapin, *The Scientific Life: A Moral History of a Late Modern Vocation* (Chicago: University of Chicago Press, 2008) 21–91.

2 ETHEREAL ENTERPRISE

1. K. Skues, *Pop Went the Pirates II* (Horning, Norfolk: Lambs' Meadow, 2009), 1–3.
2. S. Street, *Crossing the Ether: British Public Service Radio and Commercial Competition, 1922–1945* (Eastleigh, Hants: J. Libbey, 2006), 40–41.
3. See, e.g., the advertisement in *Radio Pictorial*, August 19, 1938, 20–21.
4. For Andorra, see the rather breathless S. Athiel, *Conquérants des ondes! L'Incroyable aventure de Radio-Toulouse et Radio-Andorre* (Toulouse, France: Editions Privat, 2008).
5. For Plugge, see K. Wallis, *And the World Listened: The Biography of Captain Leonard F. Plugge, a Pioneer of Commercial Radio* (Tiverton, Devon: Kelly, 2008).

6. Street, *Crossing the Ether*, 148–49.

7. R. Chenevier, "La naissance et l'histoire de Radio-Normandie," *l'Illustration*, 97:5024 (June 17, 1939); J. B. Cameron, "Radio Normandy as I saw it," *Radio Pictorial*, July 7, 1939. (Cameron was publicity manager for IBC.)

8. *This Is the I.B.C.* (London: IBC, August 1939); *Radio Normandy Programme Book* (London: IBC, July 1939), 34; Mike Leonard, *From International Waters: 60 Years of Offshore Broadcasting* (Heswall, Liverpool: Forest Press, 1996), 3–5; McKibbin, *Classes and Cultures*, 463; Wallis, *And the World Listened*, 168–69.

9. Wallis, *And the World Listened*, 168–91.

10. For Radio Luxembourg, see D. Dominguez-Muller, *Radio-Luxembourg: Histoire d'un média privé d'envergure européenne* (Paris: l'Harmattan, 2007).

11. Street, *Crossing the Ether*, 147.

12. G. A. Codding, Jr., *The International Telecommunication Union: An Experiment in International Cooperation* (Leiden: E. J. Brill, 1952), 139–40; Briggs, *History*, I, 315–18.

13. Briggs, *History*, II, 360; Dominguez-Muller, *Radio-Luxembourg*, 73–76.

14. "Radio Luxembourg: An international broadcasting problem," *Wireless World*, 23:15 (October 13, 1933), 306.

15. Briggs, *History*, II, 339–69.

16. For a general account, see G. A. Slater, "Relay," *Relay Association Journal*, 1:6 (March 1936), 14–16, 22.

17. Editorial, *Radio Relay Review*, 1:14 (November 1933), 1; Street, *Crossing the Ether*, 29.

18. G. Young, "New Year's message," *Relay Association Journal*, 1:4 (January 1936), 2.

19. Editorial, *Radio Relay Review*, 1:7 (April 1933), 1–2.

20. "Should they pick and choose?" *Radio Relay Review*, 1:11 (August 1933), 1–2.

21. G. H. Watson, "Unpopular programmes—and why they are disliked," *Relay Association Journal*, 4:3 (July 1938), 337–38; B. J. White, "Unpopular programmes," *Relay Association Journal*, 4:4 (August 1938), 346–48; *Radio Relay Review*, 1:1 (August 1932), 23.

22. H. MacCallum, "The B.B.C. point of view," *Radio Relay Review*, 1:5 (February 1933), 6–8.

23. Ullswater Committee Report (Cmd. 5091) (London: HMSO, 1936), 39, §130. In general, see Briggs, *History*, II, 356–60.

24. G. Fane, Letter to the editor, *Relay Association Journal*, 1:7 (April 1936), 16.

25. R. R. Gooding, "How to minimise disconnections," *Relay Association Journal*, 1:1 (October 1935), 22–23; A. D. Thomas, "Disconnections," *Relay Association Journal*, 1:4 (January 1936), 22; H. J. Boon, "We open a new relay station in London," *Relay Association Journal*, 1:4 (January 1936), 18–20.

26. T. Toward, "Supervising the programmes," *Relay Association Journal*, 2:2 (June 1936), 32–35.

27. J. W. C. Robinson, "New Year's message," *Relay Association Journal*, 2:9 (January 1937), 202–04, 206.

28. Eckersley, *The Power Behind the Microphone*, 195–96.

29. M. Eckersley, *Prospero's Wireless: A Biography of Peter Pendleton Eckersley, Pioneer of Radio and the Art of Broadcasting*, 3rd ed. (Romsey, Hants: Myles Books, 1999), xi–27.

30. Ibid., 149–50.

31. Ibid., 167, 187–88; McIntyre, *The Expense of Glory*, 172–73.

32. Eckersley, *Prospero's Wireless*, 337–38.

33. Ibid., 324.

34. E.L., "Concerning television," *Relay Association Journal*, 1:5 (February 1936), 10; Coase, *British Broadcasting*, 78–79. See also Eckersley's letter to *The Times*, June 22, 1939, 12.

35. See issues of the *Relay Association Journal* from 5:1 (May 1939) onwards.

36. Eckersley, *Prospero's Wireless*, 401–55.

37. R. Skidelsky, *Oswald Mosley* (New York: Holt, Rinehart & Winston, 1975), 250.

38. Ibid., 330–31.

39. H. J. P. Bergmeier and R. E. Lotz, *Hitler's Airwaves: The Inside Story of Nazi Radio Broadcasting and Propaganda Swing* (New Haven, CT: Yale University Press, 1997), 96–97.

40. W. J. West, *Truth Betrayed* (London: Duckworth, 1987), 120–24; A. De Courcy, *Diana Mosley: Mitford Beauty, British Fascist, Hitler's Angel* (London: Chatto & Windus, 2003), 179–83, 188–91.

41. Bergmeier and Lotz, *Hitler's Airwaves*, 8–9.

42. West, *Truth Betrayed*, 111–14; Eckersley, *Prospero's Wireless*, 358.

43. West, *Truth Betrayed*, 116–19.

44. *Plan de Montreux* (Berne: Bureau de l'Union Internationale des Télécommunications, 1939).

45. De Courcy, *Diana Mosley*, 195–96. It is a small but significant fact that in his utopian vision of a wired future, published several years later, Eckersley still ascribed the role of the benevolent information provider to Wire Broadcasting.

46. Eckersley, *Prospero's Wireless*, 373, 377, 411, 437, 453.

47. Bergmeier and Lotz, *Hitler's Airwaves*, 84–85, 95–96.

3 POLTERGEISTS AND POLITICS

1. L. Gordon, *The Public Corporation in Great Britain* (Oxford: Oxford University Press, 1938 [originally a 1936 D. Phil. thesis]), 1–2, 13–15, 316; Scannell and Cardiff, *A Social History of British Broadcasting.* Vol. I, 6; *Britain's Industrial Future: Being the Report of the Liberal Industrial Inquiry* (London: Ernest Benn, 1928), 63, 75; G. D. H. Cole, *Principles of Economic Planning* (London: Macmillan & Co., 1935), 121; H. Dalton, *Practical Socialism for Britain* (London: G. Routledge & Sons, 1935), 98–99, 102–04, 141–42; W. A. Robson, "The British Broadcasting Corporation," in Robson, ed., *Public Enterprise: Developments in Social Ownership and Control in Great Britain* (London: Allen & Unwin, 1937), 73–104, esp. 73–74; Sir A. Salter, "Planned socialisation and world trade," *The Listener,* December 12, 1934, 978–79; E. Goodman, *Forms of Public Ownership and Control* (London: Christophers, 1951), 20–22.

2. Sir William Beveridge, *Social Insurance and Allied Policies* (Cmd. 6404) (London: HMSO, 1942), 6–7.

3. "Contact with listeners," *The Listener,* 18:460 (November 3, 1937), 946.

4. For the IBC, advertisers were listed in an annual *Radio Normandy Programme Book.*

5. Briggs, *History,* II, 503.

6. R. Dahrendorf, *LSE: A History of the London School of Economics and Political Science 1895–1995* (Oxford: Oxford University Press, 1995), 210–23, 298; A. Ebenstein, *Friedrich Hayek: A Biography* (New York: Palgrave, 2001), 55, 59–61; R. Skidelsky, *John Maynard Keynes,* 3 vols. (London: Macmillan, 1983–2000), II, 454–59.

7. R. H. Coase, "Arnold Plant," in Coase, *Essays on Economics and Economists* (Chicago: University of Chicago Press, 1994), 176–84.

8. A. Plant, "Trends in business administration," *Economica,* 35 (February 1932), 45–62.

9. Briggs, *History,* II, 227–49; Street, *Crossing the Ether,* 138–39, 289–91.

10. H. Price and R. S. Lambert, *The Haunting of Cashen's Gap: A Modern "Miracle" Investigated* (London: Methuen, 1935).

11. Coase, *British Broadcasting,* 142–43, 145 n38.

12. R. S. Lambert, *Ariel and All His Quality: An Impression of the BBC from Within* (London: Victor Gollancz, 1940), 237.

13. Sir Ernest Benn, *Modern Government* (New York: Appleton-Century, 1936), 64.

14. Lambert, *Ariel and All His Quality,* 315–17.

15. Briggs, *History,* II, 472–76.

16. H. Jennings and W. Gill, *Broadcasting in Everyday Life: A Survey of the Social Effects of the Coming of Broadcasting* (London: BBC, 1939), esp. 7, 39–40.

17. R. Silvey, *Who's Listening? The Story of BBC Audience Research* (London: Allen & Unwin, 1974), 13–86. For insights into how radical the change was in the BBC's knowledge of listeners, compare H. Matheson, "Listener research in broadcasting," *Sociological Review*, 27:4 (October 1935), 408–22, and M. A. Hamilton, "The influence of radio on social life and habits," *B.B.C. Quarterly*, III:2 (July 1948), 93–102, esp. 100–02.

18. "Testing listeners' tastes," *The Listener*, 18:445 (July 21, 1937), 122.

19. *BBC Yearbook* (London: BBC, 1933), 72; Coase, *British Broadcasting*, 76–77; Briggs, *History*, II, 485, 494.

20. Briggs, *History*, II, 503.

21. *Report of the Special Board of Inquiry* (Cmd. 5337) (London: HMSO, 1936).

22. *Hansard*, December 17, 1936, 2727–81; Coase, *British Broadcasting*, 86–88; Briggs, *History*, II, 512.

23. F. A. Hayek, "Economics and knowledge," *Economica*, n.s. 4:13 (February 1937), 33–54; B. Caldwell, *Hayek's Challenge: An Intellectual Biography of F. A. Hayek* (Chicago: University of Chicago Press, 2004), 205–31; S. Kresge and L. Wenar, eds., *Hayek on Hayek: An Autobiographical Dialogue* (Chicago: University of Chicago Press, 1994), 92.

24. "Nazi-Socialism," in F. A. Hayek, *The Road to Serfdom: Text and Documents*, ed. B. Caldwell (Chicago: University of Chicago Press, 2007 [1944]), 245–48.

25. "Freedom and the economic system," in F. A. Hayek, *Socialism and War: Essays, Documents, Reviews*, ed. B. Caldwell (Chicago: University of Chicago Press, 1997), 181–88, 189–211.

26. Caldwell, Introduction, in Hayek, *Road to Serfdom*, 1–33, esp. 3–23.

27. M. Polanyi, *Personal Knowledge: Towards a Post-Critical Philosophy* (Chicago: University of Chicago Press, 1974 [1958]).

28. Hayek, *Road to Serfdom*, 175–77; Hayek, "Planning, Science, and Freedom" (1941), in *Socialism and War*, 213–20.

29. R. Cockett, *Thinking the Unthinkable: Think-Tanks and the Economic Counter-Revolution 1931–1983* (London: HarperCollins, 1994), 82–84.

30. Hayek, *Road to Serfdom*, 208–09; Ebenstein, *Hayek*, 56.

31. J. Shearmur, "Hayek, *The Road to Serfdom*, and the British Conservatives," *Journal of the History of Economic Thought*, 28:3 (September 2006), 309–14.

32. C. Eade, ed., *Victory: War Speeches by the Right Hon. Winston S. Churchill* (London: Cassell & Co., 1946), 186–99; M. Gilbert, *Never Despair: Winston S. Churchill 1945–1965* (New York: Houghton Mifflin, 1988), 32–42; C. R. Attlee, *Purpose and Policy: Selected Speeches* (London: Hutchinson, 1947), 3–12.

33. H. Grisewood, "Response and responsibility," *B.B.C. Quarterly*, IV:3 (October 1949), 165–69.

34. E. S. Austin, *The Times*, July 16, 1946, 5.

35. H. H. Wilson, *Pressure Group: The Campaign for Commercial Television* (London: Secker & Warburg, 1961), 135–36 and n.

36. A. C. Turner, *Free Speech and Broadcasting* (Oxford: Blackwell, 1943), 11; Sir Ernest Benn, *The B.B.C. Monopoly* (London: Society of Individualists, 1944 [1941]).

37. K. Adam, "The press, the B.B.C. and the public," *B.B.C. Quarterly*, II:2 (July 1947), 71–76, esp. 75.

38. G. Orwell, *Essays*, ed. J. Carey (New York: Knopf, 2002), 628–29, 593–94, 362, 1234. It is worth noting that Orwell resigned from the BBC's Indian service not because he believed its propagandizing efficient in any such totalitarian sense but because he thought it futile.

39. *The Economist*, October 28, 1944, 564–65; November 4, 1944, 597–98; November 11, 1944, 630–31; and November 18, 1944, 660–62. See also *The Economist*, January 5, 1946, 8, and June 29, 1946, 1035–36.

40. Sir F. Ogilvie, "Future of the B.B.C.," *The Times*, June 26, 1946, 5. Another complaint centering on the monopoly is "The B.B.C. marks time," *The Round Table*, 36 (1945–46), 323–29.

41. Wilson, *Pressure Group*, 169; A. Plant, "Property in programmes," *BBC Quarterly*, VI (Spring 1951), 18–24; Plant, "The New Commerce in Ideas and Intellectual Property" (1953), in his *Selected Economic Essays and Addresses*, 87–116; *Report of the Committee on Broadcasting, 1960* (Cmd. 1753, 1962).

42. E. F. Durbin, *New Jerusalems: The Labour Party and the Economics of Democratic Socialism* (London: RKP, 1985), 136.

43. Coase, *British Broadcasting*, 52–53, 96n, 142–43, 191, 195–96; R. H. Coase, "A B.B.C. Enquiry?" *The Spectator*, 6149 (May 3, 1946), 446–47.

44. S. Lloyd, "Minority Report," *Report of the Broadcasting Committee, 1949* (Cmd. 8116, 1950–51), 201–10; Churchill College, Cambridge: Selwyn Lloyd Papers (SELO) 6/39; Wilson, *Pressure Group*, 56–57.

45. G. Longden, "Let's Look into This: Some Thoughts on Television," MS at Churchill College.

46. G. Bell to S. Lloyd, November 24, 1953, SELO 6/44.

47. S. Lloyd, "The future of broadcasting," *National and English Review*, 136:820 (June 1951); "Monopoly in Radio?" *The Economist*, January 20, 1951, 115; "Jack" [Profumo?] to Lloyd, February 26, 1952, on "The future of British Broadcasting": Churchill, SELO.

48. Cockett, *Thinking the Unthinkable*, 102–05.

4 THE ABOMINABLE NO-MAN

1. Recommendation for O. Smedley to be awarded the Military Cross: National Archives, WO 373/49.

2. R. Brown and B. Anthony, *A Victorian Film Enterprise: The History of the British Mutoscope and Biograph Company, 1897–1915* (Trowbridge, Wilts.: Flicks Books, 1999), 67; C. Smedley, *Crusaders* (London: Duckworth, 1929), 4–5; W. H. Sherman, *Used Books: Marking Readers in Renaissance England* (Philadelphia: University of Pennsylvania Press, 2008), 170–76.

3. O. Smedley, *The Abominable No-Men* (London: Alexander Publications, n.d. [1952]).

4. "Young Liberals," *The Guardian*, March 17, 1959, 6.

5. "Differences in Commonwealth and foreign debates," *The Guardian*, September 21, 1957, 2.

6. "Free-for-all on free trade," *The Guardian*, September 20, 1958, 2; F. Boyd, "Order prevails at assembly," *The Guardian*, September 30, 1960, 1; "Common market challenge for agriculture," *The Guardian*, September 23, 1961, 3; F. Boyd, "Buoyant Liberals crush critical minority," *The Guardian*, September 23, 1961, 1.

7. *The Times*, March 5, 1954, 9.

8. *The Times*, February 19, 1966, 9.

9. P. Croome, "This man says 'Enoch Powell is my disciple,'" *Cambridge Evening News*, June 4, 1976, 23; L. Abelson, "Would you pay £29 to get rich quick?" *Sunday Express*, June 18, 1972; Prufrock, "Portrait of an English eccentric," *Sunday Times*, February 6, 1977, Business section, 72.

10. A. Fisher, *The Case for Freedom* (London: Runnymede Press, n.d. [1949]), 5, 27–30, 32, 41, 56; G. Frost, *Antony Fisher: Champion of Liberty* (London: Profile, 2002), 36–43.

11. Frost, *Antony Fisher*, 43–54.

12. IEA Papers, Hoover Institution, Stanford University, California: see, e.g., IEA 62:1, 62:3.

13. A. Denham and M. Garnett, *British Think-Tanks and the Climate of Opinion* (London: UCL Press, 1998), 83–88; Crockett, *Thinking the Unthinkable*, 122–62; Frost, *Antony Fisher*, 36–90.

14. Mont Pelerin Society Papers, Hoover Institution, box 1, folder 6; Hunold to Fisher, December 23, 1959: Mont Pelerin Society Papers, box 13, folder 7.

15. Mont Pelerin Society Papers, box 13, folder 9.

16. R. Harris, *Advertising in a Free Society* (London: IEA, 1959); R. Harris and A. Seldon, *Advertising in Action* (London: Hutchinson for the IEA, 1962); Harris and Seldon, *Advertising and the Public* (London: Deutsch, 1962).

17. Harris and Seldon, *Advertising in Action*, ix.

18. R. Harris, "Information and planning," Mont Pelerin Society Papers, box 17, folder 4.

19. This version of events derives from conversation with Mandy Fairman Dick, Fairman's widow, in December 2008. In general, see B. Sendall, *Independent Television in Britain*, 4 vols. (London: Macmillan, 1982–90), I, 118–19. For Meyer, see K. Wallis, *And the World Listened*, 69, 77, 93.

20. R. Chapman, *Selling the Sixties: The Pirates and Pop Music Radio* (London: Routledge, 1992), 61, 117–18.

21. See the interview of Crawford by Colin Nichol at http://www.off shoreradio.co.uk/odds37.htm, and B. Harte, *When Radio Was the Cat's Whiskers* (Kenthurst, Australia: Rosenberg, 2002), 177–81.

22. The name seems to have been chosen in homage to the American radio entrepreneur Gordon McLendon, who had been an owner of Radio Nord. McLendon came from the town of Atlanta, Texas.

23. See, e.g., *Daily Mail*, April 1, 1964, and *Daily Telegraph*, April 6, 1964.

24. At that time £30,000 would correspond to about $700,000 today, and Smedley's projected profits would amount to $20–$40 million.

25. Sir Noel Ashbridge, "Wavelengths: An international problem," *B.B.C. Quarterly*, II:1 (April 1947), 1–12; J. Persin, "Will space be open to piracy?" *Telecommunication Journal*, 30:4 (April 1963), 112–15; D. M. Leive, *International Telecommunications and International Law: The Regulation of the Radio Spectrum* (Leyden: Sijthoff; Dobbs Ferry, NY: Oceana Publications, 1970), 132–33, n. 84.

26. Leonard, *From International Waters*, 56–57; K. Black, *Upper Circle: A Theatrical Chronicle* (London: Methuen, 1984), 55–56, 70–73, 79–80, 117–19, 126–39, 189, 207–09, 215–16, 220–21; J. Green, *Days in the Life: Voices from the English Underground, 1961–1971* (London: Heinemann, 1988), 35–36. Compare the list in Chapman, *Selling the Sixties*, 70, which differs somewhat from that given here from Atlanta documents but is not incompatible with it. Black's memoir stops before her involvement with Project Atlanta, the story of which she promised to tell in a second volume that never appeared.

27. Why O'Rahilly chose the name Caroline soon became obscure. It has often been said that the inspiration was President Kennedy's daughter, or (more plausibly) Tory politician Reginald Maudling's. More recently it has been claimed that the name originated at *Queen* magazine in the early 1960s. For most listeners, the name, like Atlanta's, was probably a minor mystery.

28. Chapman, *Selling the Sixties*, 67–73.

29. *Daily Telegraph*, April 9, 1964; B. Jordan, "I go aboard the pirate pop ship," *Daily Mail*, March 31, 1964.

30. *Daily Telegraph*, May 14, 1964; *The Guardian*, June 2, 1964; *The Times*, April 2, 1964; *Hansard*, October 26, 1966, vol. 734, col. 1013; August 12, 1966, vol. 733, col. 435; October 19, 1966, vol. 734, cols. 199–201; December 15, 1965, vol. 722, cols. 274–75; and June 18, 1964, vol. 258, cols. 1363–66. See also L. M. Gander, "The case against Radio Caroline," *Daily Telegraph*, April 13, 1964.

31. National Archives, HO 255/1013.

32. *Daily Telegraph*, April 9, 1964, May 14, 1964, May 21, 1964; J. Stanley, "Frequencies for local broadcasting," *Daily Telegraph*, May 22, 1964; *Hansard*, June 18, 1964, vol. 258, cols. 1363–66; L. M. Gander, "Caroline's listeners," *Daily Telegraph*, May 20, 1964.

33. *Hansard*, May 12, 1965, vol. 712, col. 508, October 26, 1966, vol. 734, cols. 1008, 1011.

34. UK Ministry of Labour and National Service, *British Broadcasting Corporation and Musicians' Union: Report of the Independent Committee* (London: HMSO, 1948); Briggs, *History*, IV, 730–31; V, 509–11.

35. *World in Action*, Granada TV, May 12, 1964; *Hansard*, June 18, 1964, vol. 258, cols. 1363–64.

36. *New Society*, October 21, 1965; "Radio Babel," *Daily Telegraph*, May 18, 1964, May 11, 1964, and May 13, 1964; National Archives, CAB 130/198.

37. *Daily Telegraph*, May 27, 1964, 17; *The Observer*, May 17, 1964, May 31, 1964; *The Guardian*, May 3, 1964.

38. S. Hall and R. Hoggart, " 'Piracy' on the air," *Daily Telegraph*, May 18, 1964; *The Observer*, May 31, 1964. For Hoggart, popular literacy, and cultural studies, see T. Steele, *The Emergence of Cultural Studies: Adult Education, Cultural Politics and the "English" Question* (London: Lawrence & Wishart, 1997), 118–43.

39. Project Atlanta, Ltd., *Directors' Report and Accounts for the period ended 1st November, 1964* (April 12, 1965). I am grateful to Mandy Fairman Dick for showing me this documentation.

40. W. Altman, D. Thomas, and D. Sawers, *TV: From Monopoly to Competition— and Back?* (London: Institute of Economic Affairs, 1962).

41. D. Thomas, *Competition in Radio* (London: Institute of Economic Affairs, 1965), 1–11. For Pye, see Wilson, *Pressure Group*, 147, and M. Frankland, *Radio Man: the Remarkable Rise and Fall of C. O. Stanley* (London: IEE, 2002).

42. K. O. Morgan, *Britain Since 1945: The People's Peace* (Oxford: Oxford University Press, 2001 [1990]), 201–02.

43. Project Atlanta, Ltd., *Directors' Report and Accounts for the period ended 31st December, 1965* (April 14, 1967). I am grateful to Mandy Fairman Dick for showing me this documentation. Kitty Black believed that Project

Atlanta continued in some form as a vehicle for trading cocoa futures, and that its remaining investors eventually emerged with some profit. This is recorded in the unpublished section of the transcript of an interview with Black conducted by Colin Nichol (Nicol) on January 22, 1984; I am grateful to Mr. Nichol for permission to cite the transcript here.

5 THE TWO TOWERS

1. C. Ehrlich, *Harmonious Alliance: A History of the Performing Right Society* (Oxford and New York: Oxford University Press, 1989), 133. As far as I know, there is no good history of the impact of transistor radios in the UK, but for the United States see M. B. Schiffer, *The Portable Radio in American Life* (Tucson: University of Arizona Press, 1991), 181–89, 206–08.
2. Quoted in A. Horn, *Juke Box Britain: Americanisation and Youth Culture, 1945–60* (Manchester: Manchester University Press, 2009), 76–77.
3. D. Kynaston, *Austerity Britain, 1945–51* (London: Bloomsbury, 2007).
4. Correspondence from Dorothy Calvert, November 9, 2008.
5. Morgan, *Britain Since 1945*, 80.
6. McKibbin, *Classes and Cultures*, 394, 412–13; Green, *Days in the Life*, 28–29; A. Marwick, *The Sixties: Cultural Revolution in Britain, France, Italy, and the United States, c. 1958–c. 1974* (Oxford: Oxford University Press, 1998), 55–80; Horn, *Juke Box Britain*, 81–82, 90; M. Abrams, *The Teenage Consumer* (London: London Press Exchange for IPA, 1959).
7. A. Davies, *Leisure, Gender and Poverty: Working-class Culture in Salford and Manchester, 1900–1939* (Buckingham, Bucks: Open University Press, 1992), 89–94.
8. J. Rogan, *Starmakers and Svengalis: The History of British Pop Management* (London: Macdonald & Co., 1988), 76–115.
9. The Essoldo lease would still be in serious arrears in November 1966: C. Edwards, ed., *The Radio City Files*, 5 vols. (London: Offshore Echos, 1999), V, 12–14.
10. *The Guardian*, August 7, 1963, 2; e-mail communication from Susan Moore.
11. J. A. Posford, "The Construction of Britain's Sea Forts," in *The Civil Engineer in War*, 3 vols. (London: Institution of Civil Engineers, 1948), III, 132–80.
12. *Hansard*, June 2, 1964, vol. 695, col. 422; June 15, 1964, vol. 696, col. 144; and June 18, 1964, vol. 258, cols. 1373–74.
13. *Hansard*, July 8, 1964, vol. 259, cols. 1014–15.

14. *Daily Telegraph*, May 27, 1964, May 29, 1964.

15. "Screaming Lord Sutch latest radio pirate," *Daily Telegraph*, May 25, 1964; "Army calls Radio Sutch a trespasser," *Daily Telegraph*, May 28, 1964; *The Guardian*, June 2, 1964.

16. D. Calvert statement, June 22, 1966, DPP.

17. *Monitor: Journal of Southend & District Free Radio Campaign*, 1 (Spring 1972), at http://www.monitor.org.uk/originals/M01/0101.htm; D. Calver,t statement, DPP.

18. *Monitor: Journal of Southend & District Free Radio Campaign*, 1 (Spring 1972), at http://www.monitor.org.uk/originals/M01/0101.htm.

19. http://www.offshoreradio.co.uk.

20. S. Henry and M. Von Joel, *Pirate Radio Then and Now* (Poole, Dorset: Blandford Press, 1984), 95.

21. W. Perry, *The Open University: History and Evaluation of a Dynamic Innovation in Higher Education* (San Francisco: Jossey-Bass, 1977), 5.

22. E. L. Woodward, "General cultural development," *B.B.C. Quarterly*, III:1 (April 1948), 24–32, esp. 27.

23. Committee on Higher Education, *Report* (Cmd. 2154) (London: HMSO, 1963), 5, 267; W. A. C. Stewart, *Higher Education in Postwar Britain* (Basingstoke, Hants.: Macmillan, 1989), 99–100.

24. G. Catlin, "University of the Air," *Contemporary Review*, 198 (1960), 358–60; M. Young, "Is your child in the Unlucky Generation?" *Where*, 10 (Autumn 1962), 3–5; G. Rumble, *The Open University of the United Kingdom* (Milton Keynes, Bucks: Open University, 1982); Perry, *The Open University*, 5–9.

25. Lord Taylor, *The Years of Crisis* (London: Labour Party, 1963).

26. *The University of the Air* (Philadelphia: Triangle Publications, 1961).

27. "Speech opening the science debate at the party's annual conference, Scarborough, 1963," in H. Wilson, *Purpose in Politics: Selected Speeches* (London: Weidenfeld & Nicolson, 1964), 14–28.

28. O. Whitley, *Broadcasting and the National Culture* (London: BBC, 1965), 3–4, 6.

29. Briggs, *History*, V, 457–502; BBC, *Educational Television and Radio in Britain: Present Provision and Future Possibilities* (London: BBC, 1966).

30. Hoggart's writings on these themes are very numerous. For the BBC and "culture," see especially Richard Hoggart, *Speaking to Each Other: Essays* (New York: Oxford University Press, 1970), 131–200. For the Pilkington Committee, see Hoggart, *A Measured Life: The Times and Places of an Orphaned Intellectual* (New Brunswick, NJ: Transaction, 1994), III:59–75. On his role in establishing cultural studies, see the collection edited by Sue Owen: *Richard Hoggart and Cultural Studies* (New York: Palgrave/Macmillan, 2008), especially Stuart Hall,

"Richard Hoggart, *The Uses of Literacy*, and the Cultural Turn," 20–32.
31. R. Hoggart and S. Hall, "Against commercial radio," *The Observer*, May 31, 1964, 30.

6 "THINGS ARE GETTING HOT"

1. *Hansard*, April 7, 1964, vol. 692, cols. 784–85.
2. Chapman, *Selling the Sixties*, 74–90.
3. *Daily Telegraph*, June 1, 1965. The government was also concerned at rumors of another pirate television station. The prospective broadcaster was called Radex; funded from America and registered in the Bahamas, it was to be managed by a New Zealander, Jim de Grey. It planned to show almost exclusively American programs. But as BBC engineers pointed out, broadcasting television from a pitching ship would have been extremely difficult, so Shivering Sands would have had a major advantage in this endeavor. One reason the government (and Benn in particular) was concerned was that a TV pirate would interfere with radio observatories, which clustered around Cambridge. At one point it explained helpfully that such broadcasting could be permitted once radio astronomy was complete—*Daily Telegraph*, June 4, 1965, June 21, 1965; *Hansard*, June 30, 1965, vol. 715, cols. 84–85.
4. D. Calvert, statement, October 7, 1966, DPP.
5. *Monitor: Journal of Southend & District Free Radio Campaign*, 1 (Spring 1972), at http://www.monitor.org.uk/originals/M01/0101.htm; contract with British Sub Aqua Club, October 13, 1965, in *The Radio City Files*, II, 11.
6. J. Bugler, "Radio pirates make for port," *New Society*, October 21, 1965, 5–6.
7. *Daily Telegraph*, May 27, 1964.
8. *Daily Mirror*, September 21, 1966.
9. "Why radio pirates are growing respectable," *Sunday Times*, June 19, 1966. The deal between the PRS and Radio London was reported in every national newspaper: see, e.g., *The Times*, *Financial Times*, *Daily Telegraph*, and *The Guardian*, February 17, 1966.
10. *Hansard*, December 8, 1965, vol. 722, col. 424; National Archives, HO 255/1021.
11. National Archives, HO 255/1013; *The Times*, February 17, 1966, 7.
12. Something of the control Dorothy Calvert exercised can be seen in correspondence with the fort DJs in Offshore Echos' *Radio City Files*: e.g., D. Calvert to T. Edwards, April 12, 1966: *The Radio City Files*, III, 28–29; D. Calvert to T. Edwards, May 5, 1966: *The Radio City Files*, III, 51.
13. *Sunday Telegraph*, March 21, 1965.

14. *Hansard*, March 3, 1966, vol. 725, cols. 1557–58.
15. O. Smedley to A. C. Horsley, May 24, 1966, DPP.
16. Dorothy Calvert, MS notes, written c. June 1966.
17. To rebut such exaggerated claims, Dorothy Calvert obtained a quotation from RCA for a new version of the transmitter that priced it at £6,310. The quotation is included in the DPP file.
18. *Evening Standard*, June 27, 1966.
19. Testimonies in DPP. Most of the riggers had time on their hands because of the national dock strike underway at the time.
20. C. McCrystal et al., "Radio City widow tells of 'Keep Out' threats," *Sunday Times*, June 26, 1966, 1, 3.
21. Some have guessed that this refers to the drowning of Pepper, but I know of no evidence either that Calvert was involved in Pepper's death or that this was indeed what he meant. It is more likely that, like the nerve gas threat, it was bombast.
22. Allbeury in fact suggested Veganin, a mixture of codeine, paracetamol, and caffeine.
23. Dorothy Calvert, statement taken July 8, 1966, DPP. In my account of the events of that afternoon and evening, I have followed testimony recorded by the various participants in the following few days—including, as here, Mrs. Calvert. It is worth noting, however, that this version differs from what the Calverts themselves remember. On their account, it was Rutter who insisted that Reg go to see Smedley, and Rutter, not Wileman, who provided the address in Wendens Ambo. Calvert had not decided to go before that point, and he remained reluctant. He demurred, on grounds of feeling unwell. But then Rutter persuaded Alan Arnold to call and offer to drive. Nor did the exchange between Dorothy Calvert and Harvey take place. These differences, small in themselves, deserve to be noted because of what they imply in concert. In the family's version, far from being a venture by a desperate man, the drive to Wendens Ambo was not undertaken at Reg Calvert's instigation at all. Not for the only time in this story, the question is ultimately beyond resolution. For the professional historian it induces a vertiginous sense of the contingencies implicit in our custom of trusting to documents.

7 THE WAR AGAINST THE PIRATES

1. McCrystal et al., "Radio City widow tells of 'Keep Out' threats." n. 20, p. 282.
2. *Evening News*, June 25, 1966.

3. *Daily Sketch, The Sun*, and the *Daily Mirror*, June 27, 1966.
4. Conversation with Dorothy Calvert, December 2008.
5. "Pop pirate," preserved and made accessible by the Institut National de l'Audiovisuel: www.ina.fr. I thank Alexandre Laumonier for drawing this to my attention.
6. Economist Intelligence Unit, *The National Newspaper Industry: A Survey* (London: EIU, 1966), part II(a), 70–71, 83–84; T. Baistow, "Anatomy of a Crisis," in R. Boston, ed., *The Press We Deserve* (London: RKP, 1970), 41–56, esp. 49; B. Harrison, *Seeking a Role: The United Kingdom, 1951– 1970* (Oxford: Clarendon Press, 2009), 56–57, 392–94.
7. Brown believed that there was one exception: he thought that Calvert had assaulted Dorothy at some point in the past, and his report implies that she had told him as much. But this was never adduced in any formal setting, and she never referred to it in any statement—G. T. Brown, Report, Brief for the Prosecution at Chelmsford Autumn Assizes, 6, DPP.
8. Ibid., 11–12, DPP.
9. W. O. Smedley, "Issues raised by pop pirates," *New Outlook*, June 27, 1966, 30–34.
10. *Evening Standard*, June 23, 1966.
11. *Hansard*, July 1, 1966, vol. 730, col. 341; July 6, 1966, vol. 731, cols. 425–26; *Evening Standard*, June 28, 1966; *The Guardian*, June 29, 1966.
12. *The Guardian*, June 27, 1966; *Daily Telegraph*, June 28, 1966.
13. *Hansard*, July 13, 1966, vol. 731, col. 1439; A. W. Benn, memo to Wilson, June 11, 1965: National Archives, FO 371/181312; "Pirate Broadcasting," memo by A. W. Benn, June 28, 1966: CAB/129/125.
14. E. Short, "No One Is Going to Cock a Snook at the Law," *Daily Mirror*, September 21, 1966, 15.
15. The invocation of Puritanism doubtless intentionally raised what was one of the most contentious rifts in British culture of the period. See Harrison, *Seeking a Role*, 472–84.
16. *Hansard*, December 7, 1966, vol. 737, col. 1327; October 26, 1966, vol. 734, col. 1010.
17. *Daily Mirror*, September 21, 1966; H. Knot, "The fight for free radio: The political activation of offshore radio's fanbase, 1964–1989," *Soundscapes*, 6 (October 2003): http://www.icce.rug.nl/~soundscapes/ VOLUME06/Fight_free_radio.shtml.
18. *Sunday Times*, September 25, 1966.
19. IEA Papers, Hoover Institution, California: IEA 110. 12.
20. Nockolds & Son to Director of Public Prosecutions, August 4, 1966, DPP.

21. Conversation with Susan Moore and Dorothy Calvert, December 2008.
22. E. W. Roskill, rev., "Stevenson, Sir (Aubrey) Melford Steed (1902–1987)," in *Oxford Dictionary of National Biography* (Oxford: Oxford University Press, 2004): www. oxforddnb. com/view/article/40101, accessed June 17, 2009.
23. *The Guardian*, October 19, 1966, 5; *Daily Express*, October 19, 1966; *The Times*, October 19, 1966; Briggs, *History*, V, 567, n. 33.
24. H. G. Lillicrapp to Short, September 23, 1966; reports on Radio 390 case, December 1 and 13, 1966, National Archives, HO 255/1021.
25. D. Calvert to A. Pine, November 9, 1966, in Edwards, ed., *The Radio City Files*, V, 6. In the same useful collection (IV, 16) is a mysterious letter from an otherwise anonymous "Uncle" to "the D-J in charge," dated June 2, 1966, giving the bearer authority to land on the fort and invite a companion into the studio for an interview. The meaning is obscure—it looks almost like a coded message—but it is plausible to connect this note to the abortive Bates plot against Shivering Sands that Allbeury revealed at about that time.
26. DPP; *Evening Standard*, January 27, 1967, 1.
27. *Hansard*, June 2, 1964, vol. 695, col. 422; *Daily Telegraph*, June 1, 1964, June 19, 1964; L. M. Gander, "BBC is silent in pirates' din," *Daily Telegraph*, May 18, 1964; memo to Wilson, A. W. Benn, June 10, 1965; National Archives, HO 255/1043; Leonard, *From International Waters*, 143–54.
28. Briggs, *History*, V, 573.
29. Chapman, *Selling the Sixties*, 226–78.
30. Stewart, *Higher Education*, 111–17.
31. J. Gale, "It's five, four, three, two—Radio ONE," *The Observer*, October 1, 1967, 3; George Melly, *Revolt into Style: The Pop Arts in Britain* (London: Penguin, 1972), 194; W. Taylor, "It's Radio One-derful," *News of the World*, October 1, 1967; B. Nightingale, "The phoney revolution," *New Society*, October 5, 1967, 458–59.

8 A MAN CALLED UNCLE

1. Dorothy Calvert, conversation, December 2008; Susan Moore, e-mail communications, May–September 2009.
2. Marwick, *The Sixties*, 479.
3. See C. Fry and C. Kray, *Doing the Business: Inside the Krays' Secret Network of Glamour and Violence* (London: Blake, 1999), e.g., 85–105.
4. *The Guardian*, July 18, 1968, 1, July 20, 1968, 3; *The Observer*, July 21, 1968, 4; *The Times*, July 18, 1968, 2, July 20, 1968, 3. The James Bond

reference was Reggie Kray's, shouted out at his own trial. The literature on the Krays is large, often unreliable, and all too frequently self-serving; but for the standard interpretation, see J. Pearson, *The Profession of Violence: The Rise and Fall of the Kray Twins* (New York: Saturday Review Press, 1973), 194–226. Read's version is in L. Read and J. Morton, *Nipper Read: The Man Who Nicked the Krays* (London and Boston: Little, Brown, 1991), 154–58, 202–03. For a more contextual account, see D. Hobbs, *Doing the Business: Entrepreneurship, the Working Class, and Detectives in the East End of London* (Oxford: Clarendon Press, 1988), 54–57. Some of the official files on this episode are still secret, so it is impossible to give a definitive account yet.

5. *Hansard*, June 18, 1964, vol. 258, col. 1370.
6. B. R. Harvey, statement, June 26, 1966, DPP.
7. Compare the view of Johnny Rogan, who felt that Calvert had taken on the role of "some demented method actor": *Starmakers and Svengalis: The History of British Pop Management* (London: Macdonald, 1988), 114.
8. *Hansard*, July 3, 1967, vol. 749, col. 191.
9. National Archives, CAB 164/135; CAB 130/467.
10. J. Markoff, "Rebel outpost on the fringes of Cyberspace," *New York Times*, June 4, 2000, 10; Leonard, *From International Waters*, 169.
11. There is an interesting parallel with the scheme mooted by lead characters in Neal Stephenson's *Cryptonomicon* (New York: Avon, 1999) for a data server in the Philippines using a similar line-of-sight principle.
12. C. Hastings, "How the BBC tried to sink Caroline," *Sunday Telegraph*, February 22, 2009, 15 (a reference for which I am grateful to Richard Epstein and John Blundell); M. Kennedy, "Officials seek access to phone and email data 1,381 times a day," *The Guardian*, August 10, 2009. For D-notices at this point, see N. Wilkinson, *Secrecy and the Media: The Official History of the United Kingdom's D-notice System* (London: Routledge, 2009), 277–342.
13. A. Petridis, "Hold tight the massive," *The Guardian*, November 22, 2002, Review, 2–4; J. Hind and S. Mosco, *Rebel Radio: The Full Story of British Pirate Radio* (London: Pluto, 1985).
14. There is a huge literature on this phenomenon, but see, e.g., S. Weber, *The Success of Open Source* (Cambridge, MA: Harvard University Press, 2004), 128–56; C. M. Kelty, *Two Bits: The Cultural Significance of Free Software* (Durham, NC: Duke University Press, 2008), 64–94; and Y. Benkler, *The Wealth of Networks: How Social Production Transforms Markets and Freedom* (New Haven, CT: Yale University Press, 2006), 212–300.
15. See, e.g., F. Turner, *From Counterculture to Cyberculture: Stewart Brand, the Whole Earth Network, and the Rise of Digital Utopianism* (Chicago:

INDEX

About the Author

Adrian Johns is professor of history and chair of the Committee on Conceptual and Historical Studies of Science at the University of Chicago. He is the author of *Piracy: The Intellectual Property Wars from Gutenberg to Gates* (2010) and *The Nature of the Book: Print and Knowledge in the Making* (1998). The latter won the Leo Gershoy Award of the American Historical Association, the John Ben Snow Prize of the North American Conference on British Studies, the Louis Gottschalk Prize of the American Society for Eighteenth-Century Studies, and the SHARP Prize for the best work on the history of authorship, reading, and publishing. Educated in Britain at the University of Cambridge, Johns has also taught at the University of Kent at Canterbury, the University of California, San Diego, and the California Institute of Technology.